D1550683

Colum McCann's Intertexts

Also by Bertrand Cardin

Colum McCann: intertextes et interactions (Rennes: Presses Universitaires de Rennes, 2016)

Lectures d'un texte étoilé: Corée *de John McGahern* (Paris: L'Harmattan, 2009)

Miroirs de la filiation: parcours dans huit romans irlandais contemporains (Caen: Presses Universitaires de Caen, 2005)

(ed.), *Journal of the Short Story in English*, special issue: The 21st Century Irish Short Story, no. 63 (autumn 2014)

with Alexandra Slaby (eds), *Contemporary Issues in Irish Studies: in memoriam Paul Brennan*, special issue of *Etudes irlandaises,* nos 40–1 (spring/summer 2015)

with Sylvie Mikowski (eds), *Ecrivaines irlandaises/Irish Women Writers* (Caen: Presses Universitaires de Caen, 2014)

with Claude Fierobe (eds), *Irlande, écritures et réécritures de la Famine* (Caen: Presses Universitaires de Caen, 2007)

Colum McCann's Intertexts

Books Talk to One Another

BERTRAND CARDIN

Published in 2016 by
Cork University Press
Youngline Industrial Estate
Pouladuff Road, Togher
Cork, Ireland

British Library Cataloguing in Publication Data

A CIP catalogue record for this book is available from the British Library

ISBN: 978-1-78205-224-1

Typeset by Dominic Carroll, Ardfield, County Cork
Printed by Hussar Books, Poland

www.corkuniversitypress.com

Contents

Acknowledgements

In working on this study for the past ten years or so, I have been aided and encouraged in so many ways, and I would like to express my thanks to the following people for their support and help: Lorie-Ann Duech, Carys Lewis, Caroline MacDonogh, Alexandra Slaby and Amy Wells.

Mike Collins and Maria O'Donovan of Cork University Press and copy-editor Dominic Carroll were invaluable in guiding this manuscript through each stage, and I would like to thank them for their patience, professionalism and hard work.

Tim Knox very kindly granted permission for his photograph of Colum McCann to be used on the cover of the book.

I am extremely grateful to Colum McCann for his kindness and generosity towards me, and for his permission to quote from his published works.

Lines from the poem 'Dancers at the Moy' are reproduced with the kind permission of Paul Muldoon.

Lines from Boris Pasternak's poem 'Winter Sky', translated by Jon Stallworthy and Peter France, are reproduced with the kind permission of Jon Stallworthy and Peter France.

Lines from Wendell Berry's poem 'Rising' are reproduced with the kind permission of Counterpoint Press.

A section of this book has previously been published as 'Authorities in Crisis and Intertextual Practice: the example of Colum McCann's *Let the Great World Spin*', in Carine Berbéri and Martine Pelletier (eds), *Ireland: authority and crisis* (Bern: Peter Lang, 2015).

Introduction

We can only give what already belongs to another.

Jorge Luis Borges, *Los Conjurados/The Conspirators*

Colum McCann's 2013 novel is called *TransAtlantic*. Such a title obviously conveys notions of transfer, transport and transplantation. It is quite significant because it somehow epitomises the writer's own life and work; indeed, it corresponds to the personal experience of McCann, who, born in Ireland, lives in the US. The title also refers to the travels of his characters, who are mostly migrants. Lastly, it alludes to all kinds of dialogues and exchanges that can be noticed in his works. One of the distinctive features of McCann's works is their relationship with other texts. They establish many intertextual links. As the writer himself says, 'Mine is a text that opens up other texts.'[1] This acknowledgement can be read as an invitation to explore these 'other texts', to investigate these interrelations and examine the dialogic combination between them.

The present work confirms that 'books talk to one another',[2] as the narrator of a McCann story remarks. McCann's books are particularly talkative in their dialogues with other books. They are studied here in turn in the chronological order of their publication, from *Fishing the Sloe-black River* (1994) to *Thirteen Ways of Looking* (2015), thus covering the two decades of the writer's literary works.

This study has the advantage of filling a gap. Indeed, critical books on McCann's fiction emphasise the importance of intertextuality in this work but do not go into the subject in greater depth. They are more interested in other textual features. Therefore it seems to be useful and innovative to decode McCann's texts in the light of other texts, particularly when they quote from them or refer or allude to them.

As with any trend of literary criticism, there are limits to this reading. On one hand, an intertextual approach gives priority to *one* aspect of the text at the expense of other essential elements, but is it not peculiar to any specific approach? On the other hand, this method is sometimes criticised because of its self-reflexiveness, which can be considered as tautological. True, according to the principle of autotelism, a work of art is an end in itself, together with its own justification. But for all that, is it absolutely non-referential? Is it the evidence of the writer's lack of interest in the problems of the world? The following pages show that it is not the case concerning McCann's fiction, in which practical and educational aims are evident.[3]

An intertextual approach is valid, relevant and fruitful because most of the time it brings to light some elements that have so far remained in the shade, and which, once disclosed, make it possible to have a better understanding of the text. It also opens a whole aspect of the work that could go unnoticed to many readers. Indeed, some of them may appreciate a text without being aware of the connections it establishes with other texts. Some others may deliberately ignore this aspect or vaguely feel that there must be something interrelated but not bother to do further research. Another category of reader can also notice that there may be a connection but fail to determine the precise book it refers to or alludes to. (For example, McCann's story 'Stolen Child' refers to Yeats' poem 'The Stolen Child' and even quotes from it without naming the poet or giving the title of the poem.) All of these readers may nevertheless have a clear understanding of the text. However, they do not reach its depths, cannot fully appreciate its flavour, and therefore miss something of it. Mentions of authors, quotations, references and allusions are as many keys offered by the writer that readers may or may not use according to their literary culture and their desire to be producers of the text.

It must be borne in mind that a text is always involved in a dialogue with other texts, some more than others. Intertextual connections prove to be so numerous in McCann's fiction that it is essential to consider only a selection.

Transtextual relationships such as translations from one language to another or screen adaptations of texts are deliberately not considered in the present work because they mobilise specific notions that are not the subject of this book. By the same token, extracts from songs and evocations of music pieces common to most of McCann's novels and stories are also not studied here. Owing to my very limited skills in the field, it appears that the music world would not be as helpful as the literary universe for my analysis. Lastly, textual relationships within McCann's work – for example, the motifs that are common to several texts of his[4] – are mentioned here when they are relevant, but they do not unduly receive further attention as a rule because I consider that the fertile connections between this author's work and texts written by *other* writers are more stimulating. In my view, intertextuality contributes to opening the text on the global library. It creates associations, establishes co-presence: the intertext is 'the effective *presence* of a text in another one', according to Genette;[5] 'other texts are *present* in it, at varying levels, in more or less recognizable forms', wrote Barthes.[6] This 'relation of co-presence'[7] between texts is the subject of this study. With quotation, reference or allusion, the text appropriates other texts; with parody or imitation, it transforms and rewrites them. McCann's work is analysed here from the angle of these relations of appropriation and transformation. His novels and short stories are read and interpreted here as rewritings of episodes taken from the Bible or from Celtic legends. They are also dealt with as mirrors of the Irish sociopolitical context or as vectors of great ideological discourses. Various texts may legitimately be connected with McCann's. They constitute his intertexts – hence the emphasis on theories of intertextuality, such as influence, authority or intentionality.

Each chapter of this book can be read separately, just like the text it deals with. Therefore readers are entirely free to choose the one they want to start with. Nevertheless, it is essential to have McCann's text in mind so that the validity of the interpretation can fully be understood and appreciated. Indeed, a metatextual reading is of no interest if the text commented upon remains unknown to the reader. Ideally, McCann's work should be (re)read with a particular attention to intertextual combinations. From then on, readers will be able to compare their own discoveries with my own. McCann's work is a gold mine for whoever is keen on textual interrelations. It invites us to perform reading like a treasure hunt, to discover the detours and dialogical secrets, and to go hunting for intertexts. So let's take these ways without further delay; it is the open season.

CHAPTER 1

Parodic Transgression in the First Short Stories

'A writer has to acknowledge that we get our voice from the voices of others. It's impossible to spring into the world unformed by anyone else', Colum McCann declares in an interview with Dave Welch.[1] His remark proves that he considers polyphony as a feature of his work. Polyphony leads to the concept of textual dialogism elaborated by Mikhail Bakhtin. According to Bakhtin, any discourse is involved in a dialogue, and parody, particularly, is one of the closest interpretations of dialogism. Parody is diphonic discourse because it simultaneously refers to two enunciative acts, two contexts of utterance: the present one and a previous one. Parody is also divergent discourse because the writer expresses himself or herself with somebody else's words. This diphonic divergent discourse is the subject of the present chapter. It will help us circumscribe the nature and contents of the dialogue between McCann's and other writers' texts. The former respond to the latter, extend their memory and existence. McCann's stories echo previous pieces of writing, but they do not model themselves on them, as they divert them and impose themselves as original forms. Both convergent through imitation and divergent through the transformation they carry out, parody is a paradoxical device. In its mechanism it fits in with somebody else's discourse that it progressively diverts and deflects in order to achieve its purposes.

Parody: an Irish tradition?

Vivian Mercier maintains that parody is an Irish tradition exemplified by Joyce's work.[2] The title of his study published in 1962, *The Irish Comic*

Tradition, testifies that this literary device is anchored in a larger comic tradition. Mercier has a classical approach to parody, which he conceives as intentionally copying the style of someone famous in a way that is humorous or sarcastic. The meaning of the word 'parody' has been changing over the years. In any case, it is no longer considered only as a comic device. This aspect is replaced with something in keeping with the universe of the game with Gérard Genette, who, two decades after Vivian Mercier, defined parody as 'the playful transformation of a single text'.[3] Then, with Linda Hutcheon, parody is totally freed from these comic and playful specificities to become an ironic form: 'Parody is a form of imitation, but imitation characterized by ironic inversion ... Parody is, in another formulation, repetition with critical distance, which marks difference rather than similarity.'[4]

In its present definitions, parody does not attack, ridicule or satirise previous texts. It is not destructive, as Mercier upheld.[5] In parody, alterity is recognised, assimilated and replaced. In preference to Vivian Mercier's restrictive approach, it will be envisaged here according to Linda Hutcheon's definition, which has the advantage of taking into account the imitative and transformative compositional elements of the device. Although Hutcheon never mentions Mercier in her *Theory of Parody*, she seems, like him, to detect a tradition in Ireland that would be due to the position of the nation on the periphery of a dominant culture:

> Parody becomes the mode of the 'ex-centric', of those who are marginalized by a dominant ideology. Parody has been a favorite postmodern literary form of writers in places like Ireland or Canada working as they do from both inside and outside a culturally different and dominant context.[6]

According to this postmodern view, parody sets up an inter-discursive relationship – made of identification and distance between the dominated and the dominant – between the periphery and the core.

If there is indeed parodic tradition in Ireland, it can be seen in the very first book of young writers who are still 'on the periphery' of the literary world and for whom the imitation of famous models could be envisaged as one of the early stages of creation. Working out their own texts with the influence of predecessors, young writers would place themselves in the protective shade of one of them,[7] and create a self-reflexive work that would give their readers a feeling of déjà vu or *déjà lu*. This hypothesis could be proved by Joseph O'Connor's first collection, *True Believers*,[8] which is made up of stories the titles of which are openly parodic, such as 'The Last of the Mohicans' or 'The Wizard of Oz'. Similarly, Jamie O'Neill's first book, *At Swim, Two Boys*,[9] is, from its title onwards, an obvious parody of Flann O'Brien's novel *At Swim-Two-Birds*.[10] The same is true of Colum McCann's *Fishing the Sloe-black River*.[11] Published in 1994, this collection of short stories is not only the author's first book but also the most parodic one of his fiction.

'Sloe-black': a parodic literal borrowing

The story that gives the collection its title, 'Fishing the Sloe-black River', narrates a day off in a small town in County Westmeath where women go fishing while men play football. At the end of the day, rods are unsnapped, picnic baskets put away; couples meet up in their cars. Exchanges of information are limited to the admission that men 'really need some new blood in midfield'[12] and that women 'didn't even get a bite'.[13] Although the river they fish has the colour of a fruit – sloe black – it does not prove especially fruitful as characters systematically come back empty-handed. Its darkness may be the sign of its barrenness. The association of the water and the colour black can be read as an allusion to the dark bile of melancholy characters,[14] unless it alludes to the etymological root of the capital city of the Republic of Ireland, where half of the story plots are located. In Irish, *dubh linn* means 'black pool', words that most probably refer to the darkness of the waters in Dublin Bay. Whatever it may be, the very combination of the words sloe-black as a compound adjective to qualify a river is bound to arouse the reader's curiosity. The colour black, which is commonly associated with soot or coal, is here connected to a small, sour fruit with a dark skin in forming the unusual compound. As it happens, this original combination is inspired by Dylan Thomas' 'play for voices'.[15] Indeed, *Under Milk Wood* starts with a sentence that, as stage directions indicate, must be whispered very softly: 'It is spring, moonless night in the small town, starless and bible-black, the cobblestreets silent and the hunched, courters'-and-rabbits' wood limping invisible down to the sloeblack, slow, black, crowblack, fishingboat-bobbing sea.'[16] The adjective 'black' is recurrent here as it appears four times, either on its own or in a compound associating it with a noun in a rather conventional way ('crowblack') or in a more unusual one ('bible-black' or 'sloeblack'). This colour is justified by the background of a moonless night. The resumption of the term 'sloeblack' by McCann testifies that he is attracted by this poetic image that he uses, as does the original text, to describe a natural liquid element. The adjective depicts the sea reflecting the night sky in Thomas' play, but in McCann's story it describes a river that happens to be black because of its muddy banks and the waste it contains. The river is like the main street, 'tumbled with litter'.[17] One of the fishing women watches 'a blue chocolate wrapper get caught in a gust of wind, then float down onto the water'.[18] As can be read at a later point in the book, chocolates are branded as 'Milk Tray'.[19] Thus by their allusion to milk the pollutants in the story counterpoint the title of Dylan Thomas' play *Under Milk Wood*. Pollution contrasts with purity. 'Sloe-black' is a minimal textual fragment, a borrowed word with a parodic value: it deals with something different but in a similar way. Initially coined by another writer, this word gathers two voices that neither merge nor cancel each other out, but combine dialogically, expressing themselves together while remaining distinct, thus asserting the diphonic nature of parodic discourse.

This twofold word or compound carries a doubleness that is characteristic of parodic fiction: it is similar because it is the same word; and yet it is slightly different as it is written as a single word by Dylan Thomas ('sloeblack') and in two words connected by a hyphen by Colum McCann ('sloe-black'). This distinction is the sign of contextual displacement and of the distance kept from the prior text, which are essential elements of parody. By definition, parody is an ambivalent and paradoxical device as it plays both on resemblance and contrast, on absorption and separation. On the one hand, it conforms to the model and adopts its signifier as its own; on the other hand, it diverts the signified and provides it with another referent.

Linda Hutcheon's definition of parody as 'a repetition which marks difference rather than similarity'[20] implies that the parodist's desire for change prevails over her/his desire for imitation. Bakhtin makes similar comments when he considers the writer's assimilation of other voices as 'refraction', a phenomenon that suggests a change of direction: 'Without making common cause with these discourses, the prose writer particularly highlights them with humour, irony or parody.'[21] Unlike plagiarism – which is anchored in absolute conformity, denies any assertiveness and implies the plagiarist's dependence on his model's discourse – parody shows resistance to imitation and has an ambivalent relationship with its object, as it is both dependent on it and independent from it. Indeed, the parodist can be considered as the vassal of her/his model, but is also able to keep her/his distance from her/him and take liberties, thus enjoying the power to be both her/himself and somebody else.

Parodic transformation in 'Sisters'

The first short story in *Fishing the Sloe-black River* is called 'Sisters'. This title is obviously reminiscent of 'The Sisters', the first story in James Joyce's collection, *Dubliners*. The two stories are not only similarly titled – with the exception of the presence of a determiner in Joyce's case – but are also comparable considering the initial position they have in their respective books. Thematically, both of them are focused on the end of a life: a priest has just died in Joyce's text; a nun is dying in McCann's. The former character has never left Dublin, whereas the latter has travelled the world. Past events are remembered in both stories, creating in the present 'a communion with the past'[22] over biscuits and comforting drinks – a glass of sherry for Joyce, a cup of tea for McCann. Death is omnipresent in the two stories, most obviously through the protagonists' dead or dying bodies or their silence, but also through various symbols, such as the sunset and the colour grey, which characterises the sisters in both texts. McCann's story reworks Joyce's and transposes it one century later across the Atlantic. It establishes between them a dialogue, which is partly implicit because of its availability in the reader's memory and his or her ability to call upon what he or she has read. A phenomenon of resonance is set up and can be interpreted as the assimilation of a model and the desire to 'commune with the past'. But as the sisters in Joyce's story are described as identically united in their selfless loyalties to their brother, the sisters in McCann are depicted as fundamentally different: they embody the contrast between spirituality and carnality. The older sister is the Lord's servant who works with the poor, whereas the younger one is at the disposal of males who give vent to their lecherous fantasies with her. McCann's story diverges from the Joycean model, notably because the recontextualised universe it depicts is no longer the same. McCann's 'Sisters' transforms Joyce's 'The Sisters' with a view to showing to what extent values have changed. The river that links the stories together – as it is present from the first to the last page of the collection – is the emblem of this chronological evolution, the sign that nothing is as it used to be. Nowadays, the Irish deliberately go and live abroad. Likewise, the moral values and ideologies of Joyce's and McCann's protagonists are very different in comparison. What sisters today would be ready to sacrifice themselves body and soul to support a brother in his priestly mission? Although some common elements would tend to make us think that McCann speaks the same language as Joyce, both discourses differ. Voices are superimposed upon one another, but tunes are different. Etymologically, the parodist performs counterpoint and can even be out of tune.[23] In this case, transposition tends towards dissonance. This combination of proximity and distance highlights the paradox of parody in which Linda Hutcheon perceives an indicator of postmodernity. Postmodern parody interprets, recontextualises and transforms modern texts. Texts of the past are given a new life, rewritten with present preoccupations, and looked at critically. As Umberto Eco puts it: 'The postmodern answer to the modern consists of acknowledging that the past ... must be revisited with irony, not in an innocent way'.[24]

The mirror image of a poem by Yeats

The parodic transformation of a text from the past is noticeable in another story from *Fishing the Sloe-black River*: 'Stolen Child' recontextualises a poem by W.B. Yeats, 'The Stolen Child'.[25] As in the previous example, the titles of both texts duplicate each other, with the exception of the determiner. With this small formal distinction, the two texts appear as both similar and different. Here again the relation of co-presence accentuates an ironic, critical postmodern use of a modern text. Yeats' poem is an invitation to romantic escape in the dream Ireland of the Celtic Twilight. At the end of each stanza, fairies call the child in a chorus:

> Come away, O human child!
> To the waters and the wild
> With a faery, hand in hand,
> For the world's more full of weeping than you can understand.[26]

McCann's story recontextualises Yeats' poem in a Brooklyn children's home at the end of the twentieth century. There, Padraic, an Irish counsellor, takes a liking to a blind black girl and tells her that her name has its roots in Irish mythology, Dana being a goddess with magic powers who conquered the country with a tribe of druids. On Saturday afternoons Padraic and Dana have a walk in an area of 'basketball courts hemmed in with chicken wire, red brick tenement houses',[27] an environment that obviously contrasts with the large natural expanses of Ireland. He sometimes quotes a few lines: '*For the world's more full of weeping than you can understand*'.[28] These words are emphasised by italics that explicitly introduce them as a quotation. Although the name of its author is never mentioned, this specific typography helps readers identify the text as being borrowed from another one and sets their interpretative skills in motion. If the connection is precisely established and the source text recognised, the understanding is all the better, because, as Genette puts it, the function of one of them cannot be perceived and appreciated without having the other in mind or to hand.[29] Indeed, the story can be fully understood only if its doubleness is taken into account. This ambivalent feature works on the ironic model that, like the parodic device from which it is a structural element, marks a difference by superimposing two strata. Irony and parody proceed on two levels: one is explicit; the other is implicit. The ultimate meaning of the ironic parodic text lies in the way these two strata superimpose in some kind of textual doubleness. This is why the reader must not treat the gap between the texts with disdain. As in the poem, where a child is taken away by fairies, the girl in the story is also stolen but by her own free will and by a Vietnam veteran whose description does not liken him at all to the imaginary creatures with magical powers: as he has no legs, he moves in a wheelchair, wears a long, grey beard, and rattles a tin can in subway cars.

Because she agrees to get married – and young brides are as likely as children to be stolen by fairies, according to Yeats[30] – Dana follows her husband into 'a small hovel … a black hole of refugees and veterans',[31] a transposition of the underworld in Celtic mythology. The wedding is just a parody of legendary feasts: the guests are 'Vietnam vets with long hair'[32] or 'blind kids from the home',[33] the bride is depicted as heavily made up,[34] the car is 'a battered Oldsmobile',[35] and the party supplies 'thunderbird and dog biscuits'.[36] The dissonance between Yeats' poem and McCann's story exemplifies Hutcheon's vision of parody as 'imitation characterized by ironic inversion'.[37]

McCann's stolen child is this very Dana who had been robbed of her family when she was a little girl:

> Her father had gone out for a packet of cigarettes and never came back, her mother had taken to the little white vials. The authorities found Dana locked in a cupboard, rake-thin, blind as the mice that scuttled in nursery rhymes, while her mother sat in the corner of the room and rocked on the balls of her toes, a bouquet of crack pipes around her feet. When she saw the badges she just shrugged. *Take her, she ain't mine no more.*[38]

Here, again, the conventions of mythological legends are inverted: unlike parents of Irish folklore who do their best to keep their child with them,

Dana's mother deliberately lets her daughter go; she gives her, abandons her, tears her from the bosom of her family. Wide is the gap between the story and the initial subject, which is transformed to such an extent that it is inverted. On the ironic model of the mirror image, the device conforms to the prior text in order to transform it better. This is what Vladimir Jankélévitch calls 'ironic conformity'.[39] In a chapter of his essay dedicated to irony, the French philosopher shows that ironic conformity pretends to adopt other people's opinions in order to discredit them. Ironic conformity is the stratagem of the Trojan horse: it consists of getting on the inside to better turn everything upside down. The cunning lies in 'the contrast between a form which grammatically conforms' to the other writer's discourse – such as the resumption of a title or the quotation of a poem – and 'an intention that can be imagined as subversive',[40] like the inversion of conventions. Between the restrictiveness of conformity and the openness of irony, there is some kind of interference, of resistance, an assertion of distinctiveness, a willingness not to go on moving forward with a model, which clearly means that mythological legends, as appealing as they may be, cannot be credited today.

Hopkins revisited

Three years after the publication of *Fishing the Sloe-black River*, *Phoenix Irish Short Stories* (1997), edited by David Marcus, was published. This anthology includes a story by Colum McCann titled 'As Kingfishers Catch Fire',[41] the hypertextual nature of which is explicitly displayed through the title and the epigraph that reads:

> As kingfishers catch fire
> Dragonflies draw flames.
>   Gerard Manley Hopkins[42]

Specifying the poet's name and the verse from which the quotation is taken, the epigraph is a pact established by the writer with the reader, who is informed of a connection between the story and the poem. It officially declares a diversion from Hopkins to McCann. According to Michele Hannoosh, who wrote *Parody and Decadence*,[43] the epigraph reproduces the functioning of parody on a smaller scale: it quotes a text in a different context and endows the quotation with a new meaning that is connected with the story it introduces.

Placed apart at the commencement of the text, the epigraph signals a gap between the quoted work and the following text, but nevertheless establishes a connection between them, exactly like parody with the parodied text. Besides, it reuses a work, but its purposes are different from the ones initially set, which is the basic principle of parody.

McCann's story narrates an Irish nurse's involvement in the Korean War. The woman interprets the circle of light around the Korean soldier she looks after as a sign of his saintliness. Yet, having returned from the front, his irradiation is due only to his having been riddled with bullets and metal pieces. The luminous reflection of the divinity, which according to Hopkins' sonnet is visible in each creature, becomes the sign of vulgar war projectiles in McCann's story. Once again, removed from its original context and transplanted into a new one, the English poet's line is subjected to parodic transformation. To Hopkins' voice summoned by the paratext of the story responds McCann's voice that implies that the order of the world according to the divine will is no longer credible today. This opinion is characteristic of the contemporary Western ideologies of our postmodern era.

As Bakhtin had it, parody is an essential element of dialogic imagination. However, this figure is also in keeping with ironic conformity. As McCann's stories illustrate, parody pretends to adopt somebody else's discourse to resist it all the better, transform it from the inside, and replace its obsolete forms with new ones. The reutilisation of somebody else's discourse in a new context, with a different orientation, revitalises the parodied text and provides it with a totally new objective. Parody gives a fresh aesthetic quality to a text or a forgotten word – such as 'sloeblack' – and can be envisaged as a tribute to the source text and its author, even if the parodist does not necessarily admit it. Though sometimes akin to 'an ironically thumbed nose',[44] parody contributes to the value of the text it transforms. Referring to another text, it favours a cultural sharing between writer and reader, who are linked by complicity, like players. And as the device is playful, parody implies not only recreation – that is, the creation of something new – but also recreation in which both writer and reader may enjoy themselves.

CHAPTER 2

A Version of an Irish Myth: 'Cathal's Lake'

The last story in the collection *Fishing the Sloe-black River* is 'Cathal's Lake'. This position at the end of the book is in keeping with the recurrent motif of completion in the text. Indeed, the plot is not only situated at the end of a week and at the end of a month but also at the end of a year. On Sunday 29 December (of an unspecified year) in Northern Ireland, a teenager is shot dead by a British soldier. He is the tenth victim of the year. During the funeral but in another part of the country, for the tenth time that year, Cathal is digging the soil to exhume a swan and mysteriously let it go.

> With the mound piled high and the hole three feet deep, Cathal sees the top of a white feather. A tremble of wet soil. 'Easy now', he says. 'Easy. Don't be thrashing around down there on me.' He digs again, a deep wide arc around the swan, then lays the shovel on the ground and spread-eagles himself at the side of the hole … He reaches down into the hole and begins to scrabble at the soil with his fingernails … The clay builds up deep in his fingernails. The bird is sideways in the soil.
>
> He reaches down and around the body and loosens the dirt some more, but not enough for the wings to start flapping … He lays his hands on the stomach and feels the heart flutter. Then he scrabbles some more dirt from around the webbed feet. With great delicacy Cathal makes a tunnel out of which to pull the neck and head. With the soil loose enough he gently eases the long twisted neck out and grabs it with one hand. 'Don't be hissing there now.' He slips his other hand in around the body. Deftly he lifts the

swan out of the soil, folding back one of the feet against the wing, keeping the other wing close to his chest. He lifts the swan into the air, then throws it away from him.

'Go on now, you little upstart.'[1]

Human beings have a limited life on earth. This is why each birth involves a death. Here it is the other way round: each death involves a birth. The gift of life is responsive to each death, the number of swans on the lake being the same as the number of victims killed in one year. This strange gesture makes the protagonist an obstetrician with special training in how to care for the soil: he helps in the birth of birds and allows them to come to life. The story develops the dialectics of death and (re)birth, completion and beginning. With its reference to the creative primordial times, it can be considered as a myth, as defined by Mircea Eliade:

> A myth narrates an event which took place at the dawn of the Great Time, in the holy time of the 'beginnings'. In other words, a myth narrates how, through the prowess of Supernatural Beings, reality – whether it is a fragment of it or cosmic reality – came into existence ... A myth is always an account of a 'creation': it reports how something started to be.[2]

This definition is interesting as regards Cathal's ritual, religious and creative gesture, but also concerning the specific notion of 'literary myth', which, in the present case, goes back to original Irish folklore and mythology.

In *Understanding Colum McCann*, John Cusatis reports that 'Cathal's Lake' was completely misunderstood by its first readers: 'McCann wrote the story while auditing a creative writing class at the University of Texas and "everybody hated it". The instructor, he said "didn't get it", asking whether the protagonist was "a magician".'[3] True, the last story could seem out of place in the collection as it appeals to magic and mystery, unlike the diegetic situations of the other narratives, which are quite realistic. According to Cusatis, many readers did not catch on to this magic story because they did not see that it was connected to Irish mythology.

The prints of the Children of Lir

'Cathal's Lake' can be read as a version of a story that dates approximately from the fifteenth century and is largely based on an earlier legend, 'The Fate of the Children of Lir' ('Oidheadh Chloinne Lir') (included as an appendix in the present book).[4] Since the dawn of time, this story has been resumed, revisited and rewritten – so much so that a group of versions with a common, invariant pattern emerges. The literary myth is a narrative that transcends the individual text to be found in its different versions. As regards the story of the Children of Lir, it is taken up with variations by Irish writers such as Thomas Moore,[5] Lady Gregory,[6] Marie Heaney,[7] Greg Delanty[8] and, in this case, Colum McCann. Considered as a whole, their versions form a literary myth.

Reading 'The Fate of the Children of Lir' together with McCann's story 'Cathal's Lake' makes it possible to notice that both pieces of writing share many common features, such as their characters – which are sometimes human beings, sometimes enchanted swans – and the motifs of hatred, jealousy, violence, innocence and sacrificed youth against a background of political chaos in Ireland.

Many anthropologists, such as Claude Lévi-Strauss, maintain that the myth, with its supra-human beings, shares the same contents and themes as the tale, and that there is no real difference between them. The classification of genres is here all the more complex as 'Cathal's Lake' is identified as a short story given its presence in the collection. As a result, the question of the distinctions between myth, tale and short story – that is, if there are any – cannot be evaded.

In his *Morphology of the Folktale* (1928), Vladimir Propp analyses the formal features of Russian tales. Despite their apparent diversity, tales revolve around a small number of constant functions and roles. All of these functions and roles are not present in every tale, but no tale can be told without using at least some of these basic units: initial situation, departure, short time of happiness, misfortune, villainy (murders and trickery), information about the villainy divulged, counteraction (receipt of a magical item, prolonged struggle, progressive relief, reparation).[9] These elements form the deep structure of the tales, and they are assumed by Propp to be universal. Interestingly, they are also present in 'Cathal's Lake', which has not only motifs in common with tales but also a similar structure.

At the beginning of the story, Cathal is described as a fifty-six-year-old man, 'a big farmer with a thick chest',[10] who lives in isolation. Indeed, he is clearly depicted as separated from other humans. Loneliness is, according to Propp, a major characteristic of the tale, a specific feature that Bruno Bettelheim also mentions: 'The fairy-tale hero proceeds for a time in isolation … [he] is helped by being in touch with primitive things – a tree, an animal, nature'.[11] Cathal is the only character of the plot whose isolation is all the more blatant because he only talks to his dog or to swans, as he does not meet any other human being. His lonely condition favours his fertile imagination, illustrated by his mental pictures – 'he imagines',[12] 'he thinks'[13] – or his conjectures introduced by 'maybe' or 'perhaps', which are recurrent adverbs in the text.[14] This loneliness is accentuated by the character's environment. In the first page of the story, the day is described as 'sad', the street as 'grey'.[15] This combination of sadness and greyness contributes to providing a general effect of monotony and melancholy, which is increased by the rain[16] – hence the protagonist's sighs.[17] Cathal's ordeal, like that of the Children of Lir, seems to be a long-lasting one, as he remarks about the time he spent digging: 'All these years of digging. A man could reach his brother in Australia, or his sister in America, or even his parents in heaven or hell if he put all that digging together into one single hole.'[18] Of course, once again Cathal's tragic destiny does not superimpose only on the fate of the Children of Lir but also on that of the children of Northern Ireland, whose untimely deaths cannot but spark off anger, wailing and revolt among their relatives.[19] This motif of working the soil can be read as an allusion to Seamus Heaney's poetry, in which the term 'digging' is recurrent. Yet the word is used in its traditional realistic sense by the Irish poet, particularly when he watches his father digging for peat, whereas Cathal is involved in an unusual activity when he makes a hole in the earth. As he can give or restore life at will so mysteriously, Cathal, in accordance with the etymology of his name,[20] runs counter to the laws of nature and stands for some force of opposition. Is it because, like the Children of Lir, he is under the influence of magical powers? Has anyone cast a spell on him before the beginning of the plot? The last paragraph of the story leads us to believe so: 'Every man has his own peculiar curse.'[21] Besides, Cathal, who claims to be 'cursed to dig',[22] considers digging the soil as a real chore as it prevents him from doing more exciting activities.[23] This curse to dig the soil is, once more, anchored in the mythical time of the beginnings – more precisely in Judaeo-Christian tradition.[24] Working the land is indeed a punishment imposed on Adam, who listened to his wife and ate the forbidden fruit: 'The Lord God said to the man: "accursed shall be the ground on your account. With labour you shall win your food from it all the days of your life."'[25] This curse is clearly echoed by the story, Cathal's words – 'Christ, the things a man could be doing now if he wasn't cursed to dig' – being like an answer to God's punishment.[26] As the Children of Lir are bound to keep the shapes of swans for nine hundred unhappy years, Cathal seems to be destined to dig as long as the conflict lasts. This long ordeal is supposed to come to an end when enchantment is broken by reconciliation. Indeed, according to the tale, the wedding of 'the Woman from the South and the Man from the North' will lift the curse. By the same token, it is highly likely that once peace is established in Ireland, Cathal will not need to dig anymore. This curse does not seem to be imposed on Cathal only but on all of his fellow countrymen. Indeed, nobody can deny that, in those days, youngsters who grew up in so dangerous an environment as Northern Ireland – where they could be killed at any time – were also somehow the victims of bad luck.

The task performed by Cathal counterpoints the preceding mindless acts of violence. Like Bodb in the tale, he counteracts the evil spell and seems to perform a similar magical transformation. Cathal's shovel is his Druid wand. Playing the role of a helper and donor, he treats birds carefully, brings them calm and peace, and allows them to come to life. He deals gently with them, and makes sure that he does not hurt them as the shovel sinks into the soil. Once he reaches the bird, he scrabbles in the dirt and lifts the swan out of the soil with great care. His work is rewarded by the beauty he digs out of the soil. The swans he takes care of are symbols of resurgence. They evoke ancient myths and are reminiscent of the phoenix in particular. They do not die, but are born or reborn. Then they migrate in their first year to continue their lives elsewhere.

In the legend, Mochaomhog soothes the birds' sufferings. By the same token, Cathal allows them to glide by peacefully. After the fear, hatred and killings generated by the Troubles, the casualties turned into swans enjoy life in a comforting community, every member of which strives to make room for the newcomer. Unlike the characters they represent – who used to kill one another – swans 'never seem to quarrel'.[27] These victims of violence are liberated from their fatal conditions. Cathal digs them up and leaves them on the lake, the water of which is comparable to the bath of baptism.[28] They stay for a while on the lake before taking their flight at the dawn of a new year: 'In two days, the whole flock will leave.'[29] Why do they stay for one year? Where do they go? These questions remain unanswered, and the story goes on with a new reference to the curse, as Cathal may have to dig the soil again and again as long as the Troubles are not over: 'The digging may well have to begin all over again.'[30] A new year brings hope for the end of violence, for a peace agreement in Northern Ireland. Cathal will then be released from his curse; he will not have to dig anymore.

In 'Cathal's Lake', the Northern Irish conflict is clearly depicted as the curse, the opposing force and the crystallisation of hate and jealousy embodied by the villain Aoife in the mythological tale. The victims of violence are young Irish people who die in their human lives in order to rise again in the shape of swans, just like the victims of the mythological story. Lastly, these characters are helped and soothed by compassionate benefactors, Cathal's role being similar to Lir's, Bodb's or Mochaomhog's.

Between reality and fantasy

The underlying presence of these mythological themes raises the issue of the generic classification of the text: 'Cathal's Lake' is not only inspired by a tale but also includes outlandish and fantastic subjects, magical items and evil spells, which are characteristic of the genre. Furthermore, 'Cathal's Lake' exemplifies the formal features that Propp regards as typical of the folk tale. As a result, 'Cathal's Lake' clearly resembles a tale.

The text, however, is inserted in a collection of short stories and is supposed to be considered as such. Besides, the story depicts the reality of a situation, as with any other text in the book. Indeed, its diegesis is deeply anchored in the realistic context of Northern Ireland, as illustrated by the names of characters (Cathal) and of places ([London]Derry, Garvagh), but also by the scenery of a lake in the rain, or the ways and customs relating to everyday life.[31] The Troubles are realistically represented as well, particularly through concrete details of the belligerents' military equipment[32] and coercive intimidatory measures, such as punishments imposed on traitors that consist in the covering of their bodies in tar and feathers[33] or injuring them in the knees by shooting.[34] Although Cathal is living in an isolated house in the middle of nowhere, he is connected to the tragic events of the world around him, particularly through the medium of his radio, which regularly informs him of new killings. All of these details denote particular attention to exact documentation to get the facts right, or at least plausible, and thus contribute to making the text a short story. Nevertheless, there is nothing realistic about humans being turned into swans. Such metamorphoses evoke the magic universe of the fairy tale.

Undeniably, a text like 'Cathal's Lake' is difficult to define: the boundary between tale and short story is blurred. The two genres are barely distinguishable: both of them are elusive forms when it comes to classification. Although the short story is most of the time realistic, are there not also fantastic stories with supernatural themes? Conversely, as a rule the tale concentrates on strange and mysterious events, but 'the term has often been applied to almost any kind of narrative, whether of fictitious or actual events'.[35] Many titles of nineteenth-century collections prove that stories and tales are interchangeable terms: Hawthorne's short stories were collected in *Twice-told Tales* (1837), and Edgar Allan Poe, who was regarded as the originator of the modern short story, wrote *Tales of the Grotesque and the Arabesque* (1839), not to mention Pushkin's *Tales of Belkin* (1830) or Flaubert's *Trois Contes* (1877), which are nothing else but short stories. McCann himself does not see a huge difference among literary genres.[36] Therefore as each form cannot be clearly distinguished, 'Cathal's Lake' is to be considered as a particular text that introduces mysterious elements, even if it remains very much based on reality. The narrative thus suggests a renewed view of the world in which mystery, irrationality and strangeness are taken into account. Reality is thus transformed and invested by active subjectivity. 'Cathal's Lake' is to be considered as a compromise between tale and short story, and which depicts an alternate, paradoxical universe juxtaposing realism and fantasy. The latter is not the former's opposite but, rather, its other side. Combining the tragic events of the Northern Irish Troubles with the mysterious stories of Celtic mythology, 'Cathal's Lake' establishes a dual universe where realistic and fantastic styles coexist and keep questioning each other. The text shows the author's irony, but also his desire to overstep any opposition between reality and fantasy, history and myth, rationality and irrationality. McCann increases the porosity of the boundary between tale and short story, and accentuates their elusiveness. The text can thus be considered as a short story that is the product of a tale to such an extent that it becomes a tale itself. With so many characteristics of each genre, 'Cathal's Lake' is to be envisaged both as a tale *and* a short story.

Hybridisation, one of the characteristic features of postmodernism, favours exchanges and borrowings to make boundaries more flexible, and advocates border crossing: Edward Said argues in favour of what he calls 'the supervening actuality of "mixing", of crossing over, of stepping beyond boundaries, which are more creative human activities than staying inside rigidly policed borders'.[37] Postmodernism provides links between literature and history, fiction and reality, but also between different genres.[38] This is why there is no use trying to classify a text in a determined category. It seems to be relevant, however, to envisage 'Cathal's Lake' in the postmodern perspective of magic realism.

Magic realism mingles and juxtaposes realistic and fantastic components. Its precise observation of reality is combined with elements of myth and fantasy. The two worlds are inextricably intertwined. 'Cathal's Lake' perfectly fits into this kind of fiction, as it blends the political issues of the real world with the magic of Celtic legends. This intermingling and overlapping revive the Irish tradition of Celtic Renaissance that also established a hybrid universe inspired both from contextual reality and local mythology.

This dissolution of barriers is a characteristic feature of the Celtic world. Indeed, many Western intellectuals of the nineteenth century, in their aim to define the specificities of Celtic literatures, emphasise this ambivalence. For Matthew Arnold, the Celtic passion for nature stems from its 'mystery'. It adds 'charm and magic' to nature because imagination or melancholy, which he considers as characteristics of the Celtic world, are 'emotive, rebellious, uncontrollable reactions to the despotism of reality'.[39] Likewise, Ernest Renan combines imagination, mystery and magic with Celticism when he maintains that the Celtic race is deeply in 'love with nature and its magic, but feels sad when man can hear nature speak about his origins and destiny'.[40] And William Butler Yeats establishes his work in a specific political context and simultaneously describes local folklore, legends and myths, thus reviving sluggish cultural identity and asserting his unconditional love for his native land.

Thus in 'Cathal's Lake', McCann goes back to his forefathers' imaginary Ireland. According to Miranda Jane Green's study on Celtic myths, the lake is a dwelling place for spirits, a thoroughfare between the earthly world and the other world.[41] The two lands can be reached by means of the lake. Spirits and humans can move freely between them in the form of a swan. Swans are thus the emblems of the passageway from one world to another; they symbolise the upper state of the being who is gradually released before going back to the supreme principle behind all things. The time they spend on Cathal's lake prepares them for this world of magic, music and enchantment known as *Tír na nÓg*, the land where people cut down by death in the prime of youth remain eternally young, just like Wilfred Owen, the English poet mentioned in the story,[42] who becomes the symbol of all the young victims of conflicts as he was killed on the battlefields of the First World War when he was just twenty-five years of age. Cathal's lake is a place of purification, the anteroom of this enchanted, timeless universe where wisdom, peace, beauty, harmony and immortality can be fully enjoyed.

Moreover, as he combines realism with mystery, McCann assumes and exploits the Yeatsian heritage in a particular way. Indeed, Cathal has a gift: his mind visualises fellow countrymen who have just passed away. At the beginning of the narrative, he has a mental picture of the young man's age and look, and of the way he died: 'Cathal coughs up a tribute of phlegm to the vision.'[43] The term *vision* is significant. Indeed, it is present in the titles of the works published by distinguished writers of the Irish Literary Revival: Lady Gregory wrote *Visions and Beliefs in the West of Ireland*[44] and William Butler Yeats explained his 'mythology' in *A Vision.*[45]

Visions of everlasting Ireland

'Cathal's Lake' not only alludes to Lady Gregory's arrangement of the Children of Lir but also implicitly evokes Yeats' universe and actually bears several striking similarities to his verse; indeed, repeatedly, the swan and its luminous plumage is immortalised by the poet as the noble, stately symbol of everlasting Ireland. In some of his poems written between 1919 and 1923 – that is, at the heart of the 'Troubles' – Yeats gives a contrasting image of the white bird's quiet and graceful purity against a background of dramatic events in Ireland:

- 'The Wild Swans at Coole' portrays a beautiful, mysterious world; Coole Lake thus stands comparison with Cathal's Lake. By the water-side, the poet, in a melancholy mood, watches the swans glide by, ponders over his own weakening, over the exhaustion of his artistic inspiration, and exclaims: 'And now my heart is sore',[46] words that Cathal, deep in his thoughts, could take up in front of the birds. The two men witness acts of extreme violence, realise that everything comes to an end, and meditate upon their own mortal condition. The swans, on the contrary, seem to defy time – 'their hearts have not grown old'[47] – like the victims of terrorism who, killed in their youth, do not have the good fortune to get old. Besides, the two texts end with the swans' flight, a metaphor for a free Ireland.

- The motif of violence in Ireland is also noticeable in Yeats' 'Leda and the Swan', a poem focused on the brutal encounter between Leda and Zeus, a magician god who introduces himself as a swan to better approach the girl he woos. From this union four children came, including twins, thus similar siblings to the Children of Lir. And the poem ends with a panoramic view of destruction: 'The broken wall, the burning roof and tower/ And Agamemnon dead'.[48] In this poem, Yeats mingles realism and fantasy: Leda's rape can be interpreted as an allegory of territorial conquest. The myths of ancient Greece, together with the myths of Ireland and the poet's personal ones, stand for the poetic approach of an interrogation of the connections between the natural and supernatural, as Jacqueline Genet emphasises.[49]
- Lastly, a swan is also present in 'Nineteen Hundred and Nineteen' and reaches Heaven: 'Some moralist or mythological poet/ Compares the solitary soul to a swan'.[50] The poet, however, far from losing his way in imaginary or dreamlike reflections, does not lose contact with his real environment, as the very title of the poem testifies, 1919 being the starting point of the Irish War of Independence. On the contrary, he becomes outraged by the escalating violence between the IRA and the Black and Tans. According to him, the world is on the road to ruin if it gets tangled up in the spiral of violence: 'Violence upon the roads: violence of horses'.[51] Directly confronted to the British colonising policy, the poet perceives the prefiguration of anarchy in his country and extends it to universal dimensions, as violence is a common feature of all warring nations.

According to the same metaphoric extension of a particular situation, McCann's choice to draw inspiration from an Irish legend is significant: Lir's dislocated family, whose members are separated after acts of violence, can be interpreted as the mirror of the Northern Irish nation, which is also dislocated by hatred, jealousy and revenge. McCann may have chosen to connect 'Cathal's Lake' to 'The Fate of the Children of Lir' because he perceives in the story of this mythological family an allegory of Northern Irish society as a whole: victims of mindless, long-standing violence, the children of Northern Ireland meet the same cruel, unfair fate as the Children of Lir.

No one can deny that the partition of Ireland occurred in violence and dislocation, too. Dislocation is a term that suggests the division of a unity into different parts. It is thus adapted to colonial experience and particularly the separation of the six counties from the rest of the insular territory. This is why, according to Seamus Deane, 'almost all Irish novelists are concerned with the varieties of social or political dislocation which are an inevitable product of the country's history'.[52] The typical example of dislocation is the city called Derry by republicans and Londonderry by unionists. Two names for one place highlight the tensions between the two sides. This city symbolises violence as it witnessed significant population segregation and suffered extensive bomb damage during the Troubles. Interestingly, in 'Cathal's Lake', the narrator seems to care about showing no prejudice, as he uses both names: Derry[53] and Londonderry.[54]

The disastrous effects of the acts of terrorism visualised by Cathal vouch for the fact that murderous violence relentlessly corrupts people's everyday lives. As a result, the Northern Irish population is dislocated and deterritorialised. If citizens wish to escape chaos, they have to leave; Cathal's brother lives in Australia, his sister in America.[55]

On the one hand, dislocation describes the process of emigration and settlement of people not only after colonial invasion but also in the post-colonial era. It evokes all those people who dispersed and settled in a place where everything is to be built. On the other hand, the term also describes the personal dismantling and mental break-up that can be observed among colonised people as a result of the coloniser's disparaging attitude towards them. Psychiatrist Frantz Fanon mentions these cases of psychotic disorder in which the whole personality is dislocated once and for all.[56] In order to represent dislocation properly, McCann could not make a better choice than magic realism, which implies a change of positions, a loss of reference points. The fate of a mythological family allegorically interpreted as a whole nation appeals to an aesthetic of magnification, which is a typical feature of magic realism. Furthermore – as proven by Latin American writers who contributed to the success and development of this hybrid universe – magic realism particularly flourishes in provincial areas that are marginalised by dominant cultures. This kind of fiction thus becomes a postcolonial phenomenon.

As McCann revives the myth of the Children of Lir and revisits Yeatsian motifs in 'Cathal's Lake', he illustrates that he does not place his native land on the periphery of a dominant culture but, on the contrary, rehabilitates it at the heart of the debate. As Neil Corcoran emphasises in his study of Yeats' influence on the writers who have succeeded him – a group McCann is part of – 'Irish literature is the scene of an intertextuality in which Ireland is itself read.'[57] Like Yeats' poems, 'Cathal's Lake' shows that the present of the nation cannot be conceived if its past is not taken into account, and that reality cannot be fully apprehended and understood if it is not enriched with some irrational elements.

In the middle of surrounding chaos, Yeats found consolation in art: even if works of art are destroyed, man will always be able to create other ones. Cathal is somehow the emblem of the artist who responds to the ugliness of the world by the beauty of the dream: he gives life to some birds that are asleep in the earth. As sordid as it may be, everyday life is a source of artistic inspiration. Because an Irish boy dies on the street when a plastic bullet slams into his chest, Cathal resorts to the irrational and digs up a swan from the mud of creation. In his aesthetic purpose to release beauty, the artist has to cover the human condition in its whole, including its corruption and confusion. To some extent, Cathal is thus the twin of McCann himself and, more widely, the twin of any Irish writer who focuses on the surrounding violence he witnesses. Cathal is then given a new dimension: he represents the Irish artist who draws inspiration from the environment around him. The story can be read as a metaphor of artistic creation. As Seamus Heaney compares his own pen with the spade his father used to dig the soil and cut the turf, McCann likens his internationally known books to swans taking their flights to cover the whole world. His works, like any work of art, provide life, beauty, dreams and consolation. They respond to the strong desires of warring nations for poetry and magic.

CHAPTER 3

The Intertext or the Reflection of Dislocated Ireland: *Fishing the Sloe-black River* and *Everything in this Country Must*

Many theorists have tried to understand why the short story has flourished so much in Ireland. The connection with oral storytelling is one of the most relevant hypotheses: the short story takes its roots in a land where the spoken word has always been valued. As Declan Kiberd remarks: 'To a greater or lesser extent, each short story writer has been conditioned by the Gaelic tradition of storytelling.'[1] On the one hand, the short story permits a kind of familiarity between the writer and his reader, like the oral storyteller and his audience. On the other hand, the short story is a form you may listen to, and its length conforms to the span of attention that a listener may give to an oral narrator. According to Edgar Allan Poe, a piece of literature should be like a piece of music, 'brief enough for the single uninterrupted session'.[2]

Oral tradition is indeed particularly present in Ireland. As the country is geographically located on the edge of Europe, its inhabitants have always been interested in otherness and known 'the islander's eagerness for news from abroad'.[3] This 'otherness' not only means foreign countries but also the imaginary universe of folklore. Indeed, fairies, leprechauns and all kinds of legendary characters were actual sources of inspiration for many Irish storytellers. Besides, in chaotic periods, particularly under the colonial yoke, the spoken word remained the only means of preserving anything resembling national identity, and the act of speech was the only index of personal value and collective power. With songs and stories, Ireland could express its character.

Nevertheless, it has not always been possible for Irish artists to express themselves freely. Repeatedly throughout history they were silenced. For example, from 1922 onwards, the Irish Free State established a severe censor-ship policy that operated for several decades. And yet throughout this period many books of short stories were published in Ireland. Short-story writers are like oral storytellers: they express themselves against all the odds, even when they are incited to silence.

Like the traditional folk song, the short story thus perfectly reflects the features of the society in which it flourishes, so making it Ireland's national art form.[4] When they are collected in one volume, short stories make a book, which is a juxtaposition of different texts separated by a white page. A book of short stories is thus segmented like a broken mirror, and somehow matches the dislocated island fractured by partition. Here, again, the genre reflects the features of Irish society.

As far as McCann's short stories are concerned, they are all the more fragmentary as they contain many mentions, quotations or allusions, and repeatedly refer to texts written by other writers. The intertextual process mirrors dislocation in the literary field: inserting somebody else's text into one's own amounts to cutting, interrupting and breaking up both of them. As it perfectly fits in with Ireland and its history, with the genre of the short story and the process of intertextuality, the motif of dislocation is central to McCann's work. It is indeed a feature of the author's reality, of the narrative context, and of the character's universe. This threefold articulation – Ireland, short story, intertext – is relevant and helpful in our approach to McCann's fiction.

Individual dislocation

The dislocation of Ireland by colonial policies is depicted in many stories, particularly in the collection *Everything in this Country Must.* Indeed, the three stories of the book are all set in Northern Ireland. They focus on the troubles and tensions increased by the British presence in the North, on the disagree-ments about the Battle of the Boyne – whether it should be commemorated or not – and on the tragic outcome of the hunger strikes of republican prisoners in 1981. Northern Ireland is the focal point of the collection. The separation of the six Northern counties and their submission to an overseas authority dislocated the national territory and fuelled a long-lasting fratricidal conflict.

The three stories – the plots of which can be set in the last two decades of the twentieth century, a long time after the ratification of partition – vouch for the lasting tensions in the North. They depict divergent ideological, political and religious views, together with the hatred many Northern Irish citizens feel towards each other's distinctive groups. The system of colonial rule and its indelible sequels breaks up and dislocates not only the entire insular territory but also the national unity, which is metaphorically represented, on smaller scales, by families and individual characters, who are also divided among themselves or who witness the dislocation of their own bodies. For example, the protagonist's uncle in 'Hunger Strike', a member of the IRA who, by the side of Bobby Sands, refuses to eat, can be considered as the symbol of the whole nation. As a result of harsh colonial policies, his body suffers and dislocates, until death overcomes him. Several protagonists have bodies that do not form homogeneous wholes anymore. They can therefore be considered as emblems of the traumatic dislocation of the national unity. Like Northern Ireland, which is judged unable to manage itself, the narrator's father in 'Wood', who suffered a severe attack that left him paralysed, is depicted as being helpless and entirely dependent on his wife:

> Mammy washed her hands in the sink so Daddy wouldn't smell the wood and then she went in to wake him up and turn him so he wouldn't get sores on his body …
>
> She does that six times a day. First she tucks her hands in under his legs and she props them up with a pillow. Then she puts her hand under his back and she rolls him over. The first time she did it, he moaned. He shouted swear words and Mammy had to hold him down until he stopped, saying shush shush shush there there there love. Afterwards we went into his room and we sat on the bed beside him and said big long prayers and Daddy told us he was sorry for shouting like that, the devil got into his throat.
>
> Now he doesn't shout anymore. He just grits his teeth and looks straight ahead at the wall.[5]

The body suffers changes that spoil the way it usually works. It is made of different parts that are no longer controlled and coordinated. Likewise, Will's or Fergus' dislocated bodies[6] do not allow them to be autonomous and free to move as they want. In the story 'Along the Riverwall', the young protagonist's body is indeed completely crushed in a road accident: 'Collarbone broken, thirty forehead stitches, ribs cracked, and the third lumbar on the lower vertebrae smashed to hell.'[7] The body is literally dislocated when bones are forced out of their normal position. In such a state, Fergus cannot master it anymore, but necessarily requires somebody's help, which is implied here by the passive sentence and the receptive verb: 'When his bed was spun he could see out the window to a ripple of trees that curtsied down to the road.'[8] Symbolically, is not Fergus' dislocated body a metaphor of the division of the Irish territory, whose deprivation of autonomy is attracting a lot of unwanted attention? Lifeless, his limbs no longer respond to his brain's orders. Thus he becomes aware of all that he is not able to do anymore:

> 'How d'ya think I feel, I'm marvellous, just fucken marvellous',
> Fergus roared at the nurse one afternoon when the knowledge was
> settling in – no more slipstreaming the 45 down Pearse Street in
> the rain, or sprinting along by the brewery, slapping at dogs with
> the bicycle pump, dicing the taxis, swerving the wrong way up the
> street, no more jokes about women sitting on things other than
> the crossbar … or slagging matches along the quays with the lorry
> drivers, or simply just trundling down Thomas Street for a pint of
> milk.[9]

The recurrent phrase 'no more' emphasises the self-persuasion of the young man who is incited to realise that it is necessary to break up with the past, turn the page, live differently and envisage a new existence, as the Irish nation had to do it in other days. This mental progression leads Fergus to make a decision: he throws his bicycle into the river, as many Irish youngsters get rid of the past and consider the sufferings, victories, defeats and commemorations of their communities as empty of meaning.

The dark, gloomy river thus becomes the garbage dump for all that deserves to be forgotten. The River Liffey is reminiscent of the Lethe, the river of Hell, the waters of which, according to Greek mythology, allowed the dead souls who had drunk them to forget their lives on earth. The river becomes a place where large amounts of waste are left. It is witness to many spoiled possibilities, to many activities that are given up; as his father was unable to pay back the loan he had contracted to buy a fridge, the protagonist cannot ride his bicycle again. As a result, these objects, which keep reminding them of their incapacity, are thrown into the water.[10] Nevertheless, once he gets rid of all the spare parts of his bicycle, Fergus imagines that they are miraculously put together:

> Perhaps one day a storm might blow the whole bike back together
> again, a freak of nature, the pedals locking on to the cranks, the
> wheel axle slipping into the frame, the handlebars dropping gently
> into the housing, the whole damn thing back in one piece. Maybe
> then he can take a dive to the bottom of the slime and ride it again
> …[11]

This wish for the reformation of unity can be interpreted as a desire to reunify the now incapable parts of his body, but it may also represent the republican dream of integrity, of making the island a homogeneous whole again by joining together Northern Ireland and the Republic. It is certainly not by chance that the character who forms such pictures in his mind is called Fergus, a name suggestive of power, Fergus being a king of Ulster in Celtic mythology.

The dislocation of bodies is not always due to an accident, but it can also be the result of a typically Irish punishment, which is repeatedly mentioned in the stories: Cathal evokes an 'old man found on the roadside with his kneecaps missing';[12] Kevin remembers a female 'pusher':

> … she had ended up with bullets in both knees. After that he would
> listen to her coming along the street and the crutches struck the
> ground, a shrill metallic language. Late at night when she played
> her stereo he could hear the crutch tapping out a rhythm against
> the floor but, when she kept dealing, the vigilantes kicked her
> door down, put two bullets in her elbows and two more in her
> ankles for good measure, after which she disappeared altogether,
> and people said she'd gone to England where she was dealing from
> a wheelchair.[13]

Kneecapping was a method used in Northern Ireland, first by the IRA, then by Protestant paramilitaries. This violent punishment made its victims physically disabled for their lifetime. Actually, on both sides, retaliation kept on spreading dislocation.

These handicapped or insane characters, whose bodies or minds are dislocated, are lonely people who live on the fringes of society. They perfectly illustrate Frank O'Connor's belief that the short story is characterised by 'submerged population groups'.[14] These protagonists are anti-heroes whose bodies show the lasting damage left by traumatic events, as the scars they have on their faces testify: Flaherty has a cut at the top of his eye,[15] Osobe 'a tiny scar over his right eye',[16] Enrique 'a scar on his chin',[17] Andrew 'a big cut on [his] head',[18] Stevie is kicked by a horse above his eye,[19] while Kevin's uncle has 'a scar running a line of outrage across the bottom of his nose'.[20] The short stories depict the slices of life of isolated, marginal, subaltern characters who are not really involved in community life, which is typical of the genre.[21] As McCann explains in an interview, he is not interested in imposing a message or an ideology on his readers but in depicting the world as he perceives it, like a writer he admires very much, John Berger, who invents stories by drawing his inspiration from characters who are never allowed to speak because they are treated as outcasts.[22] Dislocation thus affects the entire diegetic universe, from the most vulnerable characters to the whole nation, not to mention the family unit. Indeed, orphan children,[23] but also young people who have broken off communications with their families after a quarrel, who do not see them anymore because they have migrated,[24] prove that domestic balance is seriously damaged. McCann's stories exemplify the absence of harmony among families; they are typical of Irish fiction, which, according to Colm Tóibín, is 'full of dislocation and displacement'.[25] Here, again, there is a close link between family and nation; indeed, considering the extent of population shifts, emigration also causes the dislocation of all types of communities.

National dislocation

Until the 1980s, many Irish people left their country for mostly economic reasons. The short story 'Fishing the Sloe-black River' raises questions that are related to this imposed migration: what is the future of Ireland if it is only peopled with elders who are doomed to fish a sloe-black, barren river? Ireland is like the football field and 'really need(s) some new blood in midfield'.[26] This hope of putting a brake on the massive emigration of the young Irish goes together with a nationalistic wish to 'fish' the six counties of Northern Ireland, the number of women on the riverside corresponding to that of the counties in the Republic – 'twenty-six of them'.[27] This desire, however, seems to be nothing else but wishful thinking, as the baskets of the twenty-six women remain empty. In the 1990s young Irish people stopped emigrating; with an unprecedented economic boom, Ireland welcomed the many foreigners attracted by the numerous job offers of the Celtic Tiger. These movements of men and women are represented in McCann's fiction through the individual destinies of some characters. Most of the time, these immigrants endeavour to forget their pasts and are not willing to narrate their personal experiences of displacement and dislocation. In 'Hunger Strike', the teenager questions Lithuanians settled in Ireland:

> Why did you come here?
> Oh, I really don't think about these things anymore.
> Why not?
> Because it's easier not to.[28]

This exchange sounds like an echo of a conversation between another teenager and a Japanese immigrant in Ireland in 'A Basket Full of Wallpaper', which is set prior to the Celtic Tiger period. The old Asian man, having found shelter in Ireland, refuses to give the reasons why he left his country, as his answers to the young man's questions show:

> 'Why did you come here?'
> 'So long ago.' … 'Don't remember. Sorry.'
> 'Were you in the war?'
> 'You ask lots of questions.'[29]

Faced with such reticence, the most eccentric rumours spread about this foreigner, who is said to be a victim of Hiroshima, a kamikaze pilot, a sadistic criminal, the son of an emperor, unless he is merely a wallpaper thief. The young protagonist and the village residents, who have never been used to coming in touch with people from other countries, associate the alien with evil, crime, illegality, whereas the poor old man does not seem to have anything to be ashamed of, given he is always humming and whistling. He merely lives as an honest worker and only wants to be left in peace. For the young man, being next to this foreign 'employer' is beneficial; indeed, although he knows nothing about the old-man's past, the protagonist takes an interest in another culture and, some years later, also has an experience abroad that makes even him lose some of his distinctive Irish characteristics. At the end of the story, the narrator is so integrated overseas that he is 'acquiring an English accent'.[30]

The social evolution of McCann's native country is mirrored by the diegetic universe. Dislocation is part of it. It is reflected in two directions – to and from Ireland – as changes of place are no longer imposed but deliberately chosen. Dislocation takes on the form of transplantation, of intentional movement, and a desire to break with the past. Unlike the previous generations, the characters of McCann's stories are attracted by foreign countries and deliberately live abroad. Just as the author himself chose to leave Ireland in order to discover the world,[31] they are intoxicated with independence, go and meet other people spontaneously, forge ties with Argentinians, Canadians and Americans. They do not feel they belong to one place, and therefore illustrate the concept of 'diaspora', as they consider themselves at home anywhere.

Since the early 1990s, this concept has been widely used to describe the process of emigration and settlement abroad of people born in Ireland. The term 'diaspora' designates not only the movement but also the members of one group who live in different parts of the world. Mary Robinson, the president of the Republic from 1990 to 1997, sought to place the diaspora at the centre of Irish consciousness, and demonstrated that living in Ireland was not necessarily a prerequisite for expressing Irish identity. The concept of diaspora gives the Irish a heightened sense of belonging to a worldwide community. It is no longer associated with collective trauma and exile. Therefore Irish identity is etymologically disseminated, displaced or dislocated. Contrary what it used to be, emigration is now intentional. The contemporary diaspora stems from a will to overcome nationalism and be part of a 'world citizenship'. Cosmopolitanism partakes of accepting oneself as a stranger and accepting the other as being like oneself – that is, a human being. It makes it possible to be free from national limitations and to make a home everywhere.

Although the narrator of the short story 'Around the Bend and Back Again' finds Ofeelia 'strange',[32] he strikes up a friendship with her and even puts himself in the wrong for her, since he lets her out of the psychiatric hospital where he is a nursing auxiliary. Transgression is a recurring motif in the collection: in addition to this protagonist, the stowaway,[33] the old man who steals clothes in a laundromat,[34] and the juvenile who has sex with a married woman and kills his rival[35] are all trespassers and law-breakers.[36] Borders are crossed and limits are constantly overstepped. In McCann's universe, strangeness is not uncanny but attractive. This is why his characters 'dis-locate', uproot themselves and move to distant countries. It is precisely because most of them can travel long distances and emigrate to the end of the world that they are so often compared to birds: one of them 'whistled like he had a bird in his throat',[37] another one's 'chest thumps like that of a small bird';[38] a character nods 'like a bird beginning to peck at a few crumbs lying on the ground',[39] and customers at the laundromat watch their clothes 'like nervous birds over crumbs'.[40] Some are described as hawks,[41] buzzards,[42] ducks,[43] others as robins,[44] wrens[45] or hummingbirds.[46] The typical character of McCann's fiction is a migratory bird, which is the subject of a meaningful comparison when it is unable to fly:

> Nearly all the kids, those forgotten blind children, the snotrags of society, the disenfranchised, the unseeing, had spent the night beating their brains against the walls, repeatedly, like birds with broken wings unable to get off the ground.[47]

The similarity confirms that the *raison d'être* of their existence is to be able to go from one place to another, whatever the reason they move and the means of transport they use. Mobility is a permanent theme in McCann's stories, as can be seen in the prepositions in their titles: through, along, around, from. Whether it is a matter of crossing, going along, around, into or out of a place, movements from one place to another are constant. The stories and their protagonists are thus made very lively and dynamic. The trips of the characters are justified by a desire to meet again a sister for the last time, to join a mistress, to steal clothes, to go to work, attend a wedding without enthusiasm, or protect oneself from acts of violence. McCann's characters travel by air, by ship or overland. The means of transport they use are varied: a pickup, a bicycle, a stolen motorbike, a wheelchair, a wheelbarrow, and they are even carried in the boot of a car. Transport is part of their lives. It is engraved on their bodies: one character had 'a pair of scars that ran like railroad tracks when he held his wrists together'.[48] A woman has 'maps of the west wrinkled on her skin'.[49] All of these characters seem to have no choice but to move, as if they were carried away on the current of the river mentioned not only in the title of the first collection but also in the first sentence of a great number of stories. The river is part of the familiar background of the protagonists. It is the emblem of transport, of movement, but also of contact and connection. As a result, the river is one of the common features linking the stories: it joins characters together and leads them to the open sea. Most of the protagonists were born in Ireland, work in the US, have love affairs with locals and foreigners. Their words and behaviours show that they care about other people, unlike their families.[50] They are characterised by travel, as is the writer himself.

Typical of the Irish diaspora, McCann is a globetrotter who crossed the US for two years, travelled in Latin America, and lived in Japan before going back to New York City, from where he regularly travels throughout the world. Travelling is a source of inspiration, a necessity in his creative process. Travelling and writing are so closely linked that travelling becomes writing and writing becomes travelling,[51] as the author explains: 'when I get into the fiction, that's when the madness emerges. And you're living with it a long time. Sometimes four hours a day. Sometimes eight hours a day, sometimes 20 hours a day, toward the end.'[52] Writing is travelling: it allows the writer to move, discover and remember, and, from then on, to create and imagine. It allows both writer and reader to escape from reality into another universe, all the more so as it establishes connections with other texts. McCann's writing invites readers to explore the large library of the world. This is why his work can be considered as transtextual,[53] more precisely intertextual, as it establishes 'copresence between two or several texts'.[54] This co-presence requires movement; besides, it implies cutting, taking and inserting excerpts into another context. The original meaning of the text quoted, mentioned or simply alluded to is thus transformed. Intertextuality partakes of deterritorialisation and reterritorialisation. It is some kind of dislocation prior to a new linking. It is both continuous and discontinuous. Using somebody else's text is extracting from it, and at the same time interrupting and fragmenting one's own by inserting the other one. Nevertheless, in spite of this discontinuity a new form of continuity is established between the quoted text and the quoting one.

As the present book proves, co-presence does not only characterise the short stories but also McCann's novels. Yet, as specified previously, these compositions of connected fragments that are collections of short stories are part of an aesthetics of discontinuity. They prove that they are characterised by dislocation not only because of their genre but also because of their intertextual features; indeed, the insertion of extracts written by others and the numerous collages and borrowings also partake of dislocation. McCann's short stories exemplify intertextual dislocation, the aesthetics of which is illustrated by those fragments borrowed from other texts that are reused in another context. As a result, they are not only 'mosaics of quotations'[55] but also mosaics of references and allusions, thus exemplifying a variety of degrees of assimilation and differentiation in the relation of co-presence between texts.

Intertextual dislocation: 'mosaics of quotation'

In McCann's stories, most quotations come from poems: in addition to reusing W.B. Yeats' lines in 'Stolen Child',[56] the first short story of the collection *Fishing the Sloe-black River* also borrows a quotation from a poem. 'Sisters' narrates Sheona's trip to her sister Brigid and their meeting. The two sisters are totally unalike: the elder one is mystic, anorexic and dying in a convent in Long Island, whereas the younger one is materialistic, full of life and takes advantage of worldly goods. Embarrassed to be a trespasser on the American territory and to knock at the door of a convent, Sheona recalls she was once implicitly compared to Mary Magdalene by the nuns of her teenage years, and relates:

> I walk towards the front entrance. Hold. Buckle. Swallow. The words of a poet who should have known: 'What I do is me. For that I came.' I rasp my fingers along the wood but it takes a long time for the heavy door to swing open.[57]

This line seems to emerge spontaneously in her mind. The quotation, given without any precision concerning its origin or author, turns out to be from a sonnet by Gerard Manley Hopkins titled 'As Kingfishers Catch Fire'. This poem is particularly appreciated by McCann, who reuses this title for one of his stories, as previously mentioned.[58] The poem dates back to 1877, the year Hopkins was ordained a priest.

> As kingfishers catch fire, dragonflies dráw fláme;
> As tumbled over rim in roundy wells
> Stones ring; like each tucked string tells, each hung bell's
> Bow swung finds tongue to fling out broad its name;
> Each mortal thing does one thing and the same:
> Deals out that being indoors each one dwells;
> Selves – goes itself; *myself* it speaks and spells,
> Crying *Whát I do is me: for that I came.*
>
> Í say móre: the just man justices;
> Kéeps gráce: thát keeps all his goings graces;
> Acts in God's eye what in God's eye he is –
> Chríst – for Christ plays in ten thousand places,
> Lovely in limbs, and lovely in eyes not his
> To the Father through the features of men's faces.[59]

Hopkins here develops the ideas of medieval theologians, such as Duns Scotus and Thomas Aquinas, for whom variety in the universe corresponds to God's desire: each thing has its *raison d'être* and its place in the divine plan. Each element of the creation is one link in the chain of beings that ranges from original chaotic emptiness to divine fullness. Anything, any creature, whether it is animal, vegetable or mineral, thus presents a facet of God's perfection. The existence of each of these components is therefore justified – hence the lines 'Each mortal thing does one thing and the same' and 'Crying *Whát I do is me: for that I came.'* The poem is a metaphorical questioning to which each creature answers with the specificity it was given by its creator. The universe of creation is thus a huge orchestra composed of innumerable instruments. In the short story, Brigid most probably adheres to this approach of a divine order of the world, although the text does not mention it explicitly. Indeed, she is a nun who is close to the poor and homeless, like the Irish saint to whom she owes her name. Sheona, on the other hand, is not part of the same orthodoxy. By making that line her motto – '*Whát I do is me: for that I came*' – she assumes what she is and what she does: she took the trouble to reach the convent to meet her sister and certainly means to achieve her aim. The steady monosyllabic rhythm of the line reveals the speaker's determination. Her words 'for that I came' play with the verb 'come', which in the story means to reach a particular point, whereas in the poem it has the meaning of coming into the world. The reunion of the two sisters after several years during which the relationship had been broken off resembles a new birth, a new beginning, a new existence. With the extract of this poem and its underlying philosophy, the short story implies that everyone has their own destiny and vocation, and can do something for the organisation of the world, whatever the ideal pursued. The sisters are not alike, but each of them has a part to play – a role, if not a mission – wherever they happen to be. At the end of the story, Sheona intends to stay by the side of her sister to support her, thus making amends for what she did not do with her dying father. Although the quotation only amounts to a few words, it evokes the whole poem and its original context, and thus invites the reader to detect the echoes between the texts.

McCann's second collection, *Everything in this Country Must*, is composed of three stories. The book includes hardly more than one quotation,[60] which can be read on the first page, since it is the epigraph. This short piece of writing is the 'quotation *par excellence*'[61] insofar as it is followed by its author's name and the title of the text it is taken from. It can thus be clearly identified as such. Besides, it is usually put at the beginning of the book, set apart from the main body of the text, as the white page between them emphasises. It has therefore something to do with dislocation. It remains outside the text and yet it is connected with it. *Everything in this Country Must* starts with a quotation from a poem by Paul Muldoon, 'Dancers at the Moy'. It is closely connected to the text, as it heralds the motifs developed in the three stories:

> Horses buried for years
> Under the foundations
> Give their earthen floors
> The ease of trampolines.[62]

To the last four lines of the poem about 'horses buried' responds the seminal sentence of the first story describing a horse caught in a river. The hectic movements of this drowning animal, struggling against the current, is the counterpoint to the static position of the horses in the poem 'buried for years under the foundations'. This echo between two voices evokes real or imminent death, a motif already implied in the title of the collection, the stories of which are set in a country where everything must die[63] – that is, the poet's birthplace, Northern Ireland. Muldoon's whole poem tackles themes that are exploited by McCann in the three stories: suffering, painful past, hunger or death. Written in 1973 in Northern Ireland – that is, at the height of the Troubles, a period of violent political tensions between British soldiers and republicans – the poem mingles history with myth when it mentions a local economic disaster. In the village where the poet grew up, Moy, County Armagh, rumour has it that some Greeks are coming to the fair to buy the horses they need for their war against the 'Regime of the Colonels'. Therefore Irish dealers bring a great number of horses to the fair so as to sell them. But, without their knowledge, peace has just been declared in Greece. As a result, no foreigner comes to the Moy. The place is soon swarming with abandoned famished horses that end up tearing one another to pieces. The disaster is transcended by time: as in a sacrificial ceremony, the bones of the horses buried under the house foundations incite the residents to dance – hence the title 'Dancers at the Moy'. The last lines of the poem, which McCann takes up at the beginning of his book, highlight the different strata of sufferings throughout the history of Northern Ireland. These historic or mythic catastrophes are sources of inspiration for Muldoon. The poem's rural background is transmuted by the surrealistic resources of folklore, parables and myths. In the Moy, a village renowned for its animal fairs, horses come flooding in from all over the island to be sold, whereas they are going to die, since 'everything in this country must'.[64] The four components – Northern Ireland, horse, river and death – are interconnected and shared by the stories and the poem, as shown by the lines preceding the ones McCann uses in the epigraph:

> The black and gold river
> Ended as a trickle of brown
> Where those horses tore
> At briars and whins,
>
> Ate the flesh of each other
> Like people in famine.[65]

In the field of intertextuality, the reference to the horses tearing one another to pieces is reminiscent of the chaos caused by Duncan's murder in Shakespeare's *Macbeth*. In the context of Irish history, it conjures up acts of cruelty, savagery, even cannibalism in times of famine. The darkness of the river, recalling the 'sloe-black river' of the first collection, mirrors this dismal universe. The black water is potentially lethal, as Katie, the protagonist of 'Everything in this Country Must', incidentally remarks: 'I put one foot on the rock in the river middle … I felt there would be a dying'.[66] The draft horse, a counterpoint to Muldoon's horses in the epigraph, is about to drown, its foreleg being trapped between rocks in the river. Ironically, just after being saved by the British soldiers, the horse is deliberately killed by Katie's father.

Water and horse are also associated in 'Wood', the second story of the collection. The young Andrew remembers seeing in newspapers some photographs of Protestant marches in Northern Ireland celebrating the Battle of the Boyne, the victory of William of Orange over the troops of James II on 1 July 1690:

> My favourite [photograph] was the two men in bowler hats and black suits and big thick ribbons across their chests. They were carrying a banner of the King on a white horse. The horse was stepping across a river with one hoof in the air and one hoof on the bank.[67]

The banner mentioned here probably duplicates an equestrian portrait of William III by Jan Wyck commemorating the landing at Brixham, Devon in 1688. Here, again, the association of horse and water is of ill omen. The commemoration of the battle of 1690 honours and remembers a victory that also meant the deaths of a great number of Catholics, which is shocking for Andrew's father though he is no Catholic himself: 'Daddy says he's as good a Presbyterian as the next, always has been and always will, but it's just meanness that celebrates other people dying.'[68] This refusal to support marches in commemoration of such episodes of Irish history incites the man, a joiner, to turn away orders connected with them. And yet now he is bedridden and unable to work, he does not know that his wife, anxious to bring in some money, agrees with the march organiser to secretly manufacture forty poles in the workshop with the help of her son Andrew, the young narrator.

Irony is omnipresent in McCann's collection. It also characterises Muldoon's universe. For example, the last four lines of the poem, quoted as an epigraph, show an ironically indifferent attitude among the Moy residents, who are dancing on the bones of dead horses, as on a trampoline. This extract is put by McCann at the beginning of his book because it condenses and reflects the universes of the poem and the collection. Both texts – written by Irish emigrants in the US and who observe the country they come from with distance – raise the issue of the way the living manage the sufferings endured by past generations. The epigraph incites the reader to see below the surface and to discover the hidden meaning of the text. The buried bones are like springs under the steps of the living – they give a rhythm to the poem and inspire artistic creation.

Intertextual dislocation: mosaics of references

Unlike the quotation, the reference does not literally resume the text it uses but makes mention of its writer, its title, one of its characters or one of its episodes.[69] Sometimes, only the writer's name is incidentally referred to: a Wilfred Owen book is tucked under a pillow,[70] a character reads Philip Larkin's poems,[71] another a play by W.B. Yeats.[72] Likewise, a specific place can explicitly refer to a writer: a Californian mountain evokes Jack Kerouac,[73] the Chelsea Hotel in New York is reminiscent of Brendan Behan,[74] and an Irish riverbank spontaneously recalls the memory of a poem by Patrick Kavanagh for Sheona, who narrates: 'naked on the side of a creek, I was quoting Kavanagh for some reason, my own love banks all green and rampant with leaves'.[75] Love banks, leaves and the colour green indeed turn out to be elements mentioned in the first line of Kavanagh's poem 'Canal Bank Walk': 'Leafy-with-love banks and the green waters of the canal'.[76]

By the same token, when he starts walking in the street, the protagonist of the short story 'Step We Gaily, On We Go', Danny Flaherty – an old Irish immigrant settled in New Orleans – remembers an essay by Henry David Thoreau, *Walking*:

> 'We should go forth', as an American poet once said, 'on the shortest journey, in the spirit of undying adventure, never to return.' But what would Thoreau know? He lived in a cabin by a lake all on his own. Flaherty, me boy, you've been reading too many books.[77]

Maybe it is precisely because he read 'too many books' that his mind is teeming with ideas, quotations and references. Indeed, his narrative is punctuated with slogans, advertisements, excerpts of old songs and Irish or American pieces of writing. When he realises he has forgotten his tweed cap in the laundromat from which he has just stolen a blouse, he retraces his steps and reaches the place, which leads him to recollect Irish cultural references:

> He shuffles towards the door, keeping his eyes down. Hup two. On the seat nearest the door he catches a glimpse of his grey tweed. Hallelujah and hail to the king. Grand job, Nora, as the saying goes. Nora being the girl that the bould Sean O'Casey left behind. He chuckles to himself. Here comes the Playboy of the Western World. Or was that Mr Synge? Onwards. Away. On yer bike. Quickly.[78]

In his inner monologue, Flaherty mentions plays, characters and writers of the country he left three decades earlier. Therefore he is not so sure that his references are reliable, all the more so as he is now not only an old man but also a former boxer who acknowledges that his nose was broken several times, which means that he was punched on the head. However, his hesitation is understandable as Nora is both a real woman belonging to the circle around the playwright O'Casey and a recurrent character in the drama of both O'Casey (Nora Clitheroe in *The Plough and the Stars*) and Synge (*Riders to the Sea* and *The Shadow of the Glen* both have Noras in their casts). A Nora can thus easily substitute herself for another Nora in Flaherty's failing memory, all the more so as O'Casey was greatly influenced by Synge. Be that as it may, *The Playboy of the Western World*, referred to here, does not include any Nora in its cast. Besides, this famous Irish play was written by John Millington Synge, not

Sean O'Casey. The old man obviously mixes up the two playwrights. Is this confusion a way to imply that famous names and titles are present in the collective memory of the Irish but that the texts are not read anymore? That the Irish people who are living abroad have no precise knowledge of the cultural specificities of their native soil?

Flaherty's mistake could also be interpreted as a warning against the possible end of the literary heritage, which may be supplanted by other, more popular media, such as Hollywood movies. In the psychiatric hospital where the story 'Around the Bend and Back Again' is set, the narrator, a male nursing auxiliary, is watching a female patient and relates: 'The way she just stares there out the window, you'd swear there was something on television in the bloody stars. Here we go with the Plough and the Stars, starring Tom bloody Cruise'.[79] The astonishing thing about this new reference to an Irish piece of writing – would the narrator be able to define it as such? – is that this play written by Sean O'Casey in 1926 was never made into a film. As a result, Tom Cruise has never been able to win fame in such an adaptation. The formal components of the reference – a title, a proper noun – are present, but they do not match, since there is no connection between them. Is this intentional? Is it a humorous way to debunk Irish cultural references? Or is there a mistake here? If it is so, whose mistake is it: the character's or the narrator's? As a matter of fact, Tom Cruise was very popular in the 1980s and 1990s, particularly when he played the leading part in *Top Gun*, a film with many spectacular manoeuvres involving Soviet and American fighter planes. As a result, it is possible to note in the narrator's words an ironic parallel between the slowness of the plough and the high speed of the plane in a starry decor. Furthermore, the stars are twice present in the title of the play, as the word 'plough' defines not only a piece of farm equipment for turning over the soil but also a group of bright stars. Lastly, as the mention of the famous American movie star immediately follows an allusion to the narrator's attraction for his patient – 'Dressing gown giving a bit of a peep there, right down to the brown of the nipple'[80] – a double entendre can be noticed here, as the narrator seems to be trying to find a sexual partner; in other words, 'cruising'. Such allusive references slightly change the intended meaning of these words, so that they mean what the speaker wants them to mean.

Nevertheless, when the work mentioned is not connected with its actual author, the reference is short-circuited. As anyone can experience in everyday life, some titles remain in the collective imagination but their authors are not precisely identified – perhaps because their works have not been read for a long time, if they ever have been by the particular character. Then these works turn out to be somewhat debunked and dislocated. Some characters – for instance, Flaherty – possibly do not remember their authors. Others do not know them because screen adaptations tend to supplant original written works. As a result, there is a change of focus that highlights the threat hanging over the book and the danger of replacing written pages with visual materials.

A similar gap can be seen in 'the wedding at Canaan'[81] that the priest mentions in his sermon. Canaan, Noah's son – who gives his name to a region in the Near East – has nothing to do with Cana, the town where, according to the Gospel, the first miracle of Jesus was performed. This episode is usually known as 'The Wedding at Cana'. Who is mistaken? Who changes Cana into Canaan? The author? The narrator? The character – the drunk priest confused about marrying a blind girl to a disabled veteran? Here, again, signifier and signified are disconnected, which is puzzling for the reader.

Intertextual dislocation: mosaics of allusions

The allusion is the minimal degree in the co-presence between two texts. It refers to another text in an indirect way. The allusion is implicit, suggestive and, consequently, more difficult to spot than any other intertextual device. It just refers to another text through some clues that are more or less detectable. The allusion does not say anything in a clear, direct way, but it can create closeness and complicity between the writer and the reader who is able to identify it. It depends much more on the reader's shrewdness than any other intertextual practices. The allusion can go unnoticed. It can also be suspected where nothing is alluded to. The perception of allusion is often subjective. This is how readers create a palimpsest as they progress in the text: they detect hidden meanings between the lines. Spontaneously, from inductive words, they freely associate words, characters or situations between the text they are reading and other texts they know, and thus establish rapprochements and connections by similarities.

In 'A Word in Edgewise', Eileen makes up her sister's face before the funeral. She recalls old memories:[82]

> Anyway, didn't Da get into awful conniptions over me knocking

the kitchen teapot over the night we came in from the dance hall? Smashed on the kitchen tiles, it did, with an awful racket … Anyway, talking of teapots, strange the way things change, isn't it? Used to be a teapot was a teapot. Nothing more and nothing less. Just teapots. But I was up and beyond in Dublin last week, baby-sitting little Kieran, his Mammy and Daddy away in London for an advertising conference. So, anyway, I took him for a walk down by the canal … we were throwing some bread to the ducks and all of a sudden little Kieran says to me, he says: 'Look at those teapots over there, Granny.' And him pointing to a couple of boys wrapped together like slices of bread underneath the Leeson Street Bridge, kissing in broad daylight. Teapots. I ask you, Moira. Apparently something to do with the way the spout curves.[83]

In addition to the sexual innuendo associating the spout with the turgescent penis, a literary allusion can be seen here. McCann's story evokes an episode in Joyce's *Ulysses* in which Leopold Bloom and Mrs Breen play a game that consists of using the word 'teapot' instead of another one, to let the audience take a guess at what is behind:

> BLOOM: Do you remember, harking back in a retrospective arrange-ment, Old Christmas night, Georgina Simpson's housewarming while they were playing the Irving Bishop game, finding the pin blindfold and thoughtreading? Subject, what is in this snuffbox?
> […]
> BLOOM: (*Meaningfully dropping his voice*) I confess I'm teapot with curiosity to find out whether some person's something is a little teapot at present.
> MRS BREEN (*Gushingly*) Tremendously teapot! London's teapot and I'm simply teapot all over me.[84]

Like Mrs Breen, Eileen – for whom the word 'teapot' only means 'homosexual' – associates the mysterious word with the capital city of England:

> They're going to enroll little Kieran in some private school on the outskirts of London. There's another one will grow up with an English accent. Dropping h's all over the place. A terrible shame.

> And he'll see more than his fair share of teapots over there, I'll tell
> you.[85]

The amusing insinuation and its veiled intertextual reference recall the very etymology of the word, 'allusion' being derived from *ludus*, which means 'play'.

Readers who are familiar with *Ulysses* can also detect another allusion to Joyce's novel in 'Breakfast for Enrique'. Like Bloom, the protagonist of the story, O'Meara, goes out to buy something to eat for breakfast. On the way, he thinks about his life with his partner, and appears romantic but also practical in his purchases, like Leopold Bloom, the main character of *Ulysses*, who, early in the morning, goes out shopping, then goes back home to cook and have breakfast with his wife Molly. Moreover, like Enrique, Molly is of Hispanic culture.[86] Besides, in both texts the protagonists prepare dishes not only for their lovers but also for cats: O'Meara in 'Breakfast for Enrique' describes 'a cat on the third floor across the street, jet black, with a dappled blue bandanna. It is forever cocking its head sideways and yawning in the window. Sometimes I bring home some sea trout and leave it on the doorstep of the house for the owner.'[87] This animal is reminiscent of Bloom's cat, which mews and brushes against the legs of his owner who is cutting a kidney for his breakfast. Here, again, allusion has something to do with dislocation, as the reading is full of meanders between subtleties.

On top of these analogies, 'Breakfast for Enrique' also indirectly refers to John Steinbeck's *Cannery Row*. The plots, characters and decors of the Irish story and the American novel show an allusive intertextual link between the two texts. 'Breakfast for Enrique' is set in a city of 'the California shore',[88] which is obviously San Francisco, as references to 'Geary Street'[89] and 'the steep hills of parked cars' show.[90] Steinbeck's novel is set at Cannery Row in Monterey, about sixty miles south of San Francisco. From 1920 to 1950, this area had a score of canning factories and industries. The local people were essentially fishermen or workers who put sardines into cans. O'Meara, the Irish protagonist of McCann's story, is a fish-gutter in San Francisco. This job is repetitive, unrewarding and often reserved for immigrants – more precisely, 'Wops and Chinamen and Polaks', as Steinbeck's novel puts it.[91] O'Meara is not only marginalised by his nationality but also by his homosexuality and his alleged laziness; referred to by the stereotype 'Paddy-boy',[92] he is also called 'bum-boy'.[93] This position of an outsider trying to integrate into a group hostile to him is also William's dilemma in Steinbeck's novel. As a watchman in a brothel, William is rejected by others who consider him to be 'a pimp'.[94]

Harassed at night by the ghost of his persecutors, O'Meara is a light sleeper. Like Mack, the protagonist of the American novel,[95] he rises early and immediately walks to the window to have a look outside. These characters who stand gazing at their environment give the narrators the opportunity to depict the gold light of the Californian coast:

> The light is like an old fisherman in a rain-slicked coat, come to look at Enrique and I, wrapped in our bedsheets.
>
> It's a strange light that comes this morning ... pushing its way through the gap and lying, with its smotes of dust, on the headboard.[96]

Daybreak favours dream and nostalgia in O'Meara, who is reluctant to go to the factory, unlike Steinbeck's characters, who run down to work as soon as the Cannery Row whistles scream. O'Meara, on the contrary, is determined to enjoy his breakfast with Enrique. This is why he goes 'to the deli, where Betty is working the counter':

> It's an old neighbourhood shop, the black and white floor tiles curled up around the edges. Betty is a large darkhaired woman ... Betty negotiates the aisles of the deli in a crabways manner, her rear end sometimes knocking down the display stands of potato crisps ... I move up and down the aisles, looking at prices, fingering the $3.80 in my pocket. Coffee is out of the question, as are the croissants in the bakery case, which are a dollar a piece ... I reach for a small plastic jar of orange juice and a half-dozen eggs in the deli fridge, two oranges and a banana in the fruit stand, then tuck a loaf of French bread under my arm ... Betty sells loose cigarettes at 25 cents each. Two each for Enrique and I will do nicely.
>
> [...]
>
> 'Can I get four of your smokes please?' I ask.
>
> Betty reaches up above her for a box of Marlboros Lights and slides them on the counter, towards me. 'My treat', she says. 'Don't smoke 'em all in one place, hon'.[97]

Interestingly, Betty's deli is the mirror of Lee Chong's neighbourhood shop, which is described on the first page of Steinbeck's novel.[98]

Both texts depict common groceries, such as delis or drugstores, in working-class areas to emphasise their customers' mediocre standard of living. Indeed, the characters have low incomes and are obliged to limit their expenditures. In this respect, both texts minutely describe what their meals are made of, and thus highlight the fact that the protagonists attach a lot of importance to food. In the deli, O'Meara remembers the breakfasts of his younger days:

> Walking down the rows of food, other breakfasts come back to
> me – sausages and rashers fried in a suburban Irish kitchen with an
> exhaust fan sucking up the smoke, plastic glasses full of orange juice,
> cornflakes floating on milk, pieces of pudding in circles on chipped
> white plates, fried tomatoes and toast slobbered with butter.[99]

The stereotype of Ireland as a country of famine is debunked here; Ireland is a place of substantial meals in the protagonist's memory. On the contrary, in the diegetic present, now he is settled in the US, O'Meara has to make do with very little, as the extract quoted above shows. Clichés are undermined in these realistic narratives, which depict the other side of the American dream.

Poverty also characterises the residents of Cannery Row. 'Whores, pimps, gamblers, and sons of bitches'[100] are so many rejects of American society. Even 'Doc' lives in a tumbledown. The doctor's presence in Steinbeck's novel counterpoints the patient's in McCann's story: Enrique is apparently suffering from AIDS and would obviously need a doctor's constant attendance. Likewise, the homosexuality of the story's characters also applies to the relationship between Frankie and the doctor. After having stolen objects to offer them to 'Doc', Frankie is questioned by the policeman in the doctor's presence and confesses that he loves him.[101]

Both texts describe the wretched lives of dropouts who continuously seek relief in drugs and alcohol. As a result, these characters witness total chaos when they wake up:

> I climb naked out of bed … The floor is cold and I step carefully.
> Last night I smashed the blackberry jamjar that used to hold our
> money. The glass splayed in bright splinters all around the room …
> I bend down and pick up the large pieces of shattered glass from the
> floor … I flick a tiny shard of glass off my finger.[102]

The somewhat sordid ordinariness of these existences is transformed at the end of the short story by the image of the starfish and its capacity to regenerate. This animal – a symbol of creative fertility and revival – closes the text with a note of optimism and hope. Likewise, *Cannery Row* mentions these 'complicated and interesting animals',[103] and explains the way they eat: 'when the tide goes out … starfish squat over mussels and limpets, attach their million little suckers and then slowly lift with incredible power until the prey is broken from the rock. And then the starfish stomach comes out and envelops its food'.[104] Beyond this naturalistic description, the reference to the starfish in both texts is significant. When they mention their strength and intelligence and their ability to heal their wounds, the two narratives imply that these sea animals are endowed with the same qualities as the human protagonists, who finally manage to survive in spite of all their difficulties.

Reading an allusion is reading texts that are superimposed on each other and deciphering the palimpsest. It is also maintaining the gap between the allusive text and the text alluded to, because within this gap lies the illumination of the text. 'Breakfast for Enrique' can therefore be read as a response to *Cannery Row*, which shows, among other things, that nothing has changed in fifty years in the microcosm of the fish gutters on the west coast of the US, the alleged land of plenty.

McCann's collections of short stories are deeply rooted in his contemporary world. They are the reflections of a 'new Ireland' that Fintan O'Toole describes as 'frantic, globalized and dislocated'.[105] They show that dislocation characterises individual bodies, but also family units and, more widely, the whole Irish nation scattered throughout the world. The motif of dislocation is not only a feature of the diegesis or the narration but also of the author's style, as the intertextual borrowings show. McCann draws on the source of anglophone literature: he refers to novels, cuts and takes up some lines from poems or plays, mentions novelists, poets or playwrights, and thus builds bridges between literary genres. Removing fragments from their original context and inserting them into his own work is a transplantation process, which nevertheless does not break the unity of the text that receives these excerpts, but makes it a harmonious whole. McCann's fiction becomes a vast network of connections that favour exchanges and dialogues. As soon as readers spot a quotation, a mention or an allusion – and most of the time the narrator helps them to do so – and takes pains to turn to the texts that are referred to, it is highly likely that they discover analogies between them. Any transplantation has an impact on what is moved. Some plants may die when they are taken out of the ground, but some others can make a fresh start once put in a different place. By the same token, for the human being emigration can lead to death or to blossoming. In the field of literature, when a fragment is taken from a text and put into another one, it is essential that the intertextual connection is identified by the reader for the graft to take. Then, once the password is known, the text is appreciated in its open relationships with the literary heritage of the world.

CHAPTER 4

The Influences of Fathers in *Songdogs*

Published in 1995, Colum McCann's first novel, *Songdogs*, is focused on the notion of return. The narrator's stay with his father in Ireland after a long absence is the opportunity for him to narrate his family's history. The backward movement is thus spatio-temporal. Conor recounts his father's youth, his parents' encounter, the early years of their married lives, his own childhood and adolescence, and his departure from Ireland five years earlier. It is only at the end of a long initiatory experience that Conor – who has become a grown man – goes back home. No sooner has he arrived than he watches his father fishing in the river and recalls a memory: 'the current was strong enough to keep him stationary. Sometimes he could stay in one spot for an hour or two, just swimming.'[1] Conor remembers swimming with his father against the current, like a salmon, which is born in fresh water, spends its life at sea, then swims up the rivers to reach its birthplace. This movement backwards opens with the very first words of the book, an epigraph quoting Francis Scott Fitzgerald's novel *The Great Gatsby*: 'So we beat on, boats against the current, borne back ceaselessly into the past.' Traditionally, the course of a river symbolises the passing of human life, but the movement here is inverted: the protagonist – though unintentionally – keeps on returning to the past. Just as efforts are necessary not to be swept away by the current, it seems difficult to resist the attraction of the past, as the narrator himself recognises: 'I cannot help this wandering backwards. It is my own peculiar curse.'[2] Floods of memories are implicitly compared to moving waters, as the protagonist is not free from their influences.

Etymologically connected to the flow, the notion of influence is interesting with regard to the concept of intertextuality. Influence perceives the relationship as creative of new texts and often adds an intergenerational aspect to the phenomenon. Indeed, influence refers to identical or similar structures, motifs and styles between works of different authors living in various periods. Therefore influence suggests affiliation in literary creation.[3] As the son comes back to his father in the characters' universe, it is legitimate to wonder whether the young writer who publishes his first novel does not also return to symbolic fathers – to the writers who preceded him – in order to draw from their works some elements that he reuses in his creative process. The effect that some writers of the past – and their works – have on McCann's novel is part of the intertextual dialogism at work in *Songdogs*. Nevertheless, the very concept of influence remains vague, subjective, hypothetical and difficult to apprehend, for how can the action exercised by a text on another be accurately determined? Is it possible to pinpoint the precise moment when an author becomes silent, to hand over to another voice? Furthermore, is any textual co-presence the sign of an influence? In order to circumscribe this delicate notion, it is necessary to rest upon reliable elements, which makes it possible to establish interconnections between *Songdogs* and previous texts.

Retrogression and retrospection: returning to the father

From the very first page of the novel, the narrator's return to his father's house discloses the ending in advance and establishes a narrative in retrospect. The narrator – Conor – is inside the narrative and recounts the story in the first person. To tell his story he lets memories emerge. His narrative is particularly focused on one character – his father.[4] Conor first refers to his own prehistory, since he starts his narrative with his father's birth: 'A russet-haired woman who only wore one sleeve on her dress gave birth to my father on a clifftop overlooking the Atlantic, in the summer of 1918.'[5] This sentence opens a long analepsis that chronologically recounts the father's story. These events can be narrated by the son only according to what he has been told, unless his own imagination fills in the gap: 'I can imagine my father back in the thirties.'[6] The period between the time of the narrative and the time of the story told is about seventy-five years – that is, the father's approximate age in the diegesis, which seems to be contemporaneous with the publishing date of the novel. Conor tells of past events until he reaches his first narrative – his return home – and thus covers the period of time from his father's birth to the *hic et nunc* of the narrative – that is, the week he spends with his father in Ireland after being away for five years. The retrospective narrative is an analepsis that is alternately connected to the main narrative. This free alternation of the past and the present is based on a regular order, as if this parallel established causal relations between diegetic periods, the present being explained by the past.

In addition to this retrospective position, it is worth mentioning that the narrative reports the young protagonist's thoughts and perceptions. As the narrative is filtered through his subjective point of view, readers stand next to him, and look and listen through his eyes and ears. As a result, they perceive the father as the son perceives him; they share his limited perspective. Readers know nothing more than the son does of what comes into the father's mind. Therefore the father is always described from the outside; his inner truth remains out of reach. The external restrictive point of view shows an undeniable prejudice and enhances the subjectivity of the son's interpretations. The father figure, however, remains the main character and the narrator's only interest; he links up the first and second narratives.[7] Either a young or an old man, he remains omnipresent; the father is indeed mentioned from the first to the last page. His presence in all of the strategic points of the narrative is highlighted by his big hands,[8] clinging to a phallic object – his fishing rod – but also by his boots, which symbolise authoritarian rule, power and repression.[9]

Relations between father and son are strained. There is no love lost between them. Commencing with the title of the novel, aggressive behaviour is implicit, songdogs being metaphorically descriptive of the protagonists. Besides, their rivalry is all the more exacerbated as the two men are the only characters of the diegetic present. The presence of grandparents, siblings or a mother would ease the tension and weaken the hostility between them. But the narrator is an only child whose mother dies prematurely. Once the mother is absent, the antagonism between the two men grows and their relationship resembles a duel. As the young protagonist is the powerless witness of his mother's decline and death, and given that he considers his father to be responsible for this irreparable loss, he signals a parricidal desire: 'I woke, tremulous, walked out into the landing and hunched down, inventing ways of killing my father: make him swallow his chemicals, thump him to a black and white pulp.'[10] This dream of massacre is sparked off by the selfishness of the father, who thinks only about his own pleasure and hobby – in this case, photography – and forgets that he is also the father of a suffering child and the husband of an unhappy, uprooted foreign woman:

> He kept a notebook with him, wrote the accounts in it. Sometimes
> he read the financial situation aloud at the dinner table, promised

that soon there would be enough for us to make our great trip to the Chihuahuan desert. 'Yes,' he'd say, 'just a few more months and another big job, we'll be on the pig's back.' Mam's lips would give a small twitch as if Mexico was sitting there, at the edge of her mouth, as if she might just be able to taste it.

But instead he built his own darkroom. He wanted to use the old cow shed, but it let in too much light, so he created it from scratch. Hired a JCB and dug out the foundations … He drained the foundation holes with an industrial hose-pump and put in pipes, dropped the cement in by himself.[11]

An objection – here introduced by the conjunction 'but', highlighted at the beginning of the paragraph, corresponding to the father's decision – always undermines the hopes and dreams of his wife and son.[12] The father's development contrasts with his family's frustration. This noticeable difference is felt to be a wrong by the boy, and upholds the Oedipal structure. As soon as his father moves away, Conor gives vent to his hatred in a cry: 'I hate him, he's a bastard! I hate him!'[13] In the wake of these events, the mother, terribly depressed, mysteriously goes missing. According to Michael, the narrator's father, she might have drowned herself. This is probably why he goes to the river every day to fish. According to Conor – the narrator and protagonist – she might have gone back to Mexico, her native country. This is why he embarks on a journey, in the hope of finding answers to his questions.

The son's initiation

Conor's trip resembles an initiation process, the stages of which correspond to those defined by Mircea Eliade.[14] *Songdogs* can thus be considered as a *Bildungsroman*. Indeed, the young protagonist is determined to break away from his previous life once and for all: 'When I left home I promised myself I'd never return.'[15] He undertakes a trip to the Americas, which allows him to achieve maturity through various ups and downs. He mingles with people from other cultures, but also feels pains in his body and mind. The young hero goes into the cosmic night mentioned by Eliade[16] through terrible ordeals that are like symbolic deaths. And at the end of these tribulations, Conor experiences a mystic rebirth:

> [I] dove in, came up laughing ... I swam for fifteen minutes ...
> suspended myself in the float ... felt strangely light in the holiness
> of silence as the water lapped over me – the light hitting my eyes
> might have come from a star long imploded – big salty crests of
> water pulling me down and shoving me upwards, throwing me
> about, exhilarated in the darkness ... I felt alive at last ... and saw
> the vision of one woman ... appearing along through the waves
> saying: *Don't be so hard on him, he's about to die* ... and I said,
> No he's not ... [and] went on swimming, saying hallelujah to the
> stars.[17]

This swim is akin to an initiation ritual, a baptism of rebirth, a ceremony that purifies and (re)introduces the neophyte not only in his human family but also in the field of spiritual values. With the knowledge he acquires from being in a lot of different situations, Conor becomes more mature and self-aware as a man – hence his joyous outburst. At the end of his trip he comes back to Ireland and considers his personal development. With his return home, Conor goes back to his father's house but not to his previous condition; he has escaped the fetters of family life once and for all. His trip is the opportunity for him to proceed to an introspective work, which results in his desire to go back home. He is prepared for reconciliation and thus confirms the functions of religions, which, according to Freud, try to solve the endless problem of guilt and alleviate the sense of doing something wrong towards the father. Driven by a feeling of ambivalent nostalgia that exceeds fear and remorse, the son goes back to his father after keeping him at a distance. Resulting from a state of distress, this return, generated by a desire for protection, accounts for the need of gratified dependence fulfilled by the divine Providence.

Nostalgia for the father is illustrated in the Gospel by the parable of the prodigal son,[18] the structure of which is comparable to the plot of *Songdogs*. Indeed, parallel readings establish mirror effects between the texts: in the Gospel, as in the novel, the young son enjoys his first taste of freedom and leaves home for 'a distant country', which can be interpreted as a lack of contact with the father's environment. Determined to make a break from his past, the young man refuses to submit to paternal authority, looks for full liberty and aims to lead his existence without being anyone's slave. His experiment causes him to take major risks and to feel emptiness. Just as the young man in the biblical story 'feels the pinch'[19] and is determined to find a job,[20] Conor lives 'in a cabin in Wyoming ... just drifting along',[21] and provides for himself by 'working jobs that hardly pay the rent'.[22] Gradually, there is a turning point in the development of the two young men, who realise that they may become strangers to themselves and finally decide to return to their fathers. They are determined to stand up: 'I stood'[23] echoes the biblical verse 'he set out for his father's house'.[24] For these subalterns who are used to bending under the paternal yoke, the vertical position is significant. Thus they can set off and meet their fathers as man to man. Their return is considered by the old man as a resurrection: 'Conor, I thought you were dead, for crissake',[25] exclaims Michael, whose words echo the father's remark in the Gospel: '[He] was dead and has come back to life.'[26] The one who was thought to be lost has been found – hence the joy of the father, whose words ring out in the Gospel according to Luke – 'let us have a feast'[27] – as in McCann's novel: 'It's nice to have ya back, Conor.'[28] This joy is not only paternal but is also shared by the son himself, who says, 'hallelujah to the stars'.[29] This song of praise is closely connected to the motif of resurrection, since 'hallelujah' is a recurrent word in the Roman Catholic Church to celebrate Easter. Therefore the beginning of the narrative emphasises antagonism and murderous rage between father and son, whereas the end achieves joyful reconciliation between the two men thanks to the son's return.

These motifs of distance and return, of repulsion and attraction, endow the father, the incarnation of the past, with a magnetic effect. The father–son relationship that the second generation tries to assume while preserving their liberty not only concerns the diegesis but also the way a young writer, who is close to his protagonist, manages his literary predecessors' heritage.

Although the prodigal son of the Bible is never mentioned in *Songdogs*, one can legitimately wonder if, in view of the cultural environment in which McCann grew up, the parable had an impact on the creation of his novel. Can *Songdogs* be read as a rewriting of the biblical text? Are common occurrences sufficient to consider that the parable exerts an influence on the novel? And if, indeed, there is influence, is the second work paying tribute to a respected precursor or, on the contrary, resisting his pervasive shadow? Referring to a specific intertextual connection, the notion of influence has been studied by the American theorist Harold Bloom, whose writings deserve to be examined as they are in keeping with the issues raised here.

The anxiety of influence

In his work published in 1973, *The Anxiety of Influence*,[30] Harold Bloom views literary history from the angle of the Oedipus complex and bases his theory of influence upon the notion of intergenerational conflict. According to his approach, any young writer lives in the shade of a famous precursor, and is thus like a son oppressed by a castrating father. Influenced by his predecessor's work, he has mixed feelings towards him: love and admiration, but also fear, jealousy and hatred. Such feelings are generated by the son's need to reject his 'father' and rebel against him to become self-sufficient and find his own voice. Influence causes an anxiety of being flooded, of being so much possessed by a precursor that one is not the fully fledged author of one's own work. Like influenza, influence gives rise to an anguish of contamination.[31] When he reads his precursor's work, the young writer is so much on the defensive that he distorts it:[32] he re-envisions, re-evaluates and revises it when he writes his own text in a bid to overcome his 'anxiety of influence'. Therefore for Bloom there are no texts but only relations between texts; meaning is a product of this interaction. This vision of the relationship between texts is obviously intertextual. Any text can be read as a revision of a previous text, an attempt to dismiss its overwhelming effect, so that the newcomer on the literary scene can find a place, occupy the ground, and open a space for his own original creative work. The young writer tries to protect himself from influences by devices comparable to defence mechanisms. He endeavours to surpass previous texts, the relationship between men of letters being envisaged by Bloom as a competition.

As *Songdogs* is focused on the relationship between father and son, Bloom's theory is appealing because it establishes the same connection on another level between McCann and his predecessors. As the son leaves home to get away from his father's hold over him – an act showing influence anxiety, among other things – and looks for his way in life 'in a confusion of love and hatred'[33] towards the old man, then manages to resolve his Oedipus conflict and make up with him, the young writer similarly claims his autonomy by publishing a work that is characteristic of his style and personality, although it is returning to its roots insofar as other texts can be recognised in it. In other words, the diegetic relationship between father and son can be interpreted as the metaphor of the intergenerational affiliation in the world of literature, as Bloom perceives it.

Now the influence the father has on his son before the latter's departure is not the same after his return. Initially the father is depicted in a vertical position of authority, whereas the son lives in submission. Five years later, when the son comes back home, he is much more powerful and has in turn become a man. The father is also different, but his change is marked by decline. His weakening, due to his ageing, makes him a vulnerable character. There is symmetry in the developments of father and son, who are exact opposites in the balance of power: the father appears to be the weaker member of the duo. Positions are exchanged, so much so that, at the end of the novel, it is the son who exercises influence over his father. He incites him to eat, to wash, and even gives him some shampoo, at his request:

> 'Conor', he said ... 'd'ya think there's any way you could put some of that shampoo on me hair?'
> [...]
> 'My arm is sore here. Can't reach up properly ...' He rubbed his shoulder. 'Maybe just help me wash it, you know.'[34]

Asking his own son something a child would ask his parents, the old man, who was up to then fierce and uncontrollable, finally lets his son dominate him, and inverts their positions. The physical attitudes of the characters are opposed to what they were before: the son has become a man and is standing.[35] At the same time the father is now submissive,[36] intimidated by the imposing threat of his son's body: 'Ya look like a bloody executioner there.'[37] In its denouement, the plot stages an ironical process of reversal. The son's hold on his father makes it possible to look differently at the writer's work in relation to his predecessors.

If McCann is influenced by the parable of the prodigal son, this does not mean that he imitates the original text. Quite the contrary, for he transforms it, rewrites it, and somewhat parodies it. While the young man in the Gospel goes back to his father in order to stay with him for good, McCann's hero stays in the house in Ireland until his visa is renewed and flies back to Wyoming once he gets the document, so again moving away from his father. Besides, when Conor is about to leave, his father does not even try to hold him back, as the popular song he hums illustrates: 'Hit the road Jack don't you come back no more no more no more.'[38]

This parodic rewriting, establishing a reversal of roles, can be interpreted along with Bloom as a defensive activity used by the young writer – in this case, McCann – to protect himself from anxiety. It allows him to escape from the threat of repetition or pastiche. Does this mean that the second writer has any influence on the first one? As the character of the son has acquired power over his father at the end of his initiation, does McCann exercise any real influence on the text he reuses? Is it still influence once there is reversibility?

It is worth analysing other examples of literary works that may have had an influence on *Songdogs* in order to check the way they are revisited in the novel. Maybe it will then be possible to determine the effect that McCann's novel has on these original texts in return.

The effect that a work has on another one is difficult to circumscribe. Influences are complex and unexpected phenomena. Yet it is very difficult for a writer to escape from the anxiety of influence, as Umberto Eco emphasises:

> In the course of my fictional work, critics have found influences of which I was totally conscious, others that could not possibly have been influences because I had never known the source, and still others that astonished me but that I then found convincing – as when Giorgio Gelli, discussing *The Name of the Rose*, spotted the influence of the historical novels of Dmitri Merezkovskij, and I had to admit that I had read them when I was 12, even though I never thought of them while I was writing the novel.[39]

As with Eco, we, the readers, are influenced by the books we have read and the books we have forgotten, but perhaps also the ones we have not read, since all of them are part of our heritage. As a result, there is more than one influence. As Eco puts it: 'the search for two-way influence is dangerous, since one loses sight of the networks of intertextuality'.[40] Whether genuine, apparent, forgotten or ignored, these influences are connected to the writer's cultural milieu, education, environment, experiences and readings. And if, as Umberto Eco remarks here, a writer may be influenced by the books he read as a child, it is worth wondering what books the young Colum McCann had in his hands. Various kinds of book were read by Irish children in the late 1960s. All of them were meant to be educational, enlightening and moralistic. Traditionally, children's books were novels for young people, but also read were concise handbooks of stories from the Holy Bible or legends from Irish mythology.

Influence of mythological legends?

Passed down through generations, Celtic tales and legends carry immemorial culture that takes root in the very life of a people and enable children to improve their knowledge of local civilisation. This mythological repertoire can be seen in *Songdogs*, which would tend to mean that the writer is somehow shaped by the young reader he was.

Michael, Conor's father, goes down to the river every day in order to fish for salmon:

> 'I'm fishing every day.
>   'Every day?'
>   'On the quest for a giant pink salmon down beyond the bend. I'd swear the fucken thing's taunting me. Up it rears every now and then and looks like it's waving.'[41]

The narrative repeatedly refers to the father's determination to catch the fish:

> He said he was going to go down to catch his fish[42] ... the old man was chasing his fish down there[43] ... He went fishing until nightfall, six hours of ferocious stupidity, for nothing this time, not a bite[44] ... he went up to the room, said he'd fish the big one tomorrow ...[45]

The father does not seem to engage in any activity other than fishing. His determination to stay every day by the river in the hope of catching the salmon is reminiscent of a famous episode of Irish mythology taken from the Cycle of Finn:

> The Fenian epic begins with the struggle of two rival clans, each of whom claimed to be the real and only Fianna Eirinn. They were called the Clann Morna, of which Goll mac Morna was head, and the Clann Baoisgne, commanded by Finn's father, Cumhal. A battle was fought at Cnucha, in which Goll killed Cumhal, and the Clann Baoisgne was scattered. Cumhal's wife, however, bore a posthumous son, who was brought up by foster-mothers among the Slieve Bloom Mountains secretly, for fear his father's enemies should find and kill him. The boy, who was at first called Deimne, grew up to be an expert hurler, swimmer, runner and hunter. Later ... he took a second, more personal name. Those who saw him

asked who was the 'fair' youth. He accepted the omen, and called himself Deimne Finn.

At length, he wandered to the banks of the Boyne, where he found a soothsayer called Finn the Seer living beside a deep pool near Slane, named 'Fec's Pool', in hope of catching one of the 'salmons of knowledge', and, by eating it, obtaining universal wisdom. The old man had been there seven years without result, though success had been prophesied to one named 'Finn'. When the wandering son of Cumhal appeared, Finn the Seer engaged him as his servant. Shortly afterwards, he caught the coveted fish, and handed it over to Deimne Finn to cook, warning him to eat no portion of it.[46] 'Have you eaten any of it?' he asked the boy, as he brought it up ready boiled. 'No indeed', replied Deimne Finn; 'but, while I was cooking it, a blister rose upon the skin, and, laying my thumb down upon the blister, I scalded it, and so I put it into my mouth to ease the pain.' The man was perplexed. 'You told me your name was Deimne,' he said; 'but have you any other name?' 'Yes, I am also called Finn.' 'It is enough,' replied his disappointed master. 'Eat the salmon yourself, for you must be the one of whom the prophecy told.' Finn ate the 'salmon of knowledge', and thereafter he had only to put his thumb under his tooth, as he had done when he scalded it, to receive foreknowledge and magic counsel.

Thus armed, Finn was more than a match for the Clann Morna … he discovered himself to his father's old followers, confounded his enemies with his magic, and turned them into faithful servants. Even Goll of the Blows had to submit to his sway. Gradually he welded the two opposing clans into one Fianna, over which he ruled, taking tribute from the kings of Ireland … destroying every kind of giant, serpent, or monster that infested the land …[47]

Undoubtedly, Michael, the old fisherman in *Songdogs*, has something in common with the Druid who lives on the riverside, obsessed by a desire to catch salmon. But he is also very close to Finn. Like him, he is the son of a warrior and is not brought up by his parents but by foster-mothers who are in charge of his education.[48] Moreover, in one of the evenings with Conor, an incident makes it possible to compare him again with the mythological character:

> His lip quivered as he moved towards the fireplace with the poker,
> knelt down, prodded softly. A few large chunks fell out on to the
> cement slab and he mashed them down with his thumb, licked at
> it to soothe the burn, spat a few pieces of ash from the end of his
> tongue.[49]

At the end of the novel, the salmon, which remained invisible for days, deigns to show itself and does a magnificent dive in the river in front of Michael and Conor, who cannot believe their eyes. This scene echoes the mythological episode, particularly through the adjectives that describe it: 'his salmon hit a zenith and it retreated headfirst into the water with a *magical* sound … *marvellous* … and he said: '… *amazing*, wasn't it?'[50]

Obviously, McCann is familiar with this story from Celtic mythology, and the extracts of his novel quoted above could confirm that his literary production is influenced by the books he read as a child. Does it mean that the legend and its author cause anxiety in him? Coming from the distant past, the legend raises the issue of authorship; indeed, it is difficult to determine the precise identity of the person who initially wrote this story. Isn't Oedipal competition to be reconsidered then? For, indeed, rebellion is not the same when it is expressed against a real or an imaginary father.

Influence is an undeniable phenomenon. However, the young author's Oedipal block and anxiety towards a castrating 'father' are questionable – all the more so when the 'father' is not clearly identified. Moreover, it must not be overlooked that influence does not affect the writers themselves but their literary works. It is not so much the writers as their texts that are influenced by the writings of their predecessors. According to Bloom, influence works in literature as in a father–son relationship. And yet influence is much more intertextual than interpersonal.

An influence of the holy scriptures?

Songdogs refers to biblical stories taken from the Book of Exodus, another work whose author is not clearly identified. Here, again, some will see the influence of the books that the writer has read. Stories from the Bible were indeed read by Irish children in the 1960s. The goal was to consolidate the foundations of Christian faith in them.

When the narrator of *Songdogs* recounts his father's origins and destiny, the history of Moses appears between the lines. Moses and Michael have much more in common than the initial letter of their names. Indeed, the two men are closely connected to fatherhood: Michael is the father of Conor, the narrator of the novel. As for Moses, he institutes a law that establishes submission to a father. In the Bible, Moses is recognised as the emblem of fatherhood. Besides, just as Moses was left to his own devices by his mother – who had to comply with Pharaoh's injunctions – the narrator's father is abandoned by his mother as soon as she has given birth.[51] The two children are taken in by women whose religions are different from theirs. The Jewish child is offered a refuge by an Egyptian woman who 'noticed the basket among the reeds',[52] as the young Irish boy is discovered by two Protestant ladies who 'saw the bundle of skin amongst some trampled flowers'[53] and carried him home. Moses and Michael have two mothers: a biological and adoptive one.[54] Discovered on the Nile, the Jewish baby is called Moses because he was drawn out of the water;[55] likewise, the liquid element is very much connected to the Irishman: 'the old man and the water are together in all of this – they have lived out their lives disguised as one another, the river and him'.[56]

Moses and Michael both leave home and experience adversity: the former faces the Egyptians' hostility, the latter joins the army during the Spanish Civil War and witnesses a scene that clearly recalls the gift of manna, the food that God sent to the Israelites in the desert after they had escaped from Egypt:[57]

> He was almost twenty-one when he stood in a Fascist camp and watched great white loaves of bread showering down on Madrid, the strangest rain the city had ever seen. The bread zipped through the winter air, over the clifftops of the Manzanares River, parachutes of it moving like snow, bombarding the city. It fell on the streets, a miracle of propaganda, beautifully arced from hidden airplanes by pilots who played at being a 1939 Jesus in the clouds.[58]

By the same token, as Moses witnesses the plague of locusts in Egypt,[59] Michael sees a similar event in Mexico: 'a curious green wind came one summer carrying swarms of locusts'.[60] Lastly, as Moses has a revelation through fire – when God speaks to him from the burning bush and asks him to liberate his people from slavery – the narrator's father, in front of the blazing darkroom, has the revelation of the liberation of his wife who deserts him. Here, again, *Songdogs* does something parodic; as in the biblical text the fire does not burn up the bush, it is particularly devastating in the novel:

> A sharp crack issued into the night with violent acceleration, a joist swinging down in a graceful arc, and then the whole roof came down with a huge splintering sound, sending sparks yawing out over the courtyard, ecstatically fizzling out towards the countryside …[61]

The fire is the sign of a presence in one case, of an absence in the other. Indeed, the fire shows the presence of God in the Bible, whereas it announces Juanita's disappearance in the novel, since the narrator's mother is never again seen after the darkroom is burnt down. Obviously, the parallel between *Songdogs* and the Book of Exodus establishes an ironic contrast. McCann re-envisions, re-evaluates and revises the biblical story in his own novel, particularly in the way his own character debunks and distorts his supposed prototype. This ironic device can also be seen in the mythological episode of the salmon of knowledge: Conor and his father do not really know what Juanita has become, perhaps because, unlike Finn, they have neither caught nor eaten the fish. McCann's rewriting does not imitate but ironically derives from the previous text and its initial meaning, a process in which Bloom would see the sign of an anxiety of being entirely possessed by a precursor, a defence mechanism from overwhelming influences, and a struggle for supremacy. Bloom would suggest that McCann revises and reinterprets his precursors' works to overcome his own anxiety of influence and to occupy the ground where powerful prede-cessors have stood. This process is what he calls 'revisionism':[62] some texts of the past are reused and their systems of ideas and principles, considered as obsolete, are transformed. This rewriting is thus affiliated with postmodern ideologies that sow feelings of doubt, reconsider historic foundations and debunk myths, as the protagonists' parodic words exemplify:

> Before he left for the river I asked him – for a bit of a joke really – if he was going to go to mass, that Mrs McCarthy might be expecting him, down there in her rosary beads and headscarf. But he shook his head sharply and all he said was: 'The Lord's my shepherd, I shall not want him.'
>
> We stood at the door and I told him that I've never been much of a man for mass, either. A bit too much like a spiritual suppository.[63]

Here, again, the parodied text is taken from the Bible. The father starts quoting

Psalm 23, which begins 'The Lord is my shepherd; I shall want nothing', but gives up and changes the second part of the verse to show that he does not support the psalmist's point of view. His reluctance to appropriate the original words creates an element of surprise, and makes him an ironist whose reaction is unexpected and paradoxical.

Whether they are taken from biblical stories or Irish legends, these references are put at the same level; the Bible is not depicted as having any kind of superiority over Celtic mythology. Once more, the narrative mirrors the era of postmodernism and relativism, which announces the demise of grand narratives and the debunking of religious creeds, which are reduced to ordinary myths.

Songdogs confirms Bloom's theory insofar as some works of precursors are indeed rewritten. Nevertheless, the psychoanalytical interpretation of this revision as a defence mechanism, as a reaction to flooding overinfluence in Oedipal competition, is controversial because, on the one hand, the 'father' is not always clearly identified and, on the other, the heritage seems to be more accepted than suffered by the successor. Indeed, the reuse of a previous text is not intended as a dismissal of the overwhelming presence of a precursor but as a decision to resume his work, corresponding to a postmodern characteristic of renewal and a desire to give a text of the past a new meaning.

An influence of the beat generation?

In the 1990s Conor recounts the route taken by his parents a long time before. He goes on the same trip, stops in San Francisco, and narrates: 'We walked to City Lights bookstore and I looked for Cici's poems among the rows of beat poets, but they weren't there.'[64] This explicit cultural reference and the following examples prove that McCann deliberately establishes a connection between his own novel and the works of the American writers Kerouac, Ginsberg and Burroughs. As he explicitly mentions them, he is not under the influence of a 'father', which would imply a passive attitude of subordination, but he '*creates his precursors*',[65] and even sets himself the task of rewriting their texts. As a result, the young writer does not suffer from anxiety.

Harold Bloom himself reconsiders this notion: four decades after the publication of *The Anxiety of Influence*, he still proves to be very much interested in influence, but not so much in the notion of anxiety, as the title of his book published in 2011 illustrates, *The Anatomy of Influence*. In it he acknowledges that 'more than forty years of wandering in the critical wilderness have tempered the anxious vision that descended upon me in 1973'.[66]

The mention of the beat generation in the novel is an element among others confirming that Kerouac's ghost is present in the textual background, and can be considered as the shadow of a father figure. Indeed, a connection can be established between *Songdogs* and the American writer's novels, such as *On the Road* or *The Dharma Bums*. Indeed, in an interview McCann reveals that, as a teenager, he enjoyed reading books that allowed him to 'travel', particularly the ones of the beat generation: 'I was reading Kerouac, Ginsberg, Burroughs, Ferlinghetti, anybody at all who would get me away from Ireland.'[67] Besides, when, in the 1980s, the young Colum McCann left his country to travel for months on the roads of America, it is highly likely that he took with him some books that mirrored his own experience, for not only are the characters he created for his novel the contemporaries of Kerouac's protagonists, they also prove to be in the same places and situations as them.

In *Songdogs*, the young Michael, who will become Conor's father, goes on a trip without any specific purpose: he leaves Ireland for Spain to fight alongside the republicans, goes to Mexico, where he gets married, takes his wife Juanita to San Francisco, then to Wyoming and New York City before bringing her back to Ireland with him. Obviously these constant movements are not justified. There is no reason for Michael to leave a place in order to go elsewhere other that his desire not to settle anywhere. This liking for the road makes the protagonists of *Songdogs* resemble the members of the beat generation, and particularly the characters of Kerouac's novels. These signs of restlessness make them 'Bohemian wanderers', 'idealistic hoboes', 'Dharma Bums'.[68]

Michael, Juanita and their friend Cici travel on the same roads and during the same years as the American founders of the beat movement, who drove at breakneck speed from coast to coast in only three days. These young people of the 1950s are thus fully fledged members of the beat generation, as their thirst for escape and eagerness for the road exemplify: 'they had no real idea where they might end up next, but they had to go somewhere'.[69] The narrator's father is described as being 'impatient with places',[70] whereas the mother put her head on Cici's shoulder and 'stared down the road'.[71] Their trips in an old car that sometimes breaks down, prompting them to hitch-hike or catch a bus in order to maintain their progress, illustrates their rejection of materialism. Besides, when Cici tries to convince Juanita to leave with her, her argument refers to this long black ribbon that is the object of a sensual metaphor: 'they'll caress the road'.[72] The relationship between Cici and Juanita is depicted as some kind of attraction: their embraces and passionate kisses or the nostalgia for the good old days, when 'there was a time of such splendid happiness',[73] would tend to prove that the two women feel drawn towards each other. The same sex attraction is also associated with the father figures of the beat generation, such as Ginsberg or Burroughs. Furthermore, in the works of McCann or Kerouac, the road is always accompanied by rhythmic sounds:

> The old man was drumming his fingers on the seat in front of him, a jazz beat ... He said 'yeah' over and over again in a slow saxophone way. It was as if New York clubs already existed in his throat. 'Yeah, yeah, yeah.' He kept on drumming and he didn't give a second thought to it.[74]

Long after, in Ireland, when an old man, Conor's father proves to be still fond of this tempo: 'Jazz bucked from the radio and he moved over to fiddle with the dial, fine-tuning it. He pecked rhythmically at the air with his head.'[75]

McCann's and Kerouac's characters also have an artistic sense in common: as Cici writes poems, Michael takes pictures. The photographs of his naked wife – considered indecent – are banned, as were many literary works by beat writers, such as Allen Ginsberg's *Howl and Other Poems*.[76] Puritan censorship is as harsh in McCarthy's America as in de Valera's Ireland, and artistic creation is therefore threatened.

Like *On the Road*, *Howl* is an emblematic book of the beat generation. This is why the use of the term 'howl' in McCann's novel is certainly not coincidental. Indeed, echoes of all these references and allusions to the beat movement can be heard in a sentence such as 'animals *howl*ed from a distance and at times Cici yammered back at them'.[77] The use of the verb can be interpreted as a hint towards Ginsberg's collection of poems.

At the end of the road, the travellers' friendship is shattered: the founders of the beat generation fall out with one another. So do the protagonists in *Songdogs*. The road trips give way to a severe nervous breakdown that Juanita, like Kerouac, does not overcome. Once a tireless wanderer, Michael, disenchanted, stops moving. He promises his wife to take to the road again as soon as they can afford it, but 'the idea of our trip to Mexico had vanished'.[78] His selfishness causes the mysterious departure of Juanita, who cannot even find solace with Cici anymore:

> How curious it is that she hasn't heard from Cici in so long. The last

time Cici wrote, she was on a train heading west, slamming through flatlands ... It was a short letter and Mam read it so often that she began to incant parts of it in her mind like a church prayer ... There is something about Cici that makes the world worth living. Mam thinks about her often ...[79]

The two friends are separated by an ocean. In Ireland, Juanita waits in vain for Cici's letters and does not even manage to get in touch with her.[80] While she is supposed to lead the life of an ordinary housewife in a country she does not like, her friend is travelling all over the US 'with a flower on her cheek, elephant flares covering her sandals, hypodermic needles stuck blithely in her arm',[81] and spending time in naturist camps, on psychedelic buses or at anti-war demonstrations. Long after, when she meets her friends' son Conor, Cici 'was a shaman of sorts'[82] 'strung out on LSD'[83] and who 'chattered with women about how to keep your gums, your fingernails, your virginity – maybe all three at once. She told stories of beat writers who had taken all three from her.'[84] Like Kerouac's dharma bums,[85] Cici is clearly depicted as the stereotype of this unconventional, provocative generation, unlike Michael and Juanita, who once back to Europe settle into a traditional lifestyle. Besides, their experience on American roads is particularly wise compared with the madness and marginality of the protagonists of *On the Road*, who were real menaces behind the wheel. Because of their excessive consumption of drugs and alcohol, Kerouac's characters alternate weddings with divorce and live in trances to such an extent that they even lapse into crime and are regularly sent to jail. This difference can be interpreted as the sign of a parodic rewriting, which is also noticeable in the description of the tower owned by Cici in the middle of Wyoming:

> For a joke a spiralling staircase was nicknamed 'Yeats' after the gyre of his poems. Cici wrote a letter of his name on every second step. She laughed that she climbed Yeats every morning, rattled him, swept him clean, descended him.[86]

W.B. Yeats published two collections of poems with the titles *The Tower* and *The Winding Stair*.[87] Here, again, there is something parodic – the girl with unbridled sexuality who 'climbs Yeats every morning and rattles him' being the exact opposite of the old Irish poet who, through his works, endeavours to escape the sensual world and reach spiritual eternity.

Although he is a partaker of influence, McCann does not show an anguish of contamination but a pleasure of enriching his own fiction with elements borrowed from other texts he could have written himself. According to E.M. Forster, a writer is influenced by a book when s/he feels that s/he could have written it.[88] This stimulating idea implies that influenced writers immerse themselves in the context of their precursors until they become them and recreate their literary works. As he was travelling all over the roads of America, did not young McCann put himself in Jack Kerouac's shoes? Forster's opinion could thus confirm that Kerouac's novels are highly influential books in the writing of *Songdogs*, and makes it possible to consider McCann as the potential writer of *The Dharma Bums* or *On the Road*.[89]

Influence is a vague concept that is difficult to comprehend. Yet the recognition of stories from the Bible or legends from Celtic mythology in *Songdogs* proves the influence of children's books on an adult's literary production. In a more or less conscious way, introducing these echoes in a first novel is, for a young writer, a way of resting on firm foundations. These texts are not reused by way of imitation but by being rewritten. And rewriting, according to Bloom, is the sign of an anxiety of influence. Yet rewriting is a creative activity that requires an active writer. In that capacity it reconsiders the notion of influence that implies the passive subordination of the submitted writer. Even if the latter is influenced without realising it, s/he is not passive since s/he changes and reworks the text. Rewriting, particularly when it is parodic, proves that the young writer does not suffer someone else's influence passively but works actively for her/his own intertextual creation.

As mentioned earlier, the word 'influence' stems from the word 'flow'; it thus contains notions of passing time and temporal memory, and implies a chronological conception of history. In this case, Kerouac's novels may be considered as flowing and seeping into McCann's, as having an effect on it, since Kerouac chronologically comes before McCann. But if McCann incites readers to revise Kerouac's work, does it mean that he has an influence over him? Only the past can influence what comes next. As a result, influence merely concerns the effect that Kerouac's book has on McCann's. This is why the concept of influence is reconsidered by intertextuality, which does not perceive textual connection in a chronological order. True, Kerouac's texts were written before McCann's, but intertextuality works both ways as it suggests a conception of literary creation in which the writer, instead of suffering an influence, changes and reworks a previous text. A parallel observation of *On the Road* and *Songdogs* highlights not only an impact of the first text on the second but also a transformation of the first text by the second. The first text can thus be read with another eye. McCann's novel adapts and rewrites Kerouac's novel, and can arouse the desire to reread it differently. With this reversibility, literary texts become active elements, the meanings of which are never fixed but always changing.

According to Bloom's approach, the word 'precursor' connotes an emphasis on conflict, the world of literature, and more generally art, being considered as a competition in which each participant tries to be more successful than the other. As a result, the relationship between a young writer and his predecessor is perceived as rivalry – *agôn* – which the American theorist considers as a central factor of our cultural tradition. Such an opinion is questionable: if there is indeed rivalry, it cannot be between writers of different generations. A game is always played between peers.[90] Aggressive behaviour could rather be envisaged between authors of the same generation who write on similar motifs. As I argued in *Miroirs de la filiation. Parcours dans huit romans irlandais contemporains*,[91] the father–son relationship is a recurrent theme in the Irish novel of the 1990s. Indeed, Colum McCann's contemporaries have, like him, made the most of the motif. And yet Michael Collins, Roddy Doyle, Dermot Bolger, Neil Jordan and Patrick McCabe pass positive judgements on their respective works, as the covers of their books testify. They speak benevolently about their fellow writers in interviews. They take part in collective books published on the initiative of one of them, and adapt their literary works for the screen after writing the script together.[92] They know one another, share their ideas, appreciate their works, and seem united by ties of friendship, if not brotherhood. Obviously, there are no relations of competition or hostility there.

The concept of influence is valuable when describing the relations between texts. It is, however, questioned and reconsidered by the notion of intertextuality, which responds to influence by refuting the author's passivity, the chronological impact of literary works and the concept of competition among writers. The young author is not subjected to influences, but produces a work that consists of drawing a series of motifs from the huge intertextual library. McCann is a free writer. He does not write under somebody's influence, which would imply that he loses a part of his freedom, but deliberately establishes a connection between his own text and previous works written by some predecessors he has selected. Thus he confirms his interest in the founding texts of

Irish culture, but also in the works written by compatriots and, more widely, Western writers, particularly American ones, who came before him. He ceaselessly returns to them, and revises them, as his complete works – and the chapters of the present work – illustrate. Indeed, all of his books refer either to biblical stories, Celtic legends or novels and poems of the anglophone literary world. With these interconnections, although McCann is the fully fledged author of his own work, he is in line with a cultural heritage: he comes to terms with the affiliation links established here, and vouches for the fact that his first novel is not so much inspired by others as part of a vast dialogue in which books talk to each other.

CHAPTER 5

Prophets of Israel in Manhattan Tunnels: a biblically informed reading of *This Side of Brightness*

The Bible is the cornerstone of Jewish and Christian cultures. It is not only a source of meditation but also a model for the expression of thought. It is a symbolic narrative of the beginning of time that initiates believers into secrets, hence its mystical nature. It has been surmised that *muein* – what initiates into secrets – was associated with *mùthos*, the word *mùthikos* ('mythical') going into Latin as *mythicus*. As a result, the Bible may be considered as telling a myth, a term of complex history and meaning. Initially the myth has its roots in the sacred; it is in league with the field of religion, but nowadays tends to denote a piece of fiction that conveys a psychological truth.

Myths continue to shape contemporary literary works. Their recurrence is creative of meaning, which, according to Paul Ricœur, is turned both towards the past and the future.[1] Thus the myth is a dynamic principle of circulation among texts. It is one of the mechanisms of intertextuality, which is often one of the basic processes of the construction and permanence of the myth.[2] Therefore engaging with a myth inevitably leads to intertextual writing, as *This Side of Brightness* illustrates.

This novel, written and published by Colum McCann in 1998, has close ties with the Bible, not only when the protagonist and his grandson go to a Baptist church to listen to 'a new young preacher ... telling the story of an ancient Egyptian king, Hezekiah'[3] but also because the plot of the novel borrows scattered elements taken from biblical episodes. The Books of Samuel, the Books of Kings and the Gospels in particular are reused and given a new life throughout the novel. These intertexts raise quite a number of questions:

70

what is the status of this rewriting? How does the novel incorporate the biblical discourse? How far is the novel fed and enhanced by these intertexts? Is there an impact on its value and the way it is read? Is there a parodic process at work?

In order to interpret the text, the mytho-critical approach is relevant. *Mythocritique* is a word coined by the French academic Gilbert Durand. It is given a broader sense by Pierre Brunel, who studies the complex relationships between myth and literature, and seeks the significant structures that come out of them. The method aims 'to disclose a relevant system of imaginary dynamisms',[4] to establish a connection between the mythic architecture of the work and the course of the narrative, and to clarify the text by the free handling of mythic figures. Brunel's study of myths in literary texts is based on three principles: emergence, flexibility and irradiation. His interpretation rests on the emergence of some explicit, mythical occurrence: a single word, a single name or a specific situation can manifest the mythical print. In addition, these mythical elements are not reproduced as such inside the work: they are modulated, inflected and adapted by the novel that lets them irradiate.

Nathan's mythic figure

The examination of mythic cases in McCann's novel first makes names emerge. Some protagonists, such as Nathan or Elijah, have prophets' names. This onomastic noteworthiness is a first mythic clue referring to the historical books of the Old Testament. Nathan is a prophet who incites the Hebrew people to wait for a king who would save the world and establish God's kingdom on earth, according to the promises he made to King David.[5] The promise mostly concerns the permanence of David's long line of descendants on the throne of Israel. David will not build a house – a temple – in honour of God's name, but it is God who will build a house – a royal dynasty – for David. The motifs of home and succession are at the heart of Nathan's prophecy. Likewise, they are an essential element in McCann's novel. Indeed, McCann reuses not only the names but also the motifs of the myth. His novel narrates the destinies of three men from successive generations: Nathan, Clarence and Clarence Nathan, whose name shows his predecessors' legacy.

Like Nathan's prophecy, the novel is focused on the motif of the house in the literal and figurative senses of the word. For the first two generations, the house refers to a precise place – an apartment in Harlem. Symbolically, 'home' means Nathan's birthplace, namely Atlanta, where Clarence, distraught, takes refuge. Finally, the motif of the house is subverted with the third generation, insofar as Clarence Nathan (or Treefrog) can only dream about his family and the home he has been expelled from, since he is homeless. He sleeps in a cubicle at the end of a beam high above the railway tracks of a Manhattan tunnel. At the end of the novel, he gets rid of his trivial possessions and goes back to the streets. With the passing generations, characters seem to distance themselves more and more from their prototypes. As a result, Clarence Nathan's homelessness and separation from his family pose a serious challenge to the ruling orthodoxy of the biblical motifs. Through this example, the novel shows that building a house or establishing a line of descent are not necessarily sources of solidity and stability, contrary to what the biblical model claims. Mythic elements are adapted and contested by McCann's novel. Even if they are recognisable, particularly through the characters' names and biblical motifs, they are always likely to be ironically reworked and transformed. The writer allows himself some freedom with the original material. This is what Brunel suggests when he perceives flexibility as a feature of the process.

The prophet Nathan, the spokesman of the holy Word of God during David's reign, is described in the Books of Samuel as a model of good behaviour, wisdom incarnate, like his namesake in the novel. Both of them have a similar function: they are determined to warn the ones who stray from the straight and narrow and encourage them to change. To do so, their attitude towards others is uncompromising: they do not hesitate to reprimand their nearest and dearest. Following the example of Nathan – who blames King David for his adultery with Bathsheba[6] – Nathan Walker sharply scolds his drug-addicted daughter-in-law and his grandson, who maintains her in dependency. Like a prophet, he induces everyone to face up to their responsibilities. Likewise, as Nathan criticises David for the murder of Uriah, Bathsheba's husband, and forecasts the death of the illegitimate child,[7] Nathan is wounded by his son's criminal acts. Biblical Nathan and novelistic Nathan are powerless witnesses of murders, crimes and misdemeanours. Both of them have premonitions, and, though they are voices in the wilderness, they predict the misfortunes that may result from such happenings.

Just like the biblical episode, the novel poses the problem of free will and shows that everyone must measure the possible effects of their acts. The tenth chapter, in which Clarence kills two men – his despicable neighbour and a policeman – and then runs off to Atlanta – where he is arrested and shot down – highlights the spiral of murderous violence. By the same token, the adulterous relationship between David and Bathsheba causes the death of the deceived husband and tragedies in the following generation.[8] Such a story shows that God does not punish men as his mood dictates, but that men are responsible for their own actions and, when they opt for violent deeds, must be reminded that murder begets murder.

This vicious circle is analysed by René Girard, for whom myths show a basic reality: cultures grow from the resolution of primal collective violence. Mimetic rivalry – this frantic desire to own what the other owns and do what the other does – is an essential driving force in human behaviour.[9] The natural violence of the relationship among humans can be solved only by the scapegoat mechanism, the designation of a person who is chased away to the desert, where the sacred burden of past violence is taken.[10] And indeed, the two protagonists of the novel – Clarence and Clarence Nathan – are clearly depicted as scapegoats, Atlanta or the cubicle in the tunnel being symbolically comparable to remote desert places resulting from terrible ordeals.

Yet as the prophet Nathan warns the people around him against their erring ways that might arouse the divine wrath, Nathan Walker asks them to give up their bad habits only for their own good, without backing up his speech with God's possible reactions, to which he shows himself quite indifferent. Indeed, after the deaths of his wife and son, Nathan notes that 'God only exists in happiness',[11] and he loses his faith:

> Walker kneels at the stone, but doesn't say any prayers. Prayers strike him as flaccid things now – useless supplications curling out only as far as the throats of men before falling back down into their stomachs. Spiritual regurgitation … You won't find me beseeching no Jesus. I'm finished with all that.[12]

Although the protagonist and the prophet have a lot in common, they are also diametrically opposed to each other, in accordance with the ironic tone employed by the narrator to re-evaluate the myth.

Elijah's mythic figure

Nine centuries before Christ, Elijah, like Nathan, does not hesitate to reproach authority figures for their idolatrous crimes. The prophet forecasts punishment to King Ahab and Queen Jezebel, who forsake the commandments of the Lord and worship Baal. Intractable, divested of any material possessions, the prophet Elijah complies with God's injunction to 'go into hiding':[13] he lives in remote areas, in ravines or caves. His story hangs over the novel as one of the characters, also called Elijah, settles in the tunnel, next to Clarence Nathan. The motif of dispossession is common to both texts: Elijah is neither an owner nor a tenant but a homeless man who finds a makeshift shelter on the fringes of society. His isolation is connected to his lack of food, water and warmth. This destitution is lessened by the helping hand of Angela, whose name makes her the reincarnation of the biblical angel who supports Elijah and brings him food when he is starving to death in the desert.[14] Nevertheless, this drifting dancer – whose body is 'a sad broken mess',[15] used and abused by men, destroyed by addictions – is an unusual angel whose features make her the opposite of a pure, innocent spirit.[16]

According to the Book of Kings, the prophet Elijah is 'a hairy man with a leather apron round his waist'[17] and who 'muffles his face in his cloak'[18] when he hears God. These details surface in the novel as Elijah covers his head: 'a blanket pulled up over his hooded sweatshirt',[19] then 'pulls the hood away from his face, revealing a long red cut on his jawbone'.[20] Clarence Nathan's body is gashed, too: 'he is broken down and headhung and dirty and covers his muscled torso with long shirts so he doesn't have to stare at his scars'.[21] In the novel, characters with prophetic names share common features with the figures of the Old Testament: like them, they wear ample clothes that allow them to cover their heads; besides, the scars on their faces are reminiscent of the incisions on prophets' foreheads – distinguishing features that, like a tattoo or a tonsure, allowed them to be easily identified. The way they cover their heads and show only a part of their faces or bodies establishes a contrast between light and darkness. This contrast is also noticeable in their dark refuge, away from the dwellings that enjoy daylight. This division between the visible and the invisible is also characteristic of the ironic process at work here. The words used do not express what they could immediately suggest. Indeed, identical names should not lead the reader astray; although characters share common features with prophets, they are also very different from them. Being a crack-smoking abuser of women who does not hesitate to kill animals as well as humans, Elijah is obviously the ironic contrast to his supposed prototype. According to the writer's usual game, the model is completely distorted. The great narratives of the Bible and their characters are genuine pretexts for parody, a particular form of expression McCann shows himself adept at dealing with. His text debunks the sacred aura of a man sent by God to make his character a total contrast to the biblical prophet, although both of them have the same name. This ironic process is part of the motif of light and darkness. It maintains a noticeable difference between being and appearing, and simultaneously contains the idea that contradictions can be reconcilable.

Treefrog: a Christlike figure

The motif of succession, mentioned above, can also be applied to Elijah, who belongs to a line of prophets. On the one hand, he is the faithful heir of Moses, particularly when he strikes the water that divides to right and left, and allows him to cross over on dry ground.[22] This episode is reminiscent of the way the survivors of the tunnel explosion in the bed of the East River make their way through the water. On the other hand, when he revives a widow's son in Zarephath,[23] Elijah announces Jesus, who, likewise, raises a widow's son to life in Nain and 'gives him back to his mother'.[24] The novel also contains many allusions to Jesus. For example, the last hours of Clarence's life are reminiscent of the Passion: like Jesus, Clarence is about thirty years of age, and he repeatedly falls down before breathing his last. Indeed, he is beaten with a club by a policeman who saw him hit McAuliffe: 'he is knocked backwards … he rises from the ground'.[25] Racked by despair, Clarence decides to run away, and in the train southwards is tempted by suicide, thinking 'he could fall right now'.[26] In Atlanta, three weeks later, Clarence is shot down by policemen.[27] The end of his life recalls the Passion, his fall being reminiscent of the road to Calvary, where, according to tradition, Jesus falls down three times. At the end of the road, Jesus is crucified – nailed to a symbolic tree.[28] Similarly, Clarence Nathan, alias Treefrog – a significant nickname – seems to climb up a metallic tree to reach his unusual shelter, the column being comparable to the trunk and the beams to branches:

> Treefrog walked along the railway tracks until he came to a large concrete column. He touched the column with both hands and waited a moment for his eyes to adjust, then grabbed onto a handhold and, with spectacular strength, hauled himself up. He walked along the beam with perfect balance, reached another catwalk and shunted himself upwards once more.[29]

Furthermore, his cubicle is described as being a safe place in a tree: the text mentions 'his nest'.[30] Lastly, there is something Christocentric about the posture of this broken man at the end of the novel: 'he stretches both arms wide and he puts one leg out in front of him and he tucks his head into his armpit'.[31] Clarence Nathan is not only dancing like the crane frozen in the river at the beginning of the novel[32] but also obviously adopting the attitude of the crucified. Besides, the narrator slapped by Dancesca mirrors Jesus ill-treated by the angry mob during his Passion:

> She just slaps me and leaves my face in my shoulder and then she moves away and the sting of her hand is in my face and I'm thinking slap me on the other side, slap me on the other side, slap me on the other side, but she's gone.[33]

It is not only his pathological obsession with duality and symmetry that incites the speaker to express this wish. Indeed, Treefrog also likens his experience to that of Jesus, and follows to the letter his advice, which ironically backs up his mental disorder. The Gospel according to Matthew says:

> You have learned that they were told, 'Eye for eye, tooth for tooth'. But what I tell you is this: Do not set yourself against the man who wrongs you. If someone slaps you on the right cheek, turn and offer him your left.[34]

By the same token, his masochistic response to his incapacity to save his grandfather evokes the stigmata of Jesus on the cross: considering that his hands failed him, he 'burnt a little hole on the back of this hand, like a crater. Then this hand.'[35] Here, again, the novel provides ironical counterpoint to the biblical episode; indeed, as Jesus heals the sick and puts new life into the dead by inciting them to 'stand up',[36] Clarence Nathan in the subway station fails to haul his grandfather up from the tracks onto the platform. Jesus 'took the girl by the hand, and she got up',[37] whereas McCann's character narrates, 'I'm reaching down to grab him ... pull him up ... and one hand slips'.[38] Such a scene revises and contests the miracle and thus attenuates the extent and importance of Jesus' authority. The protagonist of the Gospels brings dead bodies back to life, whereas 'in his notebook Treefrog writes: Back down under the earth, where you belong.'[39]

Mythic irradiating words

The ultimate word of the novel heralds the end of a world and the beginning of another. The term 'resurrection' suggests some hope for the victory of life over death. It is a mythic word with a power of irradiation. Most of the time, according to Brunel, such irradiation is carried out from a word,[40] and 'resurrection' is a very significant one. It particularly alludes to Elijah and Jesus, as we have just seen. Yet as these two biblical protagonists work miracles and restore dead bodies to life, resurrection is not treated in its literal sense in the novel as it is in the Bible. Indeed, the word is used here in its figurative sense, since it describes the way workers only just avoid death in a tunnel[41] and the way the homeless leave the underground passages to return to light and seek refuge in less remote places. Going from the literal to the figurative sense of a biblical term is a form of deterioration, of debasement, according to Denis de Rougemont, for whom the literary history of a myth is always read like 'the history of some devaluation'.[42] McCann transforms the meaning of the myth and revisits its motif from a materialistic viewpoint, as if a return from death to life could no longer be objectively envisaged today – hence this repeated remark that reflects contemporary postmodern ideology: 'our resurrections aren't what they used to be'.[43] The process of devaluation described by de Rougemont can also be observed in the ascents in the novel, which are not to be understood literally, as with the Ascension of Jesus or Elijah. Indeed, Elijah's dramatic ascent on a chariot of fire is here debased by the dark, sordid universe of an underground tunnel.

The narrative starts with an accident: as men are digging a tunnel below the East River, a hole releases the pressurised air. Despite the efforts of the workers, who do their best to stuff it, the hole grows wider and causes a blowout. Some men are trapped in the tunnel, while Nathan and two of his workmates are sucked through the soil, pebbles and river dirt, then reach the water, move up and then erupt through the surface of the river, shot out into the air on a huge brown geyser: 'they are *rising* through the river'.[44] This return to life is like a resurrection, which is referred to in the Gospel with the same verb: 'The Messiah is to *rise* from the dead on the third day.'[45] This movement upwards, to a higher position, also evokes the Ascension of Jesus, who 'was lifted up'[46] to his father. Along the river, Maura O'Leary, an Irish miner's wife, witnesses the scene: 'She notices a few scows and barges and some bits of rafted rubbish on the water. The morning sun shining wheels of light in the flow … Mules and carts beyond the edges of the banks.'[47] There is something biblical about the scenery insofar as a parallel can be drawn with Elijah's ascension:

> Elijah and Elisha went on, talking as they went, and suddenly there
> appeared chariots of fire and horses of fire, which separated them one
> from the other, and Elijah was carried up in the whirlwind to heaven.
> When Elisha saw it, he cried, 'My father, my father, the chariots and the
> horsemen of Israel!' and he saw him no more. Then he took hold of his
> mantle and rent it in two, and he picked up the cloak which had fallen
> from Elijah, and came back and stood on the bank of the Jordan.[48]

The 'wheels of light' mentioned in the novel are reminiscent of Elijah's
dramatic ascension. Nevertheless, here again are not the 'chariots and horses
of fire' somewhat debased by the 'mules and carts'? Later, at the scene of the
blowout, Nathan's grandson, like Elisha, witnesses his friend's ascension and
disappearance: 'Elijah had stood under the pipes, with steam around his feet,
and then he disappeared and left Treefrog alone. It was as if he had vanished
into the steam.'[49] Another time, 'Treefrog watches Elijah emerge through a
shaft of light.'[50] And the narrative continues:

> She moves to go below deck as the river howls and erupts. A massive
> funnel of water greets the city on one bank and Brooklyn on the
> other ... At first Maura sees only sandbags and planks of wood aloft
> on the geyser. She reels back, clutching at her stomach ... She sees
> Nathan Walker, his powerful body, and the red hat that has stayed
> on his head like an autograph, tied under his chin with a string. But
> the other two bodies are hard to make out as they crest the water,
> in their strange *ascension*.[51]

Recurrent in the novel,[52] the term 'ascension' is what Brunel would consider a
'mythic irradiating word'. In this respect, it is worth noticing that this process
of moving to a higher level applies to each of the three protagonists of the
novel, even if they also experience the opposite movement:

- Nathan goes down to work in the tunnel and it is thanks to this mirac-
  ulous rising into the air that he does not die. Nevertheless, when he
  returns down to the subway with his grandson, he does not go up to
  the platform, and falls under a train.[53]
- His son Clarence is praised to the skies in his youth and described as
  being 'so goddamn handsome',[54] but is shot down by a policeman in
  Atlanta at the age of thirty.

- Lastly, his grandson, Clarence Nathan or Treefrog, after leading a happy life with his wife and child, experiences a severe fall: thrown out of the house, he is reduced to hiding in a dark underground tunnel.

These examples show that the archetypal structure of the myth is a system of antagonistic forces, as Gilbert Durand claims.[55] Indeed, the structure of *This Side of Brightness* focuses on a bipolar relationship of opposites, particularly on upward and downward movements, as the protagonists' experiences illustrate.

For Clarence Nathan, who belongs to the third generation, the fall is to be interpreted in the biblical way. Indeed, he is comparable to Adam, who, as a punishment, is driven out of the Garden of Eden. As Adam's banishment causes death, since his disobedience puts an end to human immortality, Clarence Nathan's eviction is also some kind of social death. Besides, for both of them, the sin, or misdemeanour, is linked to sexuality. The motif of paradise lost is present in the novel, as memories show: 'those were the good times'.[56] Furthermore, as Clarence Nathan is forced to crawl on his stomach to get into his cubicle, he is obviously comparable to the serpent of Genesis.

According to Christian doctrine, Jesus redeems and saves the human kind through his death, descent into hell, Resurrection and Ascension.[57] Clarence Nathan is somehow the epitome of man in Christian theology: after a dark period, he has access to light and stands up again, as the ultimate word highlights (that word being 'resurrection'). As the term 'fall' is mentioned in the very first sentence of the novel, the last sentence heralds the hope of 'resurrection'.[58]

Like the Bible, McCann's novel aims to depict an individual or collective destiny through the exceptional development of a family or a hero. As it borrows figures, motifs and episodes from the holy book, *This Side of Brightness* can be read as a mythic narrative in which biblical allusions and references are not only mere ornaments but give shape and sense to the text, the structure of which is based on downward and upward movements. Besides, with the motifs of death, resurrection and ascension, the end of the novel is similar to the last chapters of the Gospels. Nevertheless, these words are devalued since they no longer have the extent and importance they used to have in their initial context. As he was writing this novel, McCann probably read or reread some books of the Old Testament, and anyway worked with the memories of his past readings, as he himself confirms: 'These references come naturally from my youth.'[59] For a writer who attended Catholic schools,[60] the Bible, before being an ideological reference and a useful material in his creative process, is first and foremost a memory of what he learned about religion as a child. Beyond this personal memory, the Bible is also a cultural common denominator that calls upon collective memory. As Treefrog's retreat into a dark cubicle can be interpreted as a return into Mother Earth's womb, McCann's resort to biblical intertexts can be understood as the sign of a writing haunted by nostalgia and anxious to revive the roots of Western civilisation. When he traces Treefrog's ancestry, McCann joins the tradition of holy men who wrote about the long lineage of biblical figures. Furthermore, this imagery endows his prose not only with some depth and savour but also with poetic, prophetic lyricism that has its roots in the past.

For Northrop Frye,[61] the Canadian literary theorist who wrote significant studies of the Bible, literature is an autonomous verbal structure in which the values and meanings of words are subordinate to a structure of interconnected motifs. He considers that the Bible plays the part of 'the great code' of art, all the more so as the book no longer inspires the fear of God, its reading being 'secularised' – hence the process of devaluation emphasised by Denis de Rougemont. This process is at work in *This Side of Brightness*: tradition is contested and challenged. McCann adapts the myth to the preoccupations of his contemporary society and thus debases its content: prophets and miracle-workers become archetypes of 'some terrible human degradation'.[62] Whereas Jesus shows his power over the forces of evil when he walks on the water, the characters of the novel walk *under* the river, in a dark tunnel. Stripped of its essential content, the myth is no longer a myth. Its mystic secret becomes commonplace and part of everyday life. Once devalued, the Bible becomes a flexible, adaptable material. As the significant motifs of resurrection and ascension illustrate, Christian terminology is omnipresent throughout the novel, but the words used have different meanings from the ones they had originally. Irony is the art of distrust and deviation. It always seems to be directed at alleged absolute truths, but there would be no irony without absolute truths. Maybe McCann plays with them because he believes in such values. He merely reckons that he 'wanted to write about resurrection'.[63] As he understands it, resurrection is the main desire of our contemporaries, who really want to live to the full. And all those who are involved by the side of second-class citizens, who help them stand up and fight, are somehow contributing to their resurrection. The diegetic universe of the novel is split, as the dichotomy of space shows: the haves live in the light of the surface, in 'this side of brightness', whereas the have-nots are hidden in the shade of underground passages. The novel depicts the scandal of division, of segregation, of an unfair social system. Writing on the dropouts empathetically, McCann proves that he is anxious to maintain the tradition of the social novel, which makes it possible to put his literary work 'on the ground, in the muck and the mire', and 'to restore the possibility of decency for the "ordinary" man and woman'.[64] Refusing fatality, he strives to stand by the feeble and the oppressed. He does not write about them from abstract mind visions: he met them, spent many months among them.[65] His fiction is thus given the value of testimony. For McCann, homelessness, as any kind of marginalisation, should be questioned by affluent citizens and incite them to think about, and act for, the establishment of a society that could be fair for all.

CHAPTER 6

Dancer and Readers:
framed and framing books

In McCann's fiction, *Dancer* has the special feature of being a novel whose protagonist comes from the real world and has the name of a man who really existed: Rudolf Nureyev (1938–93). Yet this name does not keep its full referentiality in fiction, according to Gérard Genette, for whom there is a clear division between the real world and the novel. The French theorist maintains that a work of fiction, even though it portrays life, does not refer to extra-textual reality. Each element borrowed from the actual world, once absorbed by fiction, becomes fictitious, like Napoleon in *War and Peace*.[1] A historical personage's name does not refer to the actual man: 'Rudi' or 'Rudolf' no longer describes historical Nureyev but a fictional, plausible character. Nureyev is thus 'fictionalised' in *Dancer*.

In order to highlight the verisimilitude of his narrative, McCann gathered a lot of information on the artist and acknowledged that, in the course of researching the book, Diane Solway's biography *Nureyev: his life* was invaluable.[2] As a matter of fact, a comparative reading of Solway's biography and McCann's novel shows many similarities: in both texts, young Rudolf is depicted as an 'overmothered son'[3] who during lonely moments finds solace in artistic disciplines – music, skating or dancing.[4] His father's activities – fishing and hunting – are, on the contrary, disliked by him: he considers them 'very uncomfortable'.[5] Weak, frail, effeminate, he is the object of scorn for the other boys, who laugh at him and often leave him hurt and humiliated.[6] In reaction to this, he becomes withdrawn and sits for hours in an observation point overlooking Ufa's railway station to watch the trains.[7] After taking part in concerts in Ufa's hospital, where children are sent to entertain wounded soldiers back from the front,[8] he takes great care to dance, without his father's knowledge, and practises every day with Anna Udeltsova, a former ballerina from Leningrad. Anna and her husband Sergei inspired the characters of Anna and Sergei Vassiliev in the novel; the first names are the same, the surnames have been changed. In reality, as in fiction, Sergei managed to survive a Siberian labour camp, but on his return to Leningrad was exiled with his wife to Ufa, a Russian city on the edge of the Ural Mountains. After being taught by Anna, Rudolf is trained by Elena Konstantinovna Voitovitch, whose full name is used in the novel. Then, in Leningrad, he works under the leadership of Aleksandr Pushkin, who puts him up. This dance instructor and his wife Xania also feature in the novel under their real identities. Conversely, Rudolf's best friend in Leningrad is a girl from Cuba, Menia, who in the novel becomes a girl from Chile, Rosa-Maria. McCann admits he has changed some names 'to protect the privacy of people living'.[9]

Some other anecdotes of McCann's novel are in accordance with Solway's biography: with his first wages Rudolf offers his mother a fur coat. He incites her to ask him if he is happy in the West in order to certify that he is. He likes telling his friends that one must not look backwards lest one should fall down the stairs. These details exemplify that fiction is in keeping with reality, though this is not always the case. Indeed, the novel can also diverge from the dancer's actual life. In his acknowledgements (at the end of the book) McCann writes: 'I have, on occasion, condensed two or more historical figures into one.'[10] For instance, though in reality Rudolf has three sisters – Rosa, Lilya and Razida – in the novel he just has one, Tamara, who was in fact, a close friend. Furthermore, according to the novel, Nureyev was born in Ufa, where he spent the first years of his life. Actually, he arrived in this town when he was four: he was born in 1938 on the Trans-Siberian Railway to Vladivostok, where his father was based as an instructor in the Red Army. Young Rudolf lived there for sixteen months. Then his family settled in Moscow, until they were evacuated in the wake of the German invasion of the Soviet Union. After one year spent in Chelyabinsk, it was only in 1942 that his family moved to Ufa. Another difference between the texts concerns Rudolf's regret, in the novel, that his father never saw him on stage.[11] This does not match reality: according to Diane Solway, Nureyev's father travelled to Leningrad in the spring of 1960 to see Rudolf dance.[12]

It is useless to extend the list of examples, which would soon become tedious. One should simply keep in mind that as the protagonist is not a person but a fictional character, *Dancer* is a biographical novel – that is, a specific subgenre in which truth and fiction are mixed. As McCann himself admits, 'some of the attributions made to public figures are exact; others are fictional'.[13] The real is thus reimagined in such a way that the discourse of fiction is a patchwork made of different elements, most of which are borrowed from reality.[14] This discourse is mixed, alternate: although it introduces recognisable signs that refer to the outside world, its status remains fictional. As it states at the commencement of the book, 'This is a work of fiction. With the exception of some public figures whose real names have been used, the names, characters and incidents portrayed are the work of the author's imagination.'

Among the connections between truth and fiction, the activity of reading is an essential one. Repeatedly in the novel, McCann turns his characters into readers of existing literary works. These references contribute to the construction of a fictional world in continuity with the actual world. The works read by characters are often referred to by authors' surnames and produce an *effet de réel* – or reality effect – that underpins the verisimilitude of the narrative. A book in a work of fiction is not only a material object but also a means of cultural exchange. It makes sense in the way it corresponds to the novel it is included in. Therefore we the readers are invited to read the inserted literary texts so as to identify the way they connect with *Dancer*. The presence of the book within the book calls upon the intertextual notion of *mise en abyme*. (*Mise en abyme* is a French expression originally used in heraldry to describe a small shield set within a larger shield bearing the same device. Equivalent formal devices have long been used in both literature and the visual arts, the obvious examples being the play within a play in *Hamlet* and Velázquez's *Las Meninas*. The expression *mise en abyme* was given a new currency by the French novelist André Gide (1869–1951), who defined it as the representation within a work of art of that work's structure. *Mise en abyme* is frequently used by the writers associated with the *nouveau roman*, and a similar self-reflexivity is typical of much postmodernist fiction.) A book read by a character can be considered as a mediator of the dialogue with the global library. Therefore a relation of comment, transformation or quotation can be established between framed and framing books.[15] This literary dialogue is the subject of the present chapter.

Reading in the Soviet bloc

If the simple fact of reading is the evidence of education, it is noteworthy that the great majority of McCann's characters have an academic standard. Indeed, most of them have books within reach. Their books contribute to the descriptions of them. Among the secondary characters of the diegesis, Sergei Vassiliev is depicted as an ardent reader. In his small flat in Ufa around 1950, one evening he welcomes his wife Anna, who has been training Rudolf, and narrates:

> Anna put on her nightgown, worn at the elbows, and perched at the very edge of the bed. I was at my desk, reading … She rose and shuffled across the room, put her arms to my shoulders …
>
> She said, Read to me, husband.
>
> I picked up the book and she said, No, not here, let's go to bed.
>
> It was a book of Pasternak's that had survived all our years, open to a poem about stars frozen in the sky. I have always adored Pasternak, not just for the obvious reasons, but because it has seemed to me that by staying in the rearguard rather than moving with the vanguard, he had learned to love what is left behind without mourning what was gone.
>
> The book was fattened from being thumbed through so much. My habit, which Anna hated, of turning down the edges of my favourite pages gave it a further thickness.[16]

We readers are given the feeling of sharing this old couple's intimacy and aesthetic sensibility. The deep inner aspect of their married life is increased by the activity of reading out loud together in the bedroom. 'The obvious reasons' probably allude to what Anna and Sergei have in common with the man of letters, who rapidly fell into disgrace for writing books that did not praise the regime. Censored, relentlessly tracked down, then required to turn down the Nobel Prize he had been awarded, Pasternak only just avoided the Gulag, and was, like Sergei and Anna, severely punished for anti-communism and anti-patriotism. There is something significant about McCann's characters reading a book written by this author: it highlights the repressive power of the Soviet regime. The theme of insubordination, implicitly evoked by the reading couple and the author they read, can also be discerned in the protagonist of the novel, Nureyev being the perfect Soviet dissident in the Stalinist era.

The 'poem about stars frozen in the sky' is most certainly 'Winter Sky' written by Pasternak in 1916 and published in the collection *Over the Barriers*, in which some characteristic features of Nureyev's destiny can be detected, particularly the fulfilment of his artistic vocation in spite of the barriers referred to in the title of the book, as the first lines illustrate:

Out of the smoky air now are plucked down
Stars for the past week frozen in flight.
Head over heels reels the skaters' club,
Clinking its rink with the glass of the night.

Slower, slower, skater, step slow-er,
Cutting the curve as you swerve by.
Every turn a constellation
Scraped by the skate into Norway's sky.

Fetters of frozen iron shackle the air.[17]

The contrast between active and passive verbs, between the skater's movements and the immobility around him, can be interpreted as the desire of the young dancer – who was first a skater – to move away from a frozen world in which no future prospects are offered. This cold, black universe, which undermines civil liberties, obviously depicts Soviet dictatorship:

Hey, skaters! There it's all the same
That night is on earth with its ivory eyes
Snake-patterned like a domino game[18]

Surveillance and espionage are parts of the tyrannical methods that make life impossible: 'tongue … is freezing tight … mouths … filled with ice'.[19] Throughout the poem, the semantic field of height opposed to the baseness of venal materialism may symbolise the young dancer's ambition to climb up the social ladder and pull himself up out of this stifling universe. Pasternak's poem can be read as a preparation of the plot of McCann's novel – a premonitory sign of the protagonist's destiny and a prospective summary of the dancer's brilliant career, as if the development of his art was written in the stars.

Later, in Leningrad, in their daughter's flat, Anna and Sergei meet Rudolf again, who has become a student in the Kirov dance school. The latter invites them to come and see him on stage in *La Esmeralda*, a ballet based on Victor Hugo's *Notre-Dame de Paris*, and Yulia, the old couple's daughter, relates: 'I had the Victor Hugo book on my shelf and in the days leading up to the dance my father read it to my mother. His was a beautiful sonorous voice and he captured nuances in the text that surprised me.'[20] As he reads aloud Hugo's novel, Sergei prepares his wife for the show, and, in his own way, stages the plot of *Notre-Dame de Paris*. The motifs of the French novel – destitution, danger, separation, condemnation, refuge, dance – are echoed by the life of the young man they are about to admire on stage. Written in Paris in a time of political chaos, during the revolution of 1830, this work causes a reflection on the everlasting opposition between power-holders and the ones who are subjected to them. The mirror effect between Victor Hugo's novel and Jules Perrot's ballet is superimposed on the reflection between included and including texts. McCann's novel looks at itself in the mirror of its intertext. Paris is a symbolic focal place of Hugo's novel. This city also plays an essential part in Nureyev's life, as it granted him political asylum, allowed him to stay in the West, and thus became the emblem of freedom.

When, in Leningrad, Yulia hears that Rudi 'defected to Paris',[21] she decides at last to leave her husband and takes a book with her: 'I packed a bag with what I imagined I would need. It included a Gorky novel with money pasted beneath the cloth cover.'[22] It is worth noticing the material evocation of the book as an object on the one hand, and its diverted function on the other, since the book is used here for other purposes than reading. Of course, the mention of the author's name makes it possible to perceive this work as a text that has not been chosen by chance.

In this excerpt, the female narrator is deeply affected by Rudolf's decision, because she thinks that she will never see him again. Having put him up in Leningrad at the request of her parents, who lived in Ufa, she became attached to him, and fell under his spell, particularly when she saw him dance in the kitchen of her flat: 'He started dancing and looked as if he was checking the span of his wings. I let him be, moving around him to clean the dishes.'[23] This comparison between a dancer and a bird on the unusual stage of a kitchen floor echoes Gorky's autobiographical novel, *My Childhood*, in which one of the characters, Tsiganok, was 'rushing madly like a kite in the middle of the kitchen, his arms swinging out as if they were wings, shifting his feet almost too fast for the eye to see. With a whoop he squatted on the floor and tossed himself about like a golden bird.'[24]

The similarity between both texts can be interpreted as an influence of the book read by Yulia on her own narrative. It is significant that she remembers this scene when she gets ready to leave the marital home and acquire her independence. The image of the bird spreading its wings symbolises the love of liberty, the desire to escape an unbearable world, described by Gorky in the first pages of his book:

> Now I see [this life] as a grim story ... As I try to bring the past to
> life I find it hard to believe that it all really happened. That dreary
> life was so full of violence that I would even like to question or
> gloss over much of it.
>   But truth is nobler than self-pity and in fact I am not writing
> about myself alone, but about that close-knit, suffocating little
> world of pain and suffering where the ordinary Russian man in the
> street used to live, and where he lives to this day.[25]

These sentences written by Gorky could very well have been taken up by
Nureyev himself. Besides, both artists have a lot in common, particularly their
rags-to-riches stories. Thanks to their brilliant artistic careers, they achieve
international fame, appear to Soviet authorities to be the enemies of the
regime, are put under surveillance, and finally go into exile in the Western
world, where they lead a nomadic existence. Their art is recognised in their
host country but banned in their country of origin.

In Gorky's novel, after this improvised dancing scene, the spectators,
gathered around the samovar, talk about a girl from Balakna whose prowess
recall Nureyev's: '[she] made people cry with joy when she danced. It really did
you good just to look at her! And I was jealous of her!'[26] says the grandmother,
who concludes irrefutably: 'Singers and dancers are the salt of the earth!'[27]

Nureyev, reader of his fellow countrymen

The books read by characters in *Dancer* are as many enclaves bearing several
similarities to it. They can be considered as 'mirror books'[28] in which characters
discover their own stories or read what the future has in store for them. These
protagonists have split personalities in front of the mirror held out by the text
they read, as they can 'become part of the book':

> You see him [Nureyev] taken under Aleksandr Pushkin's wing; you
> see him reading constantly because Pushkin has told him that to
> be a great dancer he must know the great stories and so, in the
> courtyard, he bends over Gogol, Joyce, Dostoyevsky; you see him
> curl into the pages and you think that whenever you read that book
> in the future you will be reading him.[29]

A few pages further on, 'the books he was reading'[30] are mentioned, together with the name of Dostoyevsky, whose work is passionately read by Nureyev both in fiction and in reality.[31] With its solitary heroes and extreme emotions, Dostoyevsky's work strikes a chord in Nureyev and contributes in shaping him. On the one hand, it participates in his awakening and awareness of the world; on the other, it fuels his embitterment against the world and his inclination to nihilism. In addition, Dostoyevsky's work allows young Nureyev to know more about an artist from his own country with whom he has a lot in common. Like him, he will suddenly be in the limelight and enjoy international fame. Like him, he will experience suffering and frustration imposed on him by the political regime. Like him, he will have to leave his country, go over to the other side, and become so lonely and desperate that he will suffer from hysteria and neuroses and try to find solace in extreme behaviour. Nureyev could take up Dostoyevsky's words in his memoir: 'Throughout my life, I have done nothing but going as far as possible; I have taken to extremes what you've done by halves.'[32] What he reads explains what he is. Here, again, readings significantly characterise the protagonist. A book not only makes it possible to describe its reader's culture, ideology or social class, it is also a mirror of the reader's existence.

In his will to increase his literary knowledge, Nureyev, in Paris – grief-stricken in the wake of his father's death – takes an interest in the work of another Russian writer: 'Reading the translation of Solzhenitsyn, there was a brief flicker of light on the page. The desire to resurrect Father was suddenly overwhelming.'[33] Solzhenitsyn's work is a hymn to survivors of failure and death. Any Russian reader who has left his country can perceive in it what his life would have been if he had remained the prey of Soviet absolutism. The hospital in Tashkent, where the plot of the novel *Cancer Ward* is set, obviously reminds Rudolf of the place where he used to dance as a child. The ward also recalls his father's recent death, as it heralds the end of his own life. This microcosm of a world of fear is the emblem of a society wasted by evil in which, according to the Russian writer, man has no other choice but to become a tyrant, a traitor or a recluse. Considered as a perjurer by his friends, relatives, workmates, former teachers and the Soviet authorities,[34] Nureyev, who refuses to go back home, finds food for thought in Solzhenitsyn's work.

With Hamet Nureyev's public rejection of his 'son the traitor',[35] the end of a father–son relationship is reminiscent of *Taras Bulba*, a novel by Gogol, who turns out to be one of Nureyev's favourite writers.[36] In the Ukrainian steppe, in the sixteenth century, Taras Bulba notices that one of his sons, Andrei, is rather unmanly. He sends him to a military camp for Cossack cavalrymen where boys are trained to be ardent defenders of the Orthodox faith, prepare for war, sack towns and villages, slaughter Jews and plunder Catholic monasteries. During one of these battles, Andrei enters enemy territory to find some bread for a woman he has met and loved in Kiev. This act urges him to break with his past for good; any return home to his old mother is, from then on, impossible. Considered a deserter, Andrei is disowned by his family, particularly by his father: 'Old Taras will tear a grey tuft from his scalp-lock, and curse the day and the hour he begot this son of his, the black sheep of the family.'[37] As a man of experience who is used to being in command and fuelling his bitter hatred toward the enemy, Taras Bulba interprets his son's initiative as an act of treason, and kills him with his own hands. To some extent, these blood ties can be transposed onto the relationship between Rudolf and his father: held up to public opprobrium and considered a renegade and a culprit by his father, is he not symbolically killed by him?

Like the actual Nureyev,[38] *Dancer*'s protagonist is not only an avid reader of Gogol but also quotes this author, and introduces his books in his own speech. As Yulia narrates, young Rudolf makes a strange remark when he gets into her flat in Leningrad: '*Oh don't trust that Nevsky Prospect, it's all lies and dreams, it's not what it all seems!* he said, quoting Gogol, surprising me.'[39] This quotation is extracted from the last page of the story 'Nevsky Prospect', in which the city of St Petersburg plays a major part, as indicated by the title of the book it is taken from – *Petersburg Tales*. This city (called Leningrad during most of Nureyev's life) is considered as exotic by young Nureyev, as it was by Gogol. The spontaneous association of St Petersburg with Gogol testifies that the teenager's mind is full of readings. 'Nevsky Prospect' is a short story that narrates the parallel destinies of two young men who meet and shadow two ladies on Nevsky Prospect, the main thoroughfare of St Petersburg. The first one, Piskariov, a painter, follows a brunette, but is disappointed when he notices that she lives in a squalid place. He goes back home, goes to sleep and dreams that he is the guest at a sumptuous party. There he meets a graceful dancer; surrounded by a group of admirers, she proves to be the girl he had tailed in the street. In a long, vain attempt to re-enact his dream, Piskariov loses sleep, swallows a lot of opium and puts an end to his life.

The other man, Pirogov, is attracted by a blond, married German woman.

As he knows she is alone on Sundays, he goes to her, dances with her, comes on strong, but the lady's husband catches them and beats up the lover. A few hours later, in the evening, Pirogov 'so distinguished himself in the mazurka that not only the ladies but even the cavaliers were in raptures',[40] hence the narrator's conclusion:

> How wonderfully this world of ours is arranged! How strangely, how inscrutably fate plays with us! Do we ever get what we really desire? Do we ever achieve what our powers have ostensibly equipped us for? But strangest of all are the events that take place on Nevsky Prospect. Oh, do not trust this Nevsky Prospect! I always wrap myself tighter in my cloak when I walk along it and try to ignore every object I see on my way. All is deception, all is a dream, all is not what it seems … You imagine that these two stout gentlemen who have stopped in front of a church that is being built are commenting on its architecture? Far from it: they are discussing how strangely two crows are sitting opposite each other … This Nevsky Prospect lies at all hours, but most of all … when the devil himself lights the street lamps, only to show everything in an unreal guise.[41]

Apart from the obvious connection between the diegesis of Gogol's narrative and the brilliant future that lays ahead of young Rudolf – the transition from darkness to light, the metamorphosis from poverty into splendour, the dancer's attractive qualities – the short story insists on Nevsky Prospect as a source of illusion and deceit. Illustrated by the citation of the young man as he sets foot in Leningrad, this notion of lying is recurrent in McCann's novel.

Dancer starts with a quotation from William Maxwell's novel *So Long, See You Tomorrow*, which ends with these words: 'in talking about the past we lie with every breath we draw'. The plot of this American novel – in which ties of love and friendship are suddenly broken, in which separation generates feelings of deception and treason and requires a complete change of life – is focused on the transformation of memory into imagination. By definition the past cannot be reached. It is inevitably invented, according to the narrator's admission:

> I assume that I knew all this once, since it was published in the evening paper and I was old enough to read. In the course of time

> the details of the murder passed from my mind, and what I thought happened was so different from what actually did happen that it might almost have been something I made up out of whole cloth.[42]

Expressed by the narrator of Maxwell's novel, this idea arouses a reflection on McCann's approach: maybe this citation was chosen as an epigraph to remind the reader that *Dancer* is not a biography but a biographical novel inspired from recognised facts and fictional elements. The epigraph can be read as a warning: it incites the reader not to overlook the fact that the text that follows is nothing but a story about partly imaginary characters and events, a piece of writing made of illusion, a deliberate myth that conveys the fragility of mimesis and can thus be related to a lie.

Among the *Petersburg Tales*, 'The Portrait' is also noteworthy insofar as its protagonist, like the one in *Dancer*, is an extremely talented artist who reached fame and fortune. Besides, the very notion of portrait is interesting, as each narrator in McCann's novel gives a personal outline of the protagonist, and insists on such and such aspect of his personality: his behaviour in society, his love of money, his stylish look, his art, language or fantasies. Polyphonic, the novel can be read as a multifaceted portrait of the dancer. Furthermore, the first half of the book is, to some extent, a 'portrait of the artist as a young man'.

'Westernisation' of the protagonist's readings

In the novel Nureyev also reads Joyce.[43] Here, again, both artists have a lot in common. In view of his own experience, the dancer can recognise himself in the young enuretic protagonist of the first chapter of Joyce's autobiographical novel *A Portrait of the Artist as a Young Man*, who is bullied by his comrades and teachers, vouching, if need be, for the fact that the same causes bring the same effects. Indeed, young Nureyev also endures humiliations in the classroom:

> He gets the answer wrong and Goyanov strikes his ruler hard on the desk. Three more wrong answers and he is slapped on the palm of his left hand. And then, before the right hand is hit, a puddle appears on the floor. The other children laugh when they realise that he has pissed himself … He roots himself there, touches the front of his wet pants.[44]

Wounded in their pride, these children will become creators of beauty. Yet Joyce and Nureyev understand very early on that if they stay in their fossilising milieu they will be unable to express their artistic talent. They have to escape from the nets thrown over their creative souls in order to give free rein to their art. As a result, the words of Stephen Dedalus, alias James Joyce, could very well be Rudolf Nureyev's:

> I will not serve that in which I no longer believe whether it call itself my home, my fatherland or my church: and I will try to express myself in some mode of life or art as freely as I can and as wholly as I can, using for my defence the only arms I allow myself to use – silence, exile, and cunning.[45]

The biographies provide no information about Nureyev's knowledge of Joyce's work. The same is true of Beckett, met and read by fictional Nureyev. It is thus legitimate to wonder if McCann, as an Irishman, does not call upon his fellow-countrymen's destinies and pieces of writing only because he identifies there some elements that stand comparison with what the dancer experienced. Indeed, Beckett was also an artist whose exile allowed him to show his creative genius. Moreover, his work is in line with Gogol's or Solzhenitsyn's, because it is ironic, sarcastic and despairing, like Nureyev's entertainments, which are always tinged with bitter melancholy. In a passage from *Dancer*, Rudolf, before going on stage, is relaxing in his dressing room, lying on a table, waiting to be given a massage:

> Rudi had a special stand set up in front of the massage table and he was reading a signed copy of Beckett, – *For Rudolf, all good wishes, Sam* – and Rudi was learning whole chunks of the book by heart, and later that night, at a dinner party in the Austrian embassy, he stood and performed a routine about stones in his pocket and stones in his mouth, quoted perfectly, syllable for syllable …[46]

This detailed precision makes it possible to identify the book read by Rudolf as being *Molloy*, in which the narrator remarks:

> I took a pebble from my pocket and sucked it. It was smooth, from having been sucked so long, by me, and beaten by the storm. A little pebble in your mouth, round and smooth, appeases, soothes, makes you forget your hunger, forget your thirst.[47]

Filling his mouth and pockets with pebbles is not only a pastime Molloy somehow justifies, it is also a recreational pleasure whose object is to find a way of exhausting the sixteen stones tucked up in his four pockets without ever sucking the same pebble twice – hence his ingenious calculations and inexhaustible solutions described on entire pages. Having his pockets filled with pebbles can also be a way of hastening his death if he falls into the water. This is why one of *Dancer*'s narrators observes:

> … at the wall of the river Rudi scooped up a number of pebbles, borrowed Victor's overcoat and stood precariously on the wall, launched into the speech once again, arms stretched wide, and Victor wondered what might happen if Rudi toppled into the water, if the Seine itself would dance.[48]

This whim consisting in filling one's pockets with pebbles is somehow akin to arranged suicide. The artist is always a suffering man or woman, hence the narrator's remark:

> … while walking home, he [Rudi] quickened his pace towards the Seine and talked about how he had begun to believe that there should be no unity in art, never, that perfection embalms it, there has to be some tearing, a fracturing, like a Persian carpet with a wrongly tied knot …[49]

In Nureyev's case, tearing and fracturing are caused by his isolation from his family: Rudolf is in exile, but, unexpectedly, finally manages to go back to his mother's room after a very long absence. Likewise, in Beckett's novel Molloy repeatedly wonders whether he will ever see his mother again: 'my mother could scarcely be waiting for me still, after so long'.[50] He is trapped in a circle, particularly the circle of his narrative, which starts with the end and terminates with the beginning. Interestingly, the first sentence of the text is, 'I am in my mother's room.'[51] By the same token, *Dancer* ends with Nureyev standing in his mother's room, a place he thought he would never return to. Seeking for his mother and for himself as well, looking for certainties that prove to be evasive, Molloy is a constant traveller: firstly, he rides his bicycle, then walks on crutches, and eventually crawls on the floor. Although he leads a nomadic life like Nureyev, Molloy appears as the exact opposite of the famous wealthy dancer: he is a one-eyed, toothless, crippled man, careless about his body that he fails to wash; his only possessions are crutches, pebbles and a bicycle. Nevertheless, he sometimes describes himself as a budding dancer, for

> there is rapture, or there should be, in the motion crutches give. It is a series of little flights, skimming the ground. You take off, you land, through the thronging sound in wind and limb, who have to fasten one foot to the ground before they dare lift up the other.[52]

As he again says: 'From time to time I caught myself making a little bound in the air, two or three feet off the ground at least, I who never bounded. It looked like levitation.'[53] Comparison of the framing and framed works shows a funny, ironical dialogue, 'so avid is the mind of the flimsiest analogy', as Molloy puts it.[54]

In the examples given so far, Nureyev reads in order to learn and enjoy himself. The part he plays in the world of art requires some general knowledge – hence his readings of Russian but also Western books. Yet the protagonist sets himself the task of undertaking a 'professional' reading in order to perfect his dancing performance. In his diary he mentions the preliminary stage of his show, and writes: '*Corsaire* duet with Sizova. Read Byron for texture.'[55] *Le Corsaire* is a ballet created in France in which Nureyev dances a *pas de deux* with his compatriot, ballerina Alla Sizova. It is based on a long poem by Lord Byron that tells the story of Conrad, a pirate who is loved by two girls. Before dancing this duet, Nureyev considers it useful to 'read Byron for texture'. This reading is a duty imposed on himself by his professional activity. Rudolf makes it a rule to read and appropriate the text that, like a script, is designed to be staged, and to immerse himself in the role, to identify with the corsair. To play Conrad, Rudolf must become Conrad. The characteristic features of this masculine, chivalric, exotic protagonist carried along by his passionate enthusiasm perfectly match the strong character of Nureyev, who, like him, is a suffering, despondent man. Indeed, both of them are in despair because they left a desolate woman behind them. Even if they are free, they remain grief-stricken. As Byron's poetic tale puts it:

> [...] his chains unbind;
> Once more his limbs are free as mountain wind
> But on his heavy heart such sadness sate,
> As if they there transferred that iron weight.
> No words are uttered [...][56]

The Russian dancer is a torturous charmer of the stuff Byronian heroes are made of. His romantic sadness and thirst for liberty lead to a comparison of Nureyev not only with Byronian heroes but also with Byron himself.[57] Indeed, their fates are similar: these two rebellious, eccentric artists spark off the hatred of the establishment, leave their countries once and for all, lead a nomadic existence, live in debauchery and extravagance, retreat into loneliness and isolation, and, finally, die in exile. Characterised by their taste for excess, their triumphant self-centredness, and their outrageously dramatic behaviour, they prove to be violent, overproud, unstable characters who make endless scenes and give themselves over to all kinds of pleasures. With the constant feeling that fate hangs over them, they sink into despair – hence the romantic nature of their destinies.

Throughout the novel, a phenomenon of Westernisation is noticeable, not only in the dancer's life in the wake of his emigration but also in his readings: after Gorky, Dostoyevsky or Solzhenitsyn, the reader broadens his cultural horizons and is progressively interested in Joyce, Beckett or Byron, until he reaches the highest degree of relaxation of moral standards with a libertine book intended for informed readers over eighteen.

Liberty and libertinage

As Sergei and Anna read out loud together, *Dancer* narrates a similar scene in which two other lovers, Rudolf and Erik, share the same book in bed. Staying in a villa at the seaside in Gallipoli, Rudolf remarks: 'In bed we read Flaubert's letters from Egypt. Outside the sea crashed.'[58] The book is here referred to not only by the author's surname, as is generally the case in the novel, but also by the title of the book they read. This reading is not imagined by McCann insofar as, according to Julie Kavanagh – who also wrote a biography – Nureyev in 1981 was 'inseparable from Flaubert's travel notes and letters from Egypt'.[59] These letters are an account of the tour Gustave Flaubert and his friend Maxime Du Camp made in the Eastern world in 1849 and 1850. The two young men were sent there by the French Ministry of Agriculture, but soon neglected their official tasks so as to realise their sexual fantasies. In his letters to Louis Bouilhet, his close friend in Rouen, young Flaubert, then aged twenty-seven, frankly depicts in minute detail his amazing sexual activities and orgies:

> The day before yesterday we were in the house of a woman who had two others there for us to lay ... I performed on a mat that a family

of cats had to be shooed off – a strange coitus, looking at each other without being able to exchange a word, and the exchange of looks is all the deeper for the curiosity and the surprise. My brain was too stimulated for me to enjoy it much otherwise. These shaved cunts make a strange effect – the flesh is hard as bronze, and my girl had a splendid arse.[60]

Homosexual experiences are also part of his lechery:

Speaking of bardashes, this is what I know about them. Here it is quite accepted. One admits one's sodomy, and it is spoken of at table in the hotel. Sometimes you do a bit of denying, and then everybody teases you and you end up confessing. Travelling as we are for educational purposes, and charged with a mission by the government, we have considered it our duty to indulge in this form of ejaculation … It's at the baths that such things take place. You reserve the bath for yourself (five francs including masseurs, pipe, coffee, sheet and towel) and you skewer your lad in one of the rooms. Be informed, furthermore, that all the bath-boys are bardashes. The final masseurs, the ones who come to rub you when all the rest is done, are usually quite nice young boys … They massage you, turning you over like embalmers preparing you for the tomb … Monday, my *kellaa* was rubbing me gently, and when he came to the noble parts he lifted up my *boules d'amour* to clean them, then continuing to rub my chest with his left hand he began to pull with his right on my prick, and as he drew it up and down he leaned over my shoulder and said '*baksheesh, baksheesh*'.[61]

Obviously, the erotic, bawdy content of Flaubert's letters is perfectly in keeping with the readers and their guests' sexual activities in Gallipoli: 'Pablo sat naked to play Shostakovich (badly) and his arse left a sweatstain on the piano stool.'[62] Besides, the two lovers are lying in bed when they are reading the letters from Egypt, which heralds the intensity of their sexual life. Reading together does not only create intellectual communion between them, it is highly likely that the performance of the one who reads out loud is accompanied by gestures. Once 'staged', the reading may awaken, if not stimulate, sexual relationships. As Nureyev becomes Conrad the corsair, why wouldn't he play the part of Flaubert or the bath boy? Besides, Flaubert's *Letters from Egypt* advocate frantic male sexual appetite in which Nureyev recognises himself. Therefore the fictionalisation of a real book and its reading is accompanied with *mise en abyme*. Lastly, considering the cultural background of a reader coming from the Soviet bloc, there is something daring and transgressive about reading a book that is banned at home. Reading Flaubert's *Letters from Egypt* is defying authority, responding to censorship, taking one's revenge on dictatorship and gazing at oneself in the mirror of one's own liberty.

Like historical Nureyev that biographers depict as a book-lover,[63] novelistic Nureyev is an ardent reader. In the fashionable circles of a busy society life, from show to show, from party to party, the act of reading makes it possible to pause momentarily, to do some soul-searching. It is the same with regards to the characters of *Dancer*. Whether it is solitary or dual, professional or transgressive, the reading of an identifiable text is an indirect description, a secret shared between the fictional readers and the actual readers that we are. Reading is a clue. Not only does it socially and culturally characterise a milieu, it also provides information about the reading character's psychology and personality. A book is a place of exchange, reflexiveness and self-reference. It tells a truth about its reader, to whom it holds out a mirror. Each book read by Nureyev reflects and discloses a part of his life, whether it is his art, his thirst for liberty, his painful isolation, his so-called treason or his sexual life. It is significant that the dancer's readings mirror his emigration from the Soviet bloc to the Western world, thus testifying to his desire to enlarge his horizons. It is also noteworthy that the great majority of the writers he reads – be they Russian, Irish or British – are, like him, artists disowned by the authorities of their countries and who ran away from unbearable yokes in order to enjoy individual freedom.

CHAPTER 7

Zoli: a mimetic and dialogic novel in memory of the oppressed

I sabel Fonseca is an American writer. She is the author of a non-fiction book relating to the lives of Romani people, *Bury Me Standing*.[1] In this work she describes the four years she spent travelling with Gypsies from Albania to Poland. This personal reportage is composed of vivid portraits of the individuals she met, of comments on the ways and customs of this nomadic people who managed, against all odds, to preserve their culture. It recounts the blurred, sometimes legendary origins of this community, and the hostility and violent attacks they had to handle. This hatred peaked during the Second World War with the Nazi genocide against Gypsies. Such persecutions are summed up in the title of the book, which takes up the words of a Roma activist who claims posthumous dignity as he has never been granted this right in his lifetime: 'Bury me standing, I've been on my knees all my life.'[2]

As a preamble, the book begins with the story of Bronisława Wajs (1910–87), who was born into a family of Polish Gypsy harpists, travelling with horses and caravans. At fifteen, she was married to an old musician of the clan, Dionizy. This mismatch incited her to sing by way of consolation.

Unlike the great majority of Romanies, who were illiterate,[3] Bronisława learned to read and write, and composed poems that she set to music. 'Drawing from the great Gypsy tradition of improvised storytelling, and from short simple folk songs, she composed long ballads – part song, part poem, spontaneously "enacted".'[4] Her texts, written in Romani language, are 'stylized distillations of collective experience':[5] she narrates the threats posed to her peers, the deaths of her relatives during the war, the horror of the concentration camps, her life as she was hiding in forests. The poetess became known as 'Papusza' – the doll. After the war, a Polish poet, Jerzy Ficowski, collected her song-poems, transcribed them into Polish and published them. A few years later he wrote an essay in which he approved of the 'Great Halt', a policy of the Polish government to enforce the settlement of Gypsies. As the latter were strongly opposed to this legislation, Ficowski used and exploited Papusza, made her a spokeswoman of forced assimilation, and asserted that the most compelling proof of the success of this policy was that 'her greatest period of poetry writing was around 1950, soon after she abandoned the nomadic way of life'.[6]

After the appearance of her poems, Papusza was visited by Roma emissaries who blamed her for collaborating with a *gadjo* and trying to abandon their traditional way of life; indeed, publishing her songs was contrary to their oral custom. Misunderstood and appalled by this manipulation, Papusza destroyed all her original works and tried to prevent publication of any of her compositions, but it was too late. Put on trial – she was called before the highest authority of the Polish Roma, the *Baro Shero* – Papusza was proclaimed 'unclean' and irreversibly excluded from the group. She spent several months in a psychiatric hospital, then lived alone in isolation for over three decades until her death in 1987. Discarded and sacrificed, Papusza is the archetype of the scapegoat.

This story inspired *Zoli*, Colum McCann's novel published in 2006. Bronisława Wajs, alias Papusza, is recognised as Marienka Novotna, known as Zoli. Jerzy Ficowski becomes Martin Stransky, the man who, with Stephen Swann's help, publishes the young woman's poems against her will. Like *Dancer*, McCann's previous novel, *Zoli* is made of fact and fiction. McCann explains in an interview: 'More or less the same thing that happens to Zoli in the novel did in fact happen to Papusza in the 1950s. However, I didn't want to write a nonfiction book … I wanted the liberty of imagining things.'[7] McCann started planning this novel after he found a photograph of Papusza that haunted him.[8] This picture can be seen in Isabel Fonseca's book,[9] which proved to be a seminal piece of writing in this case. As McCann puts it: 'The story of Zoli was suggested to me after reading the extraordinary study *Bury Me Standing: the Gypsies and their journey*, by Isabel Fonseca.'[10] In his research on Romani culture,[11] McCann read many books and documents at the New York Public Library, consulted maps so as to follow the routes taken by these nomadic families, and decided to meet them in Eastern Europe. His motivation for writing about this minority stems from his desire to fill in a gap: 'It struck me that this was largely an untold story.'[12] Indeed, not only are there very few writers among the Roma, which can be explained by their purely oral culture, but there are also very few grand narratives about this minority, which is nevertheless made up of thirteen million people. This lack of interest may be due to the prejudiced attitudes against them.[13] McCann himself acknowledges that he was biased against the Roma.[14] Therefore he had to fight against his own preconceived notions before getting into Gypsy camps.

As the purpose of the present book is to provide an intertextually informed reading of McCann's work, a link must be found between *Zoli* and textual interaction. Spontaneously, some nineteenth-century novels crop up in the reader's literary memory. Indeed, in view of the author's nationality, the upset protagonist tracked down by predatory criminals, the geographical area in which most of the plot takes place – the Carpathians – and the nightmarish atmosphere of the diegetic universe, Dracula's shadow hangs over the narrative: the vampire, created in 1897 by an Irishman, Bram Stoker, can be transposed onto the persecutor of Gypsies, who takes a sadistic pleasure in chasing human beings. Both of them are bloodthirsty. Their victims are also alike, the torments suffered by Mina, the female protagonist of *Dracula,* being similar to the ones experienced by Zoli.

The latter – banished, ostracised and excluded by members of her own group – also recalls another woman with a tragic destiny: the protagonist of Nathaniel Hawthorne's *The Scarlet Letter* (1850). The defamatory letter *A* that Hester Prynne bears on her dress so that her adultery is known is reminiscent of the letter *Z* that in Auschwitz was tattooed on the left arms of Gypsies, who were identified by the German word *Zigeuner.*[15] In this respect, it is probably no accident that McCann chose to give his protagonist a name beginning with the letter *Z*. From *A* to *Z*, Hester and Zoli redraw the great chain of the oppressed and humiliated, the wretched of the earth.[16] *Zoli* and *The Scarlet Letter* are novels of mental torture and agony, but both of them end with women's liberation, as Francesca and Pearl, the heroines' daughters, take advantage of their mothers' rebellion, since they leave the place of suffering once and for all, and blossom a happy marriages.

In addition to these intertextual allusions, that deserve to be developed, *Zoli* is also made of specificities that are noteworthy. Indeed, the writing of the novel is characterised by two new experiences for McCann: on the one hand, this is the first time he has written a novel in a woman's voice;[17] on the other, this is the first time he has written and published his own poems.

Writing about a poetess without quoting her poems is difficult. Yet the diffusion of her works was precisely something Papusza refused and fought against. McCann was then confronted with a dilemma: how to quote her without once again violating her wish not to be published, without siding with the ones who had 'betrayed' her. It would have been contrary to the spirit of the novel, according to McCann, who ultimately decided to write some original poems, inspired from Papusza's, and credit them to Zoli. Guided by her writing when composing his own verse, he sought to narrow as much as he could the gap between her work and his. As they belong to literature in the second degree, these poems are intertextual.

Imitative writing

McCann's poems can easily be distinguished from the text they are inserted in as they are emphasised by italics. They give the reader a glimpse of Papusza's work. They take some of its specificities, then reorganise and adapt them to Zoli's situation. They take part in the creation and reproduction of a model. McCann rewrites Papusza's poems and endeavours to make his own texts as close as possible to the spirit and letter of the original ones. His poetry, in the style of Papusza's, is clearly imitative. It is the work of a craftsman, a forge worker – hence its connection with forgery, which Gérard Genette perceives as being the basic concept of imitation:

> The simplest, purest, or perhaps the most neutral mimetic *state* is without doubt that of forgery. It can be defined as the state of a text resembling as much as possible those of the imitated corpus, without anything in it that draws attention to the mimetic process itself or to the mimetic text, whose resemblance must be as transparent as possible without designating itself as resemblance – that is, as an imitation.[18]

According to Genette, forgery is the process of imitating documents. Yet there is no intent to deceive here: true, McCann wrote poems informed by Papusza's, but his works have never been illegally represented as the original ones. This kind of imitation also differs from pastiche, which is a work written in the style of another writer in a comical or satirical tone. McCann's poems are no caricatures. They do not ridicule but, on the contrary, show admiration for Papusza's work. Besides, pastiche is nothing else but imitation of style, whereas McCann's poetry here also strives to capture the spirit of the model. His verse is respectful of the specific language and thought of the

Polish poetess. McCann's poetry explores Papusza's poems and takes up their figures, motifs, structures and vocabulary.

This imitative writing is notably characterised by repetitive elements, such as phrases, words or sounds: 'By *what is* broken, *what is* snapped, I create *what is* required ... *they broke, they broke* my little brown arm'.[19] These resumptions are also noticeable in Papusza's poems: '*the water* does not look behind ... *the water* that wanders'.[20] Imitation is also stylistic: like Papusza, McCann introduces many interjections – 'Lord!'[21] – and prosopopoeia – 'My land, we are your children.'[22] These figures of speech highlight the speaker's loneliness. Another feature the two works have in common is their repeated questioning, the interrogative form reflecting the uncertainty of the protagonists' condition: 'Where should I go? What can I do?'[23] These similarities testify that Zoli's poetry – that is, McCann's – is dictated by Papusza's style.

The imitative process also includes a resumption of motifs and themes. Semantic fields such as silence and verbalisation, and also the notion of return – whether it is to nature or to the past – are omnipresent in Papusza's verse:

> [...] water
>
> You can hear it
> Wandering
> When it wishes to speak.
> But poor thing it has no speech ...
>
> ... the water does not look behind.[24]

The same motifs can also be seen in Zoli's poems: 'The river turned'; 'And our song went into the mountains'; 'We called this song the quiet.'[25] Similarly, the motifs of loss and wandering are noticeable in both works. Once again, Zoli's words echo Papusza's, and keep their nostalgic and melancholy tone: 'the hour of our wandering has been/ And passed and been and passed again'[26] is reminiscent of 'the time of the wandering Gypsies/ Has long passed.'[27] Papusza sheds tears over a world that no longer exists:

> That of which I speak
> Has all, all passed away,
> Everything has gone with it –
> And those years of youth.[28]

As a witness of identical scenes, Zoli shares her grievous complaint: 'Look at our fallen homes/ And all the Gypsies broken!'[29] Zoli is a member of a persecuted minority who proudly claims her identity and the colour of her skin, as exemplified by the phrase 'dark father',[30] which is inspired from Papusza's line 'O forest, my father,/ My black father!'[31]

McCann does not replicate Papusza's poems but absorbs their letter and spirit to credit Zoli with some lines that are as close as possible to the original ones. Nevertheless, any imitative practice implies a gap between the two texts. Imitation necessarily means distortion, as trifling as it may be. Although it looks very close to its model, Zoli's poetry inevitably changes Papusza's by imposing its own discourse. Furthermore, the contexts of the creative process are quite different: obviously, McCann's approach, culture and sensitivity are not the same as Papusza's. Whatever efforts he made in his poems, an Irish-American in 2006 cannot write exactly as a Gypsy poetess of Eastern Europe who personally suffered from banishment and exile in the middle of the twentieth century. His text – translated and suited to another cultural and linguistic context – will always be that of a foreigner. Indeed, the text is here transposed into another language; Papusza's poems were written in the Romani language: 'The Polish poet Jerzy Ficowski collected and transcribed the stories that Papusza had painstakingly copied out in Romani, written phonetically in the Polish alphabet.'[32] Having been translated by Ficowski into Polish, the stories were later translated into English, the language that allowed McCann access to the texts, to imitate them and attribute them to Zoli. The development between the starting line – the actual poet's work – and the finish line – the fictional poet's work – is strewn with obstacles and bristling with transplantations, testifying that imitation inevitably transforms the model. It would be illusive to think that the second text is completely faithful to the first one.

Although they belong to the same genre – that is, poetry – McCann makes his own text fit Papusza's. But he also distances himself from her work, and adapts Zoli's poetry to some scenes of the novel that are not inspired by the poet's real life. For example, the death of Zoli's relatives by drowning in a lake in front of the members of the Hlinka, the local Gestapo, is imagined by McCann:

> We asked by what roads we could escape –
> They showed us the narrowest one
> [...]
> They drove our wagons onto the ice

And ringed the white lake with fires,
So when the cold began to crack
The cheers went up from the Hlinkas.
We forced our best horses forward
But they skidded, bloody, to the shore.
My land, we are your children,
Shore up the ice, make it freeze!
[…]
They loaded the railway trains
Until the springs went flat.
We heard the moaning of Gypsy children
Too hungry to sleep or dream
[…]
We were taken in through their gates
They let us up through their chimneys.[33]

A feature of this poem, which is also a characteristic of Papusza's verse, is the dichotomy introducing a Manichaean world based on a distinction between 'them' and 'us', two pronouns referring to antagonistic communities. This binary opposition is not only present in Zoli's poetry but also in her narrative:

> They cut our tongues and make us speechless and then they try
> to get an answer from us … even the worst of us has never been
> among the worst of them. They make enemies of us … They expect
> us to see the future or at least to rob its pockets. They shave our
> heads and say … why can't you just be like us?[34]

This sectarian language does not have its roots in Papusza's verse but in much older, vaguer origins.

The revival of a sectarian, ideological discourse

This dichotomic discourse rests upon a value judgement that is significant of ethnocentrism. It is used to define oneself in relation to either Gypsies or *gadji*.[35] Indeed, this essential distinction can also be noticed in Stransky's speech in which Gypsies are, this time, referred to as 'they', since the speaker is not a member of their group: 'they're the joke of the week … we can make a whole new art form'.[36] Each community seems reluctant to name the other group and contents itself with personal pronouns referring to membership – 'we' – or exclusion – 'they'. As the signifiers remain the same, the signified switch. This sectarian approach takes root in ancient culture and proves to be particularly tenacious, as Edward Said notes:

> Throughout the exchange between Europeans and their 'others' that began systematically half a millennium ago, the one idea that has scarcely varied is that there is an 'us' and a 'them', each quite settled, clear, unassailably self-evident … the division goes back to Greek thought about barbarians, but, whoever originated this kind of 'identity' thought, by the nineteenth century it had become the hallmark of imperialist cultures as well as those cultures trying to resist the encroachments of Europe … We are still the inheritors of that style …[37]

This view of the world is still perceptible in the literature, society and history of Gypsies and *gadji*. The literary text here echoes collective languages tinged with xenophobic ideology, and inserts them without any comment. It integrates stereotypical speeches corresponding to the ways of thinking of antagonistic groups. Although the field of literature is exceeded here, this process of insertion and transformation is intertextual. Indeed, in this case the literary text is connected to society through the medium of a dialogue.[38] The basic premise of the theory of intertextuality is that a text is always involved in a dialogue with other texts, whatever they are: '*any text* is constructed as a mosaic of quotations; *any text* is the absorption and transformation of another', as Kristeva puts it.[39] A text is not merely a published piece of literary writing, it also comprehends the discourses of the social and histori-cal contexts. As a result, any interaction between literature and ideology is intertextual and dialogic. This intertextual dialogism considers the other and her/his speech through the literary text and confronts a variety of points of view, of cultures, of contrasting stereotypes. For the English critic Matthew Arnold, in 1869, 'culture' implied refined feelings and lofty ideals. He defined it as 'the best that is known and thought in the world'.[40] This personal opinion created drifts, as Said explains:

> Arnold believed that culture palliates, if it does not altogether neutralize, the ravages of a modern, aggressive, mercantile, and

brutalizing urban existence. You read Dante or Shakespeare in order to keep up with the best that was thought and known, and also to see yourself, your people, society, and tradition in their best lights. In time, culture comes to be associated, often aggressively, with the nation or the state; this differentiates 'us' from 'them', almost always with some degree of xenophobia. Culture in this sense is a source of identity ...[41]

Said illustrates his point with extracts from British works by Dickens, Conrad and D.H. Lawrence. In their books he notices a hierarchical organisation in which one of the two poles is always ruling and has its own power confirmed by this way of thinking. In these authors' societies, binary opposition was widespread, particularly in the relationships between England and Ireland. For the nineteenth- and early twentieth-century Englishman involved in projects relating to the present and future of his nation – the consolidation of a large colonial empire, commercial and industrial development – the Irishman, who is perceived as pastoral, nostalgic and fatalistic, is the 'other' par excellence. Besides, unlike the Englishman – the loyal subject of a local monarch who proves to be both a political and religious leader – the Irishman is subjected to foreign political and religious authorities whose respective seats are in London and Rome. As John Wilson Foster emphasises, 'the Catholic was made inescapably Other'.[42] This view of the world not only characterises the Victorian era but can also be observed in the following decades, as contemporary Irish fiction exemplifies.[43] Therefore it is significant that this ideological speech, which can be considered as archaic, is used in *Zoli* insofar as the novel was written by an Irishman raised in a Catholic family who is assumed to feel solidarity with other minorities who suffered humiliations in the past. As McCann himself remarks about the time he spent among the Roma, it was very useful to be Irish because he did not belong to a ruling, oppressive culture.[44] His characters' ethnocentric discourse can paradigmatically be substituted, because it may correspond to what the author himself heard in Ireland. In any case, such a speech is reminiscent of the one used by all the antagonists of the world. In this respect, it is significant that the favourite book of Zoli's grandfather is *Capital*,[45] Marx's critical account of the capitalist economy centred on the idea that historical, social and political developments are driven by a dialectic of conflict between exploiting and exploited classes. Hunting any kind of alienation, the proletarian revolution envisaged by Marxist theory yearns for the gathering of all the oppressed of the world no matter where they come from; as the famous slogan puts it, 'Working men of all countries, unite!' The Irish are not different from Jews or Gypsies: all of them make common cause with the same fight against exploitation. Exploited and exploiting classes are clearly identified by Marxist philosophy as two distinct and antagonistic categories, familiar with the discourse opposing 'them' to 'us'.

Whoever the speaker and referent may be, the truth is systematically defined by 'our' truth, which consists of determining everybody's values from personal ones, in extending the principles or beliefs of one's group to humanity. The community to which 'we' belong is bound to be the one that possesses the highest values. This distinction always brings notions of purity, superiority and glorification of 'our' group and humiliation of others, 'we' being always shown to best advantage compared with 'them'.

Ironically, at the end of the novel, Francesca, Zoli and Enrico's daughter – the offspring of the union of a banished Gypsy poet and a wealthy Italian heir – shows in her speech that she does not recognise herself in her mother's origins, but that she is totally assimilated and integrated into *gadji* society, as demonstrated by her answer to her mother, who asks her:

> 'And where are ours?'
> 'Ours?'
> 'Yes, ours.'
> 'Block eight. There's a few out near the highway too. They've
> built little shelters for themselves ...'
> [...]
> 'We try to help as much as possible.'[46]

One generation is enough to reverse the situation: the mother's 'ours' are the daughter's 'others'.

The 'we'/'they' distinction is one of the ways by which otherness is defined. The notion of the other refers to one pole of the relationship between a subject and a person defined as a non-self that is different or other. The other is seen as a source of threat to the autonomy and freedom of the subject. The relationship with the other is always antagonistic, as it is based upon the dialectics in which the only possibilities are being dominated or dominant. The other is here a negative definition of otherness: it refers to what cannot be seen as identity and sameness.[47] As Said evokes in the extract quoted above, this sectarianism goes back to the distinction between the civilised Greeks and barbarians. In the *gadji's* speech, the Roma are what 'we' are not – or prefer to think we are not – that is, thieves and liars. Moreover, they ignore individual property and form small nomadic communities. Besides, they cannot read or write. As a result, are they not in contrast to the civilised people that 'we' are – in other words, savages? This idea shows through Stransky's speech when he tries to persuade Swann to record their songs:

> They're the joke of the week. Thieves. Conmen. Just imagine if we could raise them up. A literate proletariat. People reading Gypsy literature. We – you, me, her – we can make a whole new art form, get those songs written down.[48]

Considering himself as the master of these uncultivated groups, Stransky feels he has to complete '*la mission civilisatrice*'.[49] By his logic, Gypsies – whom he perceives as being behind the times, if not retarded – need to be 'educated' and introduced to civilisation.[50] Likewise, the nurse from whom Zoli refuses to take any more medicine makes a similar remark: 'She bit me, the little savage.'[51] This ethnocentric, segregationist speech is based on the same binary scheme in which the two parts are mutually exclusive – a system of 'social apartheid'[52] that leaves no room for any possible conciliation. From then on, there is nothing surprising about Zoli's self-perception: she no longer considers herself 'a Romani woman', not even a 'Gypsy', but only 'a primitive creature'.[53] Her narrative is explicit: 'the fascists hunted us to give us another dose of their hatred – we were no more than wild animals to them'.[54] Comprehended as an 'anonymous collectivity',[55] the minority group is like a herd. Therefore an individual belonging to this group is nothing but a wild beast. Is this not the case with Zoli when she devours a raw bird or is chased by a pack of hounds?[56] Not only is she driven out of the geographical borders of her territory, she is also expelled beyond the bounds of humankind in the other's language. By the same token, when Swann, in search of Zoli, faces Slovak soldiers, he gets from them a significant answer:

> I was, I told them, a translator and sociologist studying the ancient culture of the Romani people. 'The what?' they asked. 'The Gypsies.' They howled with laughter.
> A sergeant leaned forward. 'There's some up there, with the monkeys in the trees.'[57]

In the paradigm shift, the *gadjo*'s stereotypical representation of the Gypsy stands comparison with the Celtophobic English image of the Irish. Indeed, in Victorian England's colonialist thought and speech, Ireland is considered a country plagued by superstition and fanaticism and peopled with canni-bals – thus a den of savages. Confirmed by the preeminence of his nation, the Englishman considers himself as setting the standard for assessing the other nations' degree of civilisation. Consequently, regarding himself as per-fectly civilised, he identifies the other, whose initiatives and results are not so glorious, as a savage. The wild Irishman is the perfect foil to the highly civilised Englishman. This ethnocentric – more precisely, Anglocentric – speech sounds simplistic in its dichotomy, but was nevertheless widely taken up and dissemi-nated in social discourse for several centuries, particularly in the nineteenth, as confirmed by L.P. Curtis' analyses in a book on Anglo-Irish relationships, which is significantly titled *Apes and Angels*.[58] The English are referred to as 'angels' – the word being an anagram for 'angles' – whereas the Irish are cari-catured as 'apes'.

Four years before *Zoli* was published, another Irish novelist, Joseph O'Connor, went back over the representations of Irishmen in Victorian caricature in *Star of the Sea*. His novel draws its inspiration from nineteenth-century publications, particularly scientific essays on the 'Gaelic mental and physical characteristics', but also from satirical magazines, with their cari-catures pushing 'the Irish-Iberian' down to the bottom of the human scale 'between the gorilla and the Negro'.[59] O'Connor's novel perfectly transcribes these ways of thinking insofar as the plot takes place at a time when Victorian England was heavily influenced by this hostile ideology, while hungry Ireland showed scathing Anglophobia.

O'Connor and McCann show a common interest in the plights experi-enced by the victims of these xenophobic clichés relating to 'lower races' and retarded peoples, in which a cultural basis of sectarianism can be observed.[60] It is surprising, however, that in the twenty-first century some Irish writers reuse such archaic discourses and take a chance by going against the tide of their contemporaries' preoccupations. In this respect, their nationality can be considered as one of the elements that justifies this interest: as both of them come from a nation that suffered the colonial experience for a long time, they are certainly most touched by any subaltern position.[61] Furthermore, taking up these sectarian stereotypes can be a way to destroy them once and for all. The Irish intellectual Seamus Deane mentions this intricate process by which a community, attempting to discover its 'true' identity, often begins with the demolition of the false stereotypes within which it has been entrapped.[62] To do so it has to carry out a cathartic operation that consists of awakening entrenched hatreds in order to eradicate them definitively. The process is probably the same for all stereotypes affecting other communities waiting to be rehabilitated. Does not McCann wish his readers could take a fresh look at the Roma?[63]

In spite of the specificity and complexity of the stories experienced by minority groups, overlappings and interconnections can be observed. Indeed, whoever the 'others' are – whether they are members of ethnic, religious or national communities – all of them are scapegoats. All of them are symbols of the disabled, oppressed and humiliated human being. In view of the identity of the heroine of the novel and of the nationality of its author, the previous examples concern the Roma and the Irish, but the Jewish community is also concerned by such discourses promoting a static twofold system based on identity and difference, on domination and subordination. It is highly likely that an analysis of the anti-Semitic speeches of Europe in the 1930s and 1940s would vouch for it. In many respects, the Roma and Jews share common destinies: throughout history they have been persecuted, exiled or exterminated. No wonder the narrative of the restless wanderer Zoli is reminiscent of the lamentations of the Jewish people in deportation:

> … it would have been the lake that I would have visited, along the road to Prešov, the dark groves where we played the harps, and the small laneway where we danced at Conka's wedding – those days shone in my head like a bright coin … There are times I still miss the crowded days and being old does not shelter me from sadness. Once I was guilty of thinking that only good things could happen; then I was guilty of thinking they would never happen again.[64]

The exile on the waterside, shedding tears over the memories of her native land, of dances and songs accompanied on the harp,[65] is reminiscent of the Hebrews remembering the fall of Jerusalem and their exile to Babylon:[66]

> By the rivers of Babylon we sat down and wept
> When we remembered Zion.
> There on the willow-trees
> We hung up our harps,
> For there those who carried us off

Demanded music and singing,
And our captors called on us to be merry:
'Sing us one of the songs of Zion.'
How could we sing the Lord's song in a foreign land?
If I forget you, O Jerusalem,
Let my right hand wither away;
Let my tongue cling to the roof of my mouth
If I do not remember you,
If I do not set Jerusalem
Above my highest joy.[67]

This psalm, in which the dichotomy between 'them' and 'us' is once more noticeable, evokes the same motifs as *Zoli's* narrative – disruption, uncertainty and nostalgia. Exiles experience long trips, hard living conditions, difficult adaptations to foreign lands. Their terrible ordeals generate weariness, discouragement and disenchantment. Their faith becomes interrogative; doubt creeps into the hearts. These characters have no illusions about painful reality, about a possible reversal of situation; they experience a real death. Yet they do not admit defeat, and carry on fighting. The memory of all these anonymous heroes, of the huge crowd of the oppressed, humiliated and persecuted, is, to some extent, kept alive by the novel.

Individuals shape their own identities through their relationships with others. What they remember is part of a network in which memories merge and complement each other. Shared by many people, these experiences of sociability are meaningful within communities and belong to 'collective memory'. Memory is interested in local stories that are discredited, not legitimised, such as the subaltern classes' everyday lives. In contrast with the winners' narratives, memory takes the defeat into account, and revisits and envisages history in counterpoint. Memory is perceived as spontaneous, emotional and closely connected to individual identity. This is why it arouses many historians' suspicions.

Zoli can be considered as a vehicle for collective memories. Firstly, the plot refers to the Roma community, but it also honours the memory of the Jewish community, which is mentioned now and then to highlight a common feature with the Romani people.[68] In addition, as we have seen, the Irish can also be discerned between the lines. Their memory, however, is only implicitly evoked, as they are never mentioned as a community.[69] This indirect statement is significant and makes it possible to question the implicit and clarify what the text is about. According to the French critic Philippe Hamon, absence is a key concept in the relationships between text and ideology.[70] In this case, the ideology of the stereotyped representations of the Roma and *gadji* generates other implicit representations that can be perceived here. From a presumably unintentional phenomenon, the writer interweaves the history of his people with the story of his novel, thus establishing connections between text and context, and letting a social unconscious filter through the text.

The mention of *poètes maudits*

Considering their backgrounds, the novelist and his heroine both revive the collective memories of Irish and Roma minorities. In their literary productions they bring back the histories of some individual writers, particularly those who, like Zoli or Papusza, underwent persecutions. Indeed, the novel mentions characters who refer to genuine, historical artists. All of the writers mentioned in *Zoli* are political activists or witnesses of attacks, revolutions, civil wars and military uprisings either in the turmoil of Spanish dictatorship, Islamist terrorism or the Soviet regime.

Prior to the commencement of the novel, an epigraph quotes Tahar Djaout, an Algerian writer and political columnist killed at the age of thirty-nine in an attack carried out by the Islamic Salvation Front in 1993. The tone is set: when the right of expression is challenged, the assertion of a literary vocation can be fatal, as is also illustrated by the case of Federico García Lorca, the Spanish poet shot dead during the Spanish Civil War at the age of thirty-seven by Francoist armies. Significantly, his verse is read by Zoli.[71] The latter is also interested in Czech and Slovak poets, such as Jaroslav Seifert and Dominik Tatarka,[72] who, reduced to silence, had to seek refuge abroad. Buffeted by the traumas of history, these writers did battle with the authorities, worked illegally and went through the ordeals of discharge, imprisonment or exile. This is also illustrated by the Soviet poets Anna Akhmatova – whose resemblance to Zoli is striking, according to Swann[73] – and Mayakovsky, 'the greatest poet of Soviet Russia',[74] whose work is read both by Zoli and Swann.[75] 'Mayakovsky, characterized by his voice of thunder and features of bronze, was the public poet, the magnanimous heart who disrupted language and faced the most difficult problems of political poetry', wrote Pablo Neruda in his memoirs.[76] 'In revolutionary Russia, he was tracked down by jealous people until he was shot dead.'[77] The Chilean poet proves to be particularly touched by the fate and tragic end of his Soviet fellow writer, because he was himself held under house arrest, then forced to go into exile. He is still considered to be 'the poet of the humiliated and the oppressed'.[78] Therefore it is not by chance that Zoli is particularly fond of his poetry: 'Among her favourites [books] was an early Neruda, in Slovak, a copy of which she had bought for herself in a second-hand shop. She moved along, lovesongs at her hip...'[79] The fictionalisation of writers in the novel alludes to books that allowed them to reach fame. The process is intertextual, as it establishes a relationship, a *mise en abyme*, and invites readers to turn to these pieces of writing.[80] Considering the place and time they lived in, the writers mentioned in the novel have different personal and artistic developments, but all of them, like Papusza and Zoli, bitterly experienced oppression and persecution. For example, in his autobiography Neruda relates the opprobrium of his peers when he came back from his tour in the US:

> After this tour, marked by my most assertive political and poetic activity, which was intended to defend and support the Cuban revolution, no sooner had I been back home to Chile than I received this famous slanderous letter from the Cuban writers, accusing me of little less than submission and treason.[81]

The destiny of the fictitious protagonist Zoli is shared and enhanced not only by the real poet it is based on – Papusza – but also by all of these attacked, persecuted historical writers who do battles as one against everyone else. Tracked down, tormented, identifiable as 'others', they are marginalised by a system. Their 'otherness' is a constituent of their dissident writers' condition and makes them part of a persecuted minority. Once their opinions differ from those of the authorities, they are bullied, frustrated in their creativity and deprived of freedom. Therefore they either go into exile or they stay in their countries, where they are banned and imprisoned, if not murdered.

McCann's interest in marginal groups, whoever they are – including muzzled writers – can here again be interpreted as a way of establishing a connection with conditions experienced by compatriots from the same corporate body. Indeed, although the writers mentioned in *Zoli* are not Irish, most of them were gagged and reduced to silence. Now, censorship strikes a particular chord for any Irish writer: with the establishment in 1929 of the Irish Censorship Board, it was strictly enforced for many decades of the twentieth century.[82] This infringement of free expression accounts for so many artists' exile from the country. True, it is worth distinguishing permanent exile, caused by institutional repressive measures, from emigration, which is mostly due to personal reasons, yet as an Irishman living in the US, Colum McCann exploits the right to be different, and shares a peripheral position with his predecessors and characters. As he is outside the major social group, he is the 'other', the foreigner analysed by Julia Kristeva:

> Who is a foreigner? The one who does not belong to the group ... the other. It has often been noted that there are only negative definitions of the foreigner ... The foreigner is the other of the family, the clan, the tribe. At first he blends with the enemy. External to my religion, too, he could have been the heathen, the heretic ... he was born on another land.[83]

Living abroad, McCann is confronted with being himself 'other'. He is thus connected to the margins by his identity not only as a foreigner but also as a writer who, as some claim, often shows solidarity with dropouts. Indeed, the Irish novelist William Trevor considers that writers have to remain outside society in order to observe it better: 'All fiction writers, indeed all artists, are by definition outsiders. We are outside society because society is our raw material, and we write about it. It's dangerous to come too close, even to the edge of it.'[84] Seamus Deane also feels that the association of literature and marginality is an absolute necessity: giving the example of Francis Stuart and Beckett, who 'ratified their social delinquency, made contact and even identification with a community of outcasts the central preoccupation of their work', he insists on 'the necessity for the artist to make contact with the outcast and despised'.[85] In the wake of his famous predecessors, McCann extends the tradition of the Irish writer who does not see the point of writing about what he is supposed to know – in this case, the Dublin suburban middle classes – but much prefers to recount the stories of others, particularly the rejected or the common people with no voice. What's more, McCann positions himself at the border of his society, which perceives the outcast as an inferior: as he makes a character living at the periphery of the community of 'ordinary' citizens the protagonist of his novel, he contributes to the restoration of the outcast's dignity, and does the exact opposite of what society does. In McCann's view, 'the writer must work in opposition'.[86] This rehabilitation of the outcast by literature is the opportunity for him to raise social problems. *Zoli* can thus be read as a social novel, as its author confirms:

> I consider myself as a social novelist. It is not really fashionable now
> as it used to be until the 1930s or 1940s, in a tradition which goes
> from Zola to Steinbeck, via Dreiser. Through their writings, these
> authors tried to influence society and bring about some change in
> people's awareness.[87]

Steinbeck and Theodore Dreiser were all the more able to 'influence society' as they were themselves somewhat on the fringes of American society due to their distinct affinity with the Communist Party. No wonder these novelists are also mentioned in the text: not only are they read and translated by Swann,[88] they also say something about the author.

Intertextual dialogism between individuals can allegorically be transposed onto dialogism between communities. True, the protagonist of the novel is an individual, a Gypsy woman excluded from her group. But she is also the symbol of the Roma community and, more widely, the emblem of all the persecuted writers of the world. In McCann's opinion, it is 'normal to look at minorities as monoliths';[89] there are no differences between them. This prolonged metaphor mobilises the motif of memory, whether it is collective, cultural or reflexive. Through the process of imitative writing, the revival of sectarian ideological discourses and the mention of *poètes maudits*, the intertextual novel is both connected with the world and with literature itself, particularly with the history of literary outputs. Though autotelic or self-centred, the intertextual novel is not fruitless. On the contrary, it generates revitalisation. *Zoli* is a compromise between novelty and repetition. In this novel, McCann replicates, reformulates and revises some elements of a work to finally create an original text. From borrowed components he constructs a totally new literary work, and invents an emblematic character. McCann establishes a chain between Papusza and Zoli's stories, and perceives himself as a link in this chain insofar as he makes his voice heard, a voice that appeals to the reason of his readers and enlightens them as to the world, a voice that induces to perceptiveness, to the elimination of simplistic stereotypes that stir up archaic antagonisms. The novel incites its readers to think about the living conditions of all these men and women who are still expelled, humiliated and persecuted because they are despised, if not hated. The novel restores dignity to these ordinary individuals who are generally neglected by citizens and authorities. It proves that literature has the capacity to change the world. *Zoli* is what is commonly called a committed novel. The Sartrean notion of commitment reflects the writer's necessary involvement in the situation that both defines and restricts his fundamental freedom. For Sartre, to write is to name and unveil the world, and to project an image of being in the world.[90] The writer thus assumes a specific position within the context of a sociopolitical reality and is said to be committed to the extent of being lucidly conscious of involvement in the world. For the committed writer, words are not simple things; they are instrumental signs that name the world with a view to changing it. McCann is clearly affiliated with this movement, and can thus be considered a committed writer. He refuses to write 'tepid exercises in entertainment',[91] but considers his books as spaces of free expression that allow him to confront the major issues of his time and take a stand on them. In his opinion, his function is to awaken his readers' consciences. The committed writer thus plays a political role that is perceptible in his discourse. Besides, is there any language that is totally apolitical?[92] As a committed writer, McCann politicises his discourse, analyses citizens' relationships with society, and dissects the influential systems of ideas and principles in order to increase his readers' awareness of a specific issue. He thus confirms that the political aspect does not pollute the literary one, but is, as Aristotle claimed, in command of all human activities.

CHAPTER 8

The Recreation of Voices in *Let the Great World Spin* – the paratext: authorities in crisis

J ust like the text, the book as an object has particular signs that call for response and interpretation. Let us imagine the potential reader's first contact with this novel published in 2009 and written by a certain Colum McCann, a writer s/he has never before heard of. With the author's name the reader is informed about a few specific features concerning his identity: the writer is a man of Irish stock. Yet the reader may not perceive the Catholic connotation of the name. Indeed, Colum or Colm comes from Colomba or Colomban, an Irish monk of the sixth century who spread the Good Word on the European mainland. This holy man is characterised by purity and missionary enthusiasm, as the Gaelic etymology of the name testifies, *Colum Cille* meaning 'the dove of the Church'. Colum is particularly venerated by the Irish Catholic Church. As for McCann, it is the name of a family from the province of Ulster that has its own coat of arms on a shield, with a helm topped by a fish surrounded by oak leaves, under which a small red wolf is usually found, the very name of McCann meaning 'the son of the wolf cub'. The McCanns were lords of Clanbrassil, County Armagh. While the first name and surname of the author are evocative of Ireland, the picture or design on the book cover, whatever the edition, depicts New York City and more particularly the Manhattan skyline. Thus the cover of the book allows the reader to make the connection between Ireland and the US.

As for the title of the novel, *Let the Great World Spin* metaphorically evokes a content that is difficult to grasp, the main subject being the 'great world' – what is more, a world that the addressee of the message is supposed to 'let spin'. This title is somewhat enigmatic and probably connotative. Indeed, the rhythm of these five monosyllables provides the phrase with a poetic touch that incites the reasonably cultured reader to put forward the hypothesis that this title draws its inspiration from another work and that it may be a quotation. If our reader leafs through the end of the book, the author's note confirms that the title comes from Alfred Lord Tennyson's poem 'Locksley Hall'.[1] Then, if the reader turns the first page of the book, s/he can read an epigraph, a short quotation of two sentences placed within quotation marks, followed by the name of its author, Aleksandar Hemon, and the title of the book it is taken from, *The Lazarus Project*.[2] Lastly, in her/his discovery of the paratext of *Let the Great World Spin*, the reader who turns a new page notices a dedication to John Berger and Jim Harrison, two writers frequently mentioned by McCann in his interviews.

As a result, in the first three pages of the book, no fewer than five authors are explicitly or implicitly conjured up. All of them write in English, whether they are British, Irish or American by birth or adoption. Apart from Tennyson, all of them were still living at the time of publication, though not all were well-known writers. By anchoring his novel in the great network of the universal library, Colum McCann apparently does not want the spotlight to be on his own text only, as he, as a writer, does not feel himself to be in a position of power. As he fits himself into a community of men of letters, he testifies that the value of his text is due not only to himself. McCann is an author, but is he in a position of authority, as the extension of the word could imply?

Definitions

The word *auctor* refers to the founder, the originator, the person who starts and establishes, the great or sovereign author being, according to tradition, none other than God the Creator himself, who, at the origin of the world, gives birth and growth. By extension, *auctor* becomes the one who starts and develops a piece of work, acquiring the meaning of the organising principle, the orchestrator of the text, which is the general sense of the word today. The Latin word *auctoritas* is derived from *auctor*. In its original meaning, authority means being an author. It also refers to the credit or credibility of a writer or a text, and to the power to make decisions and influence other people. The scriptures, for example, are authoritative because they have this power. Progressively, the word 'authority' has come to refer to the strength of a reference or quotation being used as a model, but also characterises someone who is strong and powerful, who enjoys legal ability, official responsibility and moral superiority.

Even if the word 'authority' has taken on new meanings, the notions of strength, power and superiority remain. Yet are they really suitable for the author? Does the author actually have power and authority? And if they do, is it not by misuse of language? For what is this power resting on? True, the author is the legal owner of their text; they give official permission for the text to be published, literally *author*ise it and can vouch for what they have written. Nevertheless, are they not first and foremost promoted by what makes them an author – that is, their originality, their uniqueness, their *authorship*? And in the case of McCann, his interest in intertextual practice? By selecting a line to make it the title of his novel, McCann acknowledges that Tennyson's poetry has prestige and authority. As we can see, the intertextual practice appeals to the concept of authority – be it authorial or textual authorities. But is not the authority of the quoting author put in the shade by that of the quoted author, and vice versa? What part does authority play in an obviously intertextual work of literature? The articulation between authority and intertextuality deserves to be studied so as to determine if these two concepts are compatible or, on the contrary, mutually exclusive, if there is reciprocal dependence, interaction between them, if authority is inversely proportional to the degree of intertextuality, or if authority is greater in a text without intertextual 'co-presence'.[3] In other words, is intertextual practice a sign that authority is in crisis?

Intertextuality: an offspring of authorities in crisis

It may be useful not to forget that intertextuality established itself in the discourse of literary criticism in a context of crisis. As Antoine Compagnon recalls – it was in 1968 – the author's overthrow, which indicated the transition from systematic structuralism to deconstructive post-structuralism, was on an equal footing with the anti-establishment rebellion of those days.[4] The concept of intertextuality stems from the death of the author. It results from her/his questionable authority, and it is indeed the author who sparked the controversy over the text in the 1960s. Two theories conflicted on this matter: on the one hand, the defenders of literary history traditionally viewed the author as the ultimate 'explanation' of a work; on the other, a new generation of critics suggested that the interpretation of the *oeuvre* should no longer be sought on the side of the artist who had produced it, but that the reader should take over as the prime source of power in a text. As a spokesman for this approach, Roland Barthes writes in a key passage that the text liberates an absolutely revolutionary activity that could be called counter-theological, since refusing to decide on the meaning finally amounts to refusing God.[5] Barthes here alludes to the etymology of the word *auctor*: for him, refusing God is denying the omniscient and all-pervading presence and influence of the author in a work of literature. The death of the author gives rise to the birth of the reader, the plurality of the text and the freedom of commenting on it, particularly of acknowledging it as a 'tissue of quotations'.[6] Intertextuality is an effect of the death of the author and an offspring of authorities in crisis. Today, with hindsight, common sense prompts us to moderate the radical stance of the death of the author and to admit that the creator of the text cannot be completely overlooked. Just as there is no author without literature, there is no literature without an author. A literary text is attributed to the person who wrote it and registered under their name. Any quotation, any reference leads to author figures whose names cannot be cut from the texts they are associated with. The author is not once and for all sentenced to death by literary criticism, but her/his status is different. The death of the author gives rise to new approaches of the author, but also of authority, which now tends to be replaced by authorship.

The concept of authorship

As authority imposes an author who holds power over her/his text, authorship considers her/him as having a regulatory function on it without claiming to determine its meaning. The concept of authorship makes it possible to maintain the presence of the author without believing in their power and hermeneutic utility. The very status of writing is questioned: what justifies that the author is as s/he is? What is their position towards their text? Authorship questions the text, refers to its possible conditions, and would tend to mean that being an author is nothing else but making one's discourse coherent and assuming responsibility for it. It amounts to making a connection between a text and a name, because authorship supposes the author's uniqueness.

So the question that is raised here is as follows: with five different authors conjured up in the first three pages of *Let the Great World Spin*, is McCann's authorship still valid? Is the only author of the text the man whose name is mentioned on the cover of the book? Or the one who wrote down the title first? In this case, Tennyson would be credited with it, for by the use of quotations McCann is not really the person who wrote the text as he is not objectively the only one who wrote it down, even if his name only is displayed on the cover of the book. Who is the originator of the message 'let the great world spin'? Are there as many authors as quotations? It must be admitted that the boundaries of authorship are often blurred.

Although this is the first time one of his books has brought together a quotation title, an epigraph and a dedication to writers,[7] McCann often signs and authorises dialogic texts – 'mosaics of quotations',[8] as the present work testifies. Because writing also means rewriting, McCann himself acknowledges that he does not write on his own – 'The fact of the matter is that there are many hands tapping the writer's keyboard'[9] – and authorship is inconceivable for him without disrupting the authority of his single voice and calling upon other voices. In this respect the paratext is quite significant as it makes it possible to construct the authority of the text. Indeed, as authorial authority is questionable insofar as it provides the author with the power to hold *the* meaning of the text, textual authority, on the other hand, seems to be more relevant as it refers to the author's capacity to freely produce her/his own text without claiming to detain its only valid explanation.

The authority of the text

Harold Bloom contends that any text is a response to a previous one.[10] It implies that a writer has to negotiate with her/his predecessor's authority. When he quotes a line by Tennyson, McCann enhances the aesthetic prestige of the poem that he conceives as a model of beauty. The authority of the text is the cause of an intertextual practice that rests on a text endowed with consideration. Of course, as it is the title, the name of the author of the original quotation is not immediately mentioned, but this absence of signature highlights the authority of the text. And even if the reader does not know the exact source of the quotation, s/he is nevertheless likely to recognise the intertextual effect. In order to exist, intertextuality needs to be identified as such by the reader. According to Riffaterre, readers recognise it when they come up against the meaning of the text, when they do not manage to grasp what it refers to, but the recognition already contributes to establishing meaning.[11] Besides, the author's note that provides the reader with the precise reference to

Tennyson's poem at the end of the book makes it possible to check the validity of the intertextual reading. Tennyson's poem is an authority, and by using the authority of another text, McCann turns textual authority into the means of his own intertextual practice.

As it is put at the beginning of a piece of writing, the epigraph is also in authority. It establishes a Chinese-box structure, a *mise en abyme*, since McCann's whole novel is a development of this quotation that is, to some extent, the embryo of the text: 'All the lives we could live, all the people we will never know, never will be, they are everywhere. That is what the world is.'[12] 'All the lives we could live' refers to the heterogeneous destinies of the numerous characters of the novel: a French walker on a cable between the Twin Towers, an Irish religious man in the squalor of the Bronx, an African-American prostitute driven to despair because of her inability to protect her grandchildren, mothers of missing soldiers in Vietnam gathered in a luxury apartment in Park Avenue – an odd collection of characters whose voices are mixed to catch and recreate the effervescence of New York City in the 1970s. Polyphonic, the novel is full of a plurality of independent voices with various tones and accents that reveal different social classes and ethnic minorities. In this web of convergences, it depicts the big city as the meeting place of the whole universe, as the term 'world' featured in both the title and epigraph implies. New York City is a kaleidoscopic microcosm, a miniature replica of the great world. By the same token, although the diegesis lasts three decades and is essentially anchored in the 1970s, the chronology spans a greater period of time. Indeed, the simple mention of the Twin Towers of the World Trade Center strikes a particular chord among us, readers of the twenty-first century. The choice of the line 'Let the great world spin' is, in this respect, all the more significant as Tennyson's poem, before this quotation, mentions 'Pilots of the purple twilight dropping down with costly bales'. These words, which can be considered as premonitory, did not fail to draw McCann's attention, and probably proved to be decisive in his intertextual choice.

Tennyson as author of *Let the Great World Spin*

Tennyson's art is a jewel of perfection in which the poet gives vent to his melancholy, thoughtful emotion that echoes the great Romantics who came before him. In 'Locksley Hall' particularly, Tennyson shows he can be misled by the mirage of progress offered by the material prosperity of the nineteenth century.

Two tendencies are reflected in his verse: one is optimistic and hopeful, the other clear-sighted and disenchanted. His belief in progress is constantly tinged with scepticism. Against a background of pessimism about the absurdity of life, he celebrates progress in a disillusioned voice, and tackles all that drives the human being to despair, considering that he often proves to be in a situation with no other solution but violence in all forms, including war. These remarks do not fail to take on another meaning in the light of the events that led to the destruction of the Twin Towers, a catastrophe broadcast live before the eyes of millions of dumbfounded viewers who, like the poet in his days, wondered if they were not under illusion and could have taken up his words as their own: 'Eye, to which all order festers, all things here are out of joint'. These echoes justify the presence of the poet who expresses himself in *Let the Great World Spin* and somewhat becomes the author of the novel, like a ghost who suddenly comes back to life, as Harold Bloom contends.[13] *Let the Great World Spin* contains undeveloped potential texts, but also revives other texts that remain within the realms of possibility.

The novel is divided into four books and each book is composed of chapters, each of which is given a title. The titles of three chapters are quotations from 'Locksley Hall'. The last part of the first book takes over and develops the title of the novel: 'Let the Great World Spin Forever Down'. The second book ends with a section whose title 'The Ringing Grooves of Change' completes the initial quotation of the poem:

> Forward, forward let us range,
> Let the great world spin for ever down the ringing grooves of
>   change.

The final section, in the fourth book, is titled 'Roaring Seaward, and I Go', which are the last words of the poem.

These inter-titles, these quotations evenly distributed across the whole novel, confirm Bloom's theory and lead the reader to think that Tennyson could be considered as the author of the novel because he *could* write such a text today. Novel writing would then be contemplated as the reactivation of a possible text that had been abandoned in the past of creation. The haunting, recurrent echoes of Tennyson's voice make him the virtual novelist; in any case, one of the authors invited by McCann to take part in the dialogue. Starting with the cover of the book, there is ambiguity, as the literal text conceals another text from which it borrows its title, a title that refers both to the diegesis of the novel and to the work within the work. The polyphonic characteristic of the text raises the problematic dimension of the very definition of authorship. The cover of the book mentions only one name but this name assumes a somewhat collective writing. In addition to the ghostly shadow of the poet in the novel – which, to some extent, makes Tennyson the author of *Let the Great World Spin* – what is more surprising is the opposite movement in this intertextual practice; indeed, Colum McCann can also be envisaged as the author of 'Locksley Hall'.

McCann as author of 'Locksley Hall'

Besides the poetic quotations in the novel, astonishing allusions to some scenes of the novel can also be picked up in the poem. Thus not only does the poem have an influence on the novel and seem to contain the seeds of it but the reading of the poem in the light of the novel also allows us to detect new elements in 'Locksley Hall'. For example, Philippe Petit, the man who walked on a cable between the towers of the World Trade Center one summer morning in 1974, could probably repeat Tennyson's words:

> Comrades, leave me here a little, while as yet 'tis early morn:
> Leave me here, and when you want me, sound upon the
>   bugle-horn.

In his motivation to achieve this exploit one thousand feet above the ground, would he not say, along with the poet:

> There methinks would be enjoyment more than in this march
>   of mind,
> In the steamship, in the railway, in the thoughts that shake
>   mankind.
>
> There the passions cramp'd no longer shall have scope and
>   breathing space …

The novel provides an explanation that allows the reader to interpret the poem otherwise. The intertextual game makes it possible not only to update the older text but also to establish interaction between present and past literary works. Likewise, many lines perfectly suit some characters of the novel, who could take them up as their own to narrate their experiences, whether it is Corrigan, Jazzlyn, Gloria or Claire. The following lines could very well come out of tearful mothers mourning for their sons who died in Vietnam:

> Where is comfort?
> [...]
> Comfort? comfort scorn'd of devils!
> That a sorrow's crown of sorrow is remembering happier
>   things
>
> Drug thy memories, lest thou learn it, lest thy heart be put to
>   proof,
> In the dead unhappy night, and when the rain is on the roof.

The intertextual practice is amazingly productive, because not only does the first text direct the reading of the second but the first one can also be read in the light of the second. The traditional notion of influence founded on the metaphor of a flow, on a chronological linear conception of history, is here denied: the intertextual connections are considered apart from any chronological link. Instead of being under somebody's influence, the writer absorbs and transforms the previous text. In this case Tennyson's poem transforms McCann's novel, which modifies it in return. As a result, the meanings of the texts are to be found in the interdependent connections they establish with one another. Outside chronological linearity, texts are the active, productive elements of a large system; they refer to one another and can be understood only through one another. They are a common good from which anyone can draw. As any text is likely to be taken up, it cannot be limited to what its author actually wrote, but it keeps on being written by the authors who quote and rewrite it. Thus 'Locksley Hall' is not only Tennyson's work but the uncompleted amount of its intertextual journey made by adding its past and future variants together. Among these variants, McCann's novel reworks it and gives it a new meaning. This meaning is to be searched first in the dialogic connection between them. It circulates from one text to another. It is no longer what the author of the first text meant, as it is not what the author of the second text means. The meaning results from interaction between both. Interaction establishes some discontinuity, which is characteristic of intertextuality. In reaction against the authority of linearity, *Let the Great World Spin*

– which can be described as kaleidoscopic or postmodern – on the one hand makes up a whole and provides continuity, but on the other fragments and interrupts the text it quotes. Any intertextual connection both respects the quoted text by using it again and, at the same time, gives it a rough handling, as it breaks it up by introducing discontinuity. Therefore intertextuality may in essence be considered as a crisis that is, by definition, some form of discontinuity introduced in a process that had so far been continuous. Playing with the dialectic of continuity and discontinuity, McCann's novel partakes of repetition and alteration, of authority and transgression. It appeals to texts, negotiates with their authority, and establishes polyphonic dialogues. This plurality shows his will to disrupt monolithic unicity and makes *Let the Great World Spin* – as any postmodern, intertextual work – a protesting, anti-establishment novel.

Hemon *author*ised by McCann

In *Paratexts: thresholds of interpretation*, Gérard Genette remarks that when the title of a book is a quotation, the supporting epigraph is imperative to give some justification.[14] *For Whom the Bell Tolls* by Ernest Hemingway, for example, starts with a few lines by John Donne from which the novel borrows its title. Here, though, the title is not justified by the epigraph but by intertitles. Besides, McCann chose to put at the beginning of his book a short extract from a novel by a certain Aleksandar Hemon published in 2008 – that is, a few months before *Let the Great World Spin*, which, though it was written by another hand, echoes the title. As mentioned earlier, the resumption of the term *world* is a parallel that makes sense. What's more, the identity of the quoted author is as important as the quotation itself: the writer mentioned is supposed to vouch for the text it precedes. And yet here, on the contrary, McCann himself, the author of the novel, surprisingly seems to be the one who vouches for the short piece of writing that is put at the beginning of his book, because, unlike Tennyson, Aleksandar Hemon is not a well-known writer.

Hemon was born in Sarajevo and stayed in Chicago for a few months in 1992. As he was living in the US, Sarajevo was besieged and he could no longer go back home. Three years later, Hemon published his first book in English (*The Question of Bruno*). *The Lazarus Project* is his third novel. It narrates the journey of a Bosnian exile in the US, Vladimir, who wants to write the story of Lazarus, a young Jewish Ukrainian killed in Chicago in shady circumstances by a police officer a century earlier, in 1908. With a friend of his, a photographer, Vladimir crosses Ukraine and other Eastern European countries to finally reach Bosnia. He is so haunted by the war and the madness of the world that Tennyson's line 'Let the great world spin' would be perfectly suitable to entitle Hemon's novel. *The Lazarus Project* has a lot in common with *Let the Great World Spin*: both of them are postmodern novels teeming with ideas, alternating fiction with illustrated facts, reflections on the past and the present, on life and the world, on the native land and the country of adoption. Hemon and McCann are two divided writers whose identities are questioned by their dislocation. They are neither rooted nor uprooted, neither sedentary nor nomadic, but exiles. This is why McCann is familiar with Irish as well as American culture. He looks at his adopted culture through the lenses of his native culture and vice versa, and devotes himself to maintaining the gap between both. This dual membership establishes a dialogue that is mirrored in his literary work by intertextual practice. According to McCann, being nationalist, sectarian and proud of oneself is as ridiculous as an author declaring her/himself as the only holder of authority. This is why he is so attached to this phenomenon of cross-fertilisation[15] among literary texts.

The Lazarus Project is a book that McCann read and appreciated – hence his decision to quote a sentence of the novel at the beginning of his own text. Writing and reading are intertwined. The writer is first a reader, and his taste for a text that so simply and sincerely expresses the interest he shares in others, in their lives, in the world, justifies his decision to insert a quotation of this novel in his own. But whereas Tennyson's poem is considered as a founding text, Hemon's quotation is valued differently here, in spite of the authority conferred upon it by its specific position. Although the quoted author's reputation is not really established, his text is given authority insofar as its extract provides the epigraph to the novel. Just as McCann in his interviews mentions the names of authors to make them known because he considers that they are not estimated at their true value, he chooses to cite *The Lazarus Project* in order to show the importance he attaches to the text and so reinforce its authority. If he is endowed with any power, the author can suggest perspectives and increase the authority of someone else's text. Once a text is the subject of intertextual practice, it is given authority. When it is quoted in an epigraph, this authority is all the stronger. Authority becomes a consequence of intertextuality. By quoting a text with lesser prestige, McCann lends credit to Hemon's text and *autho*rises its author. Thus in the paratext of *Let the Great*

World Spin, the title exemplifies that intertextual practice can be founded by authority, whereas the epigraph proves that authority can also be founded by intertextual practice.

McCann *author*ised by Berger and Harrison

Let the Great World Spin is dedicated to two authors: John Berger and Jim Harrison. In view of these writers' respective dates of birth, 1926 and 1937, the dedication, written by an author who was himself born in 1965 – that is, one generation later – can be read as a tribute from a son to his father. Indeed, when he mentions Berger as his 'master',[16] McCann recognises him as a mentor and model, a symbolic father. Gerard Genette also sees a connection between father and son in the paratextual references to writers of the previous generation: 'The young writers … give themselves the consecration and unction of a … prestigious filiation.'[17] The paratext displays an affiliation, which establishes a tradition of men of letters from the nineteenth-century ancestor to the novel writer and his fellow author quoted in the epigraph, via their fathers, whom they consider as their masters. McCann discloses a close relationship with these writers through the medium of his dedication.[18] Though it is not specified if this relationship is a purely artistic connection between writer and reader or a tie between men who personally know and appreciate one another, the dedication nevertheless keeps its function as moral, intellectual and aesthetic support. As McCann has emphasised in interviews, he admires Berger and Harrison – and admiration is, according to Neil Corcoran, a response to a predecessor's work[19] – for their attention to the world, for their acute sight of the real, for their courage, too. Indeed, these writers fight with the arms of fiction; they are committed, resistant to the established order, to the authorities' speeches and ideologies: they are protesters. They lend their support to the common people, to the outcasts, to those who are overlooked by society and share with them, as Berger puts it, 'the same respect for the Earth, the same sense of precariousness, the same concern when you look at the sky' without ever lapsing into maudlin realism or moralising pathos. These writers are reporters who open their eyes and ears,[20] just like McCann himself, who seems to be their worthy heir. Finding his place in this literary tradition, McCann promotes his own text and presents it as the fruit of a work that aims to be like Berger's and Harrison's productions. In theory, these two writers beforehand authorised McCann to mention them in his dedication. Somehow or other they are responsible for the novel that pays tribute to them, and they show their support and contribution to it. To some extent they also vouch for the book that they most probably read and could have written themselves. The relationship between writers and readers is both reflexive and symmetric. Because s/he is an interpreter, any reader is also somehow the author of the text. Even if s/he is not a writer, even if the novel is not dedicated to her/him, s/he is nevertheless invested with an authority, because s/he can indefinitely interpret the text. Promoted the producer of the text, s/he is also the producer of the *meaning* of the text and, thus, somehow its author. The difference between writing and reading is then abolished and gives the reader an authority that the author was formerly credited with.

Conclusion

The motif of connection or connectedness starts with the illustration of the cover of *Let the Great World Spin*, which, from below, depicts a tiny silhouette walking on a cable between the World Trade Center Twin Towers. It is prolonged by the paratextual components of the novel. The latter are places of connection, of *mise en abyme*: as the title is connected with the text it introduces, but also the one it quotes, the epigraph is connected with the title and the text, as the dedication shows a connection among authors. These relationships confirm that McCann does not give his name to one text alone but to a connection between texts. His name becomes the pivot on which the practice of literature revolves, a means of intertextuality that incorporates his work in a particular connection with other texts. This source of fruitful exchanges revitalises the notion of authorship, which is no longer envisaged as a distinctive mark but as the connecting mirror effect between them. As discussed earlier, intertextuality is subsequent to a crisis of authority, as its birth immediately follows the death of the author. And yet intertextuality is all the more connected with authority crisis as it also shatters the authority of the text. In this case, would the authority of the intertext be conceivable? As the authority of the author is replaced by the authority of the reader, the authority of the text could also be replaced here by the plural, shared authority of the intertext. The word, however, does not seem to be appropriate anymore; indeed, authority, in this case, is scattered in a multiplicity of texts called upon in an unceasing movement to such an extent that it finally dissolves and no longer makes any sense. Again as discussed earlier, intertextuality *is* crisis: it introduces discontinuity in a continuous process. And yet, as with any crisis, it does not remain boxed in but suggests revival and resumption. Intertextuality is free, rebellious and intractable. It oversteps any notion of hierarchy, of authority as it oversteps any spatio-temporal limit, since the national borders do not make sense anymore, since the present and the past interact and make the literary work immortal. As Genette contends in *Palimpsests*, intertextuality constantly relaunches old works in a new circuit of senses,[21] confirming the idea developed by Borges, for whom literature is inexhaustible insofar as one book already is.[22] This book does not only have to be re-read but also rewritten. In a utopian vision, all publications are but one endless big book and all authors are one. If it is so, the principle of contemporary writing ties up with the question raised by Foucault, who himself borrowed the expression from Beckett: 'What does it matter who is speaking? Someone said: what does it matter who is speaking?'[23]

CHAPTER 9

The Recreation of Voices in *Let the Great World Spin* – the text: 'as if anticipating the fall'[1]

With twelve different narrative characters, *Let the Great World Spin* establishes a chorus of various voices that provides the novel with a fragmented postmodern structure. These voices assume the narration in the first or third person and capture snapshots of the lives of characters of different nationalities, ethnic groups or social backgrounds: an anonymous high-wire walker; Irish social worker John Corrigan and his brother Ciaran; a mother and her daughter, Tillie and Jazzlyn Henderson, both prostitutes; two young artists, Lara and Blaine; a wealthy couple, Claire and Solomon Soderberg, whose son died in Vietnam, just like the three children of Gloria, an African American woman living in the Bronx. To these voices can be added those of narrators coming from other novels referred or alluded to here. These voices are renewed, recreated and recontextualised by the intertextual borrowing. Indeed, the vocal and textual connections, symbolised by the funambulist's wire, allow readers to make cross-readings, to leave one text and come back to it after checking a detail in another one, as the walker comes and goes on his tightrope: 'There he goes again. He's walking across again … That's his sixth or seventh time across.'[2] The acrobatic feat described here was in fact performed on 7 August 1974 by Philippe Petit, a French funambulist who walked high above the ground between the towers of the World Trade Center. This location, the focal point of the plot line, establishes a link between McCann's novel and other texts that take an interest in it. This building obviously crystallises 9/11 fiction, and *Let the Great World Spin* can be considered as being part of it. Indeed, 9/11 texts share one common motif, among others: the fall. Of course, retrospectively, any evocation of the

Twin Towers inevitably refers to their temporary existence and their dramatic collapse. The theme also suggests the body's fall – that is, Philippe Petit's possible failure, but also, twenty-seven years later, the leap into the void from the blazing skyscrapers by scores of desperate people. Nevertheless, although McCann's novel shares common features with other books, *Let the Great World Spin* includes specificities that deserve to be highlighted. Indeed, the parodic process at work in the text also contributes to making the fall a crucial motif. Here, the diversion – a distinctive characteristic of the process – illustrates a downward movement that reveals a lower stylistic level. As a result, McCann's novel approaches the motif of the fall both literally and figuratively.

'The collision point of stories'

Among the intertextual references underlined by critics, *Let the Great World Spin* is compared to *The Great Gatsby*. As Sheila Hones remarks in her study of McCann's novel, echoes of *Gatsby* reverberate throughout the third chapter of Book One, 'A Fear of Love'.[3] Although the plot takes place in the early 1970s, Lara and Blaine feel a particular attachment to the 1920s lifestyle: Lara cuts her hair 'flapper-style';[4] both of them listen to jazz music,[5] live in 'a cabin built in the 1920s, out of red cedar' 'an hour and a half from New York City'[6] and drive 'an antique 1927 Pontiac Landau',[7] the car that crashes into the van, causing Corrigan and Jazzlyn's deaths. This fatal car accident is obviously reminiscent of the crash that kills Myrtle Wilson in *Gatsby*. Similarly, in both cases Lara and Gatsby are both prepared to lie in order to take responsibility for the accidents in which they were involved as passengers, although the characters they are speaking to are not taken in.[8] These echoes between the two novels re-enact the crazy atmosphere of the Roaring Twenties in which the thirty-year-old protagonists get intoxicated.[9] Besides, the female narrator of the third chapter of *Let the Great World Spin* explicitly compares her couple to the famous writer and his wife: 'We were the edge, the definers. We had developed our idea to live in the Twenties, a Scott and Zelda going clean.'[10]

Apart from these common features, the particular place of the fatal car crash narrated in *Gatsby* is interesting for the reader who has in mind McCann's novel and the background of 9/11 fiction:

> This is a valley of ashes – a fantastic farm where ashes grow like wheat into ridges and hills and grotesque gardens; where ashes take

the forms of houses and chimneys and rising smoke and, finally, with a transcendent effort, of ash-grey men, who move dimly and already crumbling through the powdery air.[11]

Indeed, this description of a landscape of death and devastation would be perfectly suitable for depicting the streets of Lower Manhattan just after the destruction of the Twin Towers. Likewise, the horrific events that occurred in New York City on that fateful day are indirectly but intentionally referred to by McCann's novel. The diegesis of this novel – starting in 1974, as the construction of the Twin Towers had just been completed – implicitly refers to their destruction. Inserted in the novel, the photograph of an aircraft flying over the World Trade Center on 7 August 1974,[12] the day when Philippe Petit performed his prowess, is inevitably superimposed on the staggering pictures of the 2001 attacks. This photograph is commented upon by Jaslyn[13] in the last chapter of the novel, in 'October 2006' – that is, five years after the disaster:

> A man high in the air while a plane disappears, it seems, into the
> edge of the building. One small scrap of history meeting a larger
> one. As if the walking man was somehow anticipating what would
> come later. The intrusion of time and history. The collision point
> of stories. We wait for the explosion but it never occurs. The plane
> passes, the tightrope walker gets to the end of the wire. Things
> don't fall apart.[14]

Separated by a time gap of twenty-seven years, these two exceptional days that drew the whole world's attention to the Twin Towers are also compared by the narrative:

> One of those out-of-the-ordinary days that made sense of the slew
> of ordinary days. New York had a way of doing that. Every now
> and then the city shook its soul out. It assailed you with an image,
> or a day, or a crime, or a terror, or a beauty so difficult to wrap your
> mind around that you had to shake your head in disbelief.[15]

So 7 August 1974 looks like 11 September 2001 – the day is described as being sunny and promising: 'That morning glided by, like most good mornings do.'[16] When Philippe Petit is making preparations for his feat, he learns by heart the plans of the building, the stairwells, the guard stations, and secretly sends some friends who sneak into the other tower to put the cavallettis in place and winch the wire tight: 'It was like they were planning a ... raid.'[17] Such a remark, concerning a harmless, spectacular feat of daring, reverberates in a sinister way, considering the subsequent events. By the same token, the mention of colonies of birds that fly into the World Trade Center buildings[18] and are found dead on the pavement gloomily echoes the tightrope-walker's possible fall, which is expected, anticipated, even cynically hoped for:

> Many of the watchers ... really wanted to witness a great fall, see someone arc downwards all that distance, to disappear from the sight line, flail, smash to the ground ... Some blessed themselves. Closed their eyes. Waited for the thump ... a shout sounded across the watchers, a woman's voice: God, oh God, it's a shirt, it's just a shirt ... It was falling, falling, falling.[19]

All of these details contribute to making *Let the Great World Spin* a 9/11 novel. In this category, Don DeLillo's narrative describes how 'A shirt came down out of the high smoke, a shirt lifted and drifting in the scant light and then falling again, down toward the river'.[20] In the same novel, *Falling Man*, the protagonist witnesses shocking scenes: 'figures in windows a thousand feet up, dropping into free space'.[21] Jay McInerney's *The Good Life* mentions 'bodies raining down on the plaza. Falling slowly and then suddenly exploding like rotten fruit on the concrete.'[22] In John Updike's *Terrorist*, Ahmad and Charlie are watching Lower Manhattan from Jersey City and talking about the attacks that destroyed the towers: 'A lot of the people killed in them lived in Jersey. I pitied them. Especially those that jumped. How terrible, to be so trapped by crushing heat that jumping to certain death is better.'[23] As for the narrator of Joseph O'Neill's *Netherland*, he 'only [has] to think of the waving little figures who were visible for a while and then not'.[24]

'The body's fall'[25] mentioned by the preacher at Jazzlyn's funeral, as opposed to the triumphant spirit, has nothing figurative here but is meant in its literal sense. Fall and death are inextricably linked. For Philippe Petit, his body's fall would inevitably have put an end to his life. Similarly, the people trapped in the blazing towers who threw themselves out of windows by force of circumstance irreparably rushed towards their deaths. The phrase 'body's fall', used in physics to illustrate the law of gravity, here characterises a deliberate free fall into space. The notion of fall and the word itself are recurrent in

McCann's novel,[26] as well as throughout 9/11 fiction, particularly in DeLillo's novel, eloquently titled *Falling Man* in reference to a performance artist who, dressed in a suit, stands on the rail of a bridge, a balcony or a building roof, then falls headfirst and remains dangling at the end of the strand of a safety harness, a few feet above the ground:

> Was this position intended to reflect the body posture of a particu-
> lar man who was photographed falling from the north tower of the
> World Trade Center, headfirst, arms at his sides, one leg bent, a
> man set forever in free fall against the looming background of the
> column panels in the tower?[27]

Like Philippe Petit, this artist conjures up these terrible moments when people were forced to jump off the blazing towers. Like him, he is under arrest, but the charges against him are dismissed.

'Things fall apart'

Right from the first pages of the Bible, the fall is linked to death, the mortal condition of the human race being the effect of Adam and Eve's fall. Although the word is not used in the Bible, the Fall defines the story of how evil came into the world because Adam and Eve did not comply with the divine orders. As a result of their sin, they are expelled from the Garden of Eden and condemned by God: 'You shall gain your bread by the sweat of your brow until you return to the ground; for from it you were taken. Dust you are, to dust you shall return.'[28] In Judaism and Christianity, the fall, inseparable from sin and guilt, introduces chaos within creation. In many Western literary texts, the fall is connected to the anguish of demerit, disorientation and powerlessness, all the more so when it is collective – for example, in a context of war. And the 9/11 attacks can accurately be interpreted as a declaration of war.[29] Be that as it may, it is a fact that the texts that deal with these events frequently repeat the motif of the lethal fall in a variety of forms. Many of them – such as DeLillo's, McInerney's, O'Neill's or Updike's novels – narrate the events of that tragic day and their aftermaths: the destruction of the towers, the wandering of dazed characters in the streets covered with dust and ashes, the psychological damage – anguish, insomnia, nightmares – and the protagonists' desire to leave the city but also to be more mindful of their fellow citizens.

These narratives are focused on the events themselves and the ensuing trauma, whereas McCann's novel pays particular attention to what happened *before* the attacks, and this is where its real originality lies. In 'Literature and Trauma', an article published in 2007 – that is, two years before the publication of *Let the Great World Spin* – McCann wrote that he did not want to read any new article about the World Trade Center. Six years after 9/11, he tended to close up each time he heard about it. He could not bear 'the machine that fuels grief'.[30] As he had in mind a plan for his novel, he rejected writing a detailed narrative about the catastrophe. He wanted to show that it is possible to write otherwise on 9/11 – hence his oblique approach to the events. Apart from the last chapter, the plot of which takes place in 2006, the diegesis of the novel unfolds prior to the destruction of the Twin Towers, to which it only alludes. *Let the Great World Spin* does not recount the disaster as such. The novel focuses on the newly built towers and is essentially based on dramatic irony,[31] McCann and his readers being aware of the temporary existence of these skyscrapers. Yet the temporal ellipsis between 1974 and 2006 passes the narrative of the World Trade Center collapse over in silence, although the motif of the fall permeates the story.

The collapse even echoes other falls. The words used by Jaslyn when she is watching the picture of a plane flying over the building, 'things don't fall apart'[32] – which takes up somewhat the story of Gloria, who was born during the Great Depression, at a time when 'things were falling apart'[33] – can be read as an allusion to Nigerian Chinua Achebe's novel *Things Fall Apart*, to which McCann paid tribute in 2008 on the fiftieth anniversary of the book's publication.[34] The subject of this novel, the plot of which is located in pre-colonial Africa, is the disruption of a whole people caused by the arrival of foreign missionaries and colonisers. The book draws its title from W.B. Yeats' work. Indeed, 'The Second Coming', a poem extracted from the collection *Michael Robartes and the Dancer* (1921), starts with these words, resumed by the epigraph of Achebe's novel:

> Turning and turning in the widening gyre
> The falcon cannot hear the falconer;
> Things fall apart; the centre cannot hold;
> Mere anarchy is loosed upon the world.[35]

Once again, when he writes 'things fall apart', McCann recalls the Irish poet's work. As Yeats was writing 'The Second Coming' in 1919 – that is,

following the First World War and a few years after the 1916 Easter Rising
in Dublin – he had been the sad witness of a chaotic, terrifying situation.[36]
Likewise, Achebe, McCann and any writer dealing with 9/11 narrate an
outburst of anarchic, devastating violence in their own style. The poem ends
with the progress of a monstrous beast, the symbol of the 'second coming',
foreshadowing the reversal of the poet's contemporary period and the establishment of a new, destructive era. This animal is reminiscent of the Beast of
the Apocalypse,[37] the dark view of the world depicted by Yeats being similar
to certain scenes of apocalyptic horror. In this respect it is worth stressing
that 9/11 fiction frequently refers to the end of the world: *The Good Life*, for
example, mentions 'this new apocalypse',[38] and narrates the way survivors meet
in a lunar landscape of ashes and flames 'as if they were the last two people
on earth'.[39] As a nod in the direction of Yeats, 'everything's falling apart' is a
phrase that can also be picked up in DeLillo's or McInerney's novels.[40] Besides
– and interestingly – just after 9/11, Yeats' poem is once more used to interpret
the events, as the narrative of *The Good Life* puts it:

> [Russell] had spent a good part of the morning answering E-mails
> from around the globe – assuring everyone that he'd survived. He'd
> deleted five copies of Auden's 'September 1, 1939', and three of
> Yeats' 'The Second Coming', as well as two copies of an E-mail
> labeled 'SATAN'S FACE?'[41]

Satan is the fallen angel par excellence, according to the Book of Revelation.
Hurled towards the earth with his angels, his fall leads to the creation of Hell,
but it also symbolises God's victory over the forces of evil. The last book of
the Bible contains many divine messengers who prove to be bearers of glad
or bad tidings.

From then on, it is hardly surprising that 9/11 literature is haunted
by these mediators between God and men. In McCann's novel, characters
are often compared to these celestial creatures: for the down-and-outs in
Brooklyn, Corrigan is a 'mad, impossible angel';[42] Philippe Petit is an 'angel
or devil'.[43] When he walks on a wire, the scene is surreal to such an extent
that the watchers can hardly believe it. Besides, if he fails he becomes the
fallen angel, strictly speaking, like the falling man whose photograph made
the front pages of the newspapers on the day following the attacks. Lianne,
the protagonist of DeLillo's novel, remembers 'he was a falling angel and his
beauty was horrific'.[44] In *The Good Life*, Luke tells his mistress Corrine, 'When

I saw you, I thought for a second maybe I had died back there, that you were an angel.'[45] In O'Neill's *Netherland*, the narrator's neighbour dresses up as an angel whose wings, either white or black, make him a messenger of good or bad news. A mystical, religious atmosphere permeates 9/11 literature, probably because of the omnipresence of death. McInerney compares Manhattan's vast, blighted landscape to 'the ruins of Babylon'[46] in which his protagonist, 'staggering up West Broadway, coated head to foot in dun ash, looked like a statue commemorating some ancient victory'.[47] This statue in the background of a destroyed city is certainly the one McCann refers to in New York that 'kept going forward precisely because it didn't give a good goddamn about what it had left behind. It was like the city that Lot left, and it would dissolve if it ever began looking backwards over its own shoulder. Two pillars of salt. Long Island and New Jersey.'[48] Lot, Abraham's nephew – the only just man in a city of sinners and guided by two angels – escaped the destruction of Sodom, whereas 'his wife looked back and turned into a pillar of salt'.[49] Writers dealing with 9/11 are interested in history through the stories relating the way their characters are affected by the trauma. Although they imagine them in their own style, the vast majority describe them with recourse to biblical references and allusions.

Distance and debasement

When Judge Solomon Soderberg returns home from court, after hearing the wire-walker who was summoned for putting people's lives in danger, his situation is similar to that of his famous namesake: he is in front of two women who beg him to speak. On the one hand, Claire, his wife, on the other, the latter's friend, Gloria, a working-class woman and a member of the club of mothers grieving for their sons fallen in Vietnam, and the narrator of the couple's dialogue:

> 'Guy walked a tightrope,' he said. 'World Trade.'
> 'We heard.'
> [...]
> 'I got to charge him.'
> 'You did?'
> 'Came up with the perfect sentence too.'
> 'He got arrested?'

'Quick shower first. Yes, of course. Then tell you all.'

'Sol,' she said, pulling his sleeve.

'I'll be right out, tell you everything.'

'Solomon!'

He glanced at me. 'Let me freshen up,' he said.

'No, tell us, tell us now.' She stood. 'Please.'

He flicked a look in my direction. I could tell he resented me, just being there, that he thought I was some housekeeper ...[50]

Solomon, the king of Israel, remains famous for the wisdom and skill he displayed when passing sentence in a case in which two women both claimed they were an infant's mother. One of them accused the other of letting her own child die out of carelessness and taking her own baby to replace it. Solomon ordered that the child be cut in half and that one half be given to each woman. Then the genuine mother revealed herself: she was the one who wished for the child to be given alive to another woman instead of letting it die.[51] In McCann's novel the extract quoted above is ironic insofar as the two mothers do not have to stand up for their sons and to speak in favour of their lives anymore as they are already dead.

This ironic distance characterises postmodern parody, which is noticeable in other examples. As a reference to the paintings hung on the walls of the Soderbergs' apartment in Park Avenue, the chapter is titled 'Miro, Miro on the Wall'. It echoes Snow White's stepmother's famous words 'Mirror, mirror on the wall, who's the fairest of them all?', a question paradoxically changed here into 'Miro, Miro on the wall, who's the deadest of them all?'[52] Beauty is replaced by death. The quotation is given a new context, a different environment. Its initial meaning is deliberately distorted. Since her son's death, Claire Soderberg has been suffering from depression. She strikes up a friendship with Gloria, who shares her grief, since her three children were also killed in battle. Claire wonders:

Perhaps she could hire Gloria. Bring her in. Odd jobs around the house. The bits and pieces. They could sit at the kitchen table together and wile away the days, make a secret gin and tonic or two, and let the hours just drift, her and Gloria, at ease, at joy, yes, Gloria, in excelsis deo.[53]

These last four words – the Latin translation of 'Glory to God in highest Heaven'[54] – form a ready-made phrase inserted into Christian liturgy to praise the divine holiness. Here, doxology is belittled by a process of debasement, Gloria being an old black woman of the people, who, far from living in the ethereal atmosphere of 'highest Heaven', contents herself with the eleventh floor of a Bronx council flat with 'window bars', 'rats out by the rubbish' and 'streetwalkers out by the underpass'.[55]

Here, postmodern parody marks 'its paradoxical doubleness of both continuity and change, both authority and transgression'.[56] Indeed, the words used here remain the 'original' liturgical ones, but they are twisted, as the model is clearly transformed. The high style of the sacred phrase is distorted to depict a trivial subject. This downward movement is emphasised by the serious nature of the parodied text. The reusing of words that first belong to a formal, elevated register is making fun of the hierarchy of styles and can be considered a form of burlesque. In this instance, making a trivial subject seem grand in such a way as to satirise the original style is a good example of a mock-heroic device. This stylistic contrast partakes of entertainment and irony.

This subtle balance between close resemblance to the original and a deliberate distortion of its principal characteristics can also be noticed when Corrigan is watching his brother among the down-and-outs. Obviously, the latter is in love with Adelita, and the narrator remarks:

> … with Adelita it was different – she wasn't pushing any greed or climax. *This is my body, it has been given up for you.*
>
> Later, around noon, I found Corrigan in the bathroom, shaving in the mirror. He had been down to Bronx county courthouse, where most of the hookers had already been released on time served. But there were outstanding warrants in Manhattan for Tillie and Jazzlyn.[57]

The sentence in italics literally takes up the words Jesus said to his disciples when he broke the bread at the Last Supper and gave his life to save mankind before dying, thus concretely showing God's love for his people and establishing the Eucharist in Christian tradition. Here, again, the scriptures are undermined by mock-heroic debasement. Reusing the words of Jesus in another context introduces a gap between a trivial situation and a high style that is a feature of parody. This mixture of tones makes up a palimpsest and partakes of intertextuality. In this new context, which is much more materialistic and commonplace than the original one, words lose their prestige and are ironically debunked, their sacred aura being taken away.

Parody is an insolent device that is fundamentally double and divided: it combines tradition with novelty, the familiar with the unusual in humorous, recreational, ironic and subversive purposes. Its imitative use of eminently 'serious' work in an ironic way questions stereotypes and gets rid of the constraints of the elevated style, those obstacles that block the pleasure principle, such as high, lofty, lyrical sentiments. Parody is based on an ironic view of life that characterises Irish literature from Sterne to Beckett. True to Joycean tradition, it enjoys shocking for pleasure, playing with paradox and scandal. This subversion of authority is carnivalesque in the sense given to the word by Bakhtin: carnivalisation describes the penetration or incorporation into everyday life of specific features of carnival – the disruption of values, the turning upside down of the hierarchical scale – and its shaping effect on language and literature. The carnivalesque element is characteristic of burlesque and mock-heroic parody. According to Bakhtin, the device is liberating, dynamic and subversive. It disrupts authority and introduces alternatives. Moreover, it ignores all kinds of borders – in the present case, the one between the sacred and the profane. With the introduction of carnivalesque features, any kind of formal, dogmatic culture becomes debunked and demystified in an ironic way. These combinations confirm the etymology of the word, parody being a song (*ôdè*) sung 'beside' (*para*) the original. As a result, the excerpts cited above can be read as descants of the scriptures that they quote to give them a meaning that is not the one they are supposed to have. Parody establishes a mirror effect in which the repeated image is reversed. In addition, it ironically distorts the intentions of the canon by suggesting that the scriptures depict an ideal that is not appropriate in our contemporary lives. As Tillie puts it: 'There aint no burning bushes and there aint no pillars of light.'[58] Parody distinguishes itself from religious quotations but nevertheless keeps referring to them. Paradoxically, it contests a model that it takes up, renews and illustrates. Parody both incorporates and challenges that which it parodies, which makes it a postmodern form where the dialogical relation between identification and distance is permanent.

Although most of its plot unfolds before that fateful day, *Let the Great World Spin* is a 9/11 novel. In comparison to the other novels that deal with the events, this anteriority makes the novel particularly original. In allusive advance, McCann manages to create a new form to narrate a trauma. He stays away from the disaster scene, but implicitly introduces it and lets it reverberate in his reader's mind. This way of writing about a shocking event is specific to the author, who keeps on refusing to make his work a mirror of the horrors of his days. Indeed, McCann could not imagine writing a novel that would be a fictionalised commentary for the pictures broadcast live by the TV channels of the whole world. Through some individual examples, he chooses to make the most of a common feature of 9/11 texts and write particularly about the body's fall, suggesting that the death of a son on a battlefield or the death of a brother or a lover in a car crash is, for the victim's friends and relatives, as tragic an event as a huge dramatic terrorist attack. This motif of the fall is intensified by the parodic tone and particularly the mock-heroic device that mirrors the textual semantic contents. Although it is everywhere, the motif is not the sign of a decline from which it is impossible to recover; indeed, there is still a potential of hope that makes it possible to cope and overcome the ordeal. In this respect Philippe Petit's prowess is emblematic; as Eoin Flannery puts it: 'all characters are funambulists, they all are forced to take risks and are all delicately perched between life and death, and hope and despair.'[59] The novel can thus be read as 'an allegory about human suffering'[60] with which all beings are inevitably confronted, and 'how that suffering can be alleviated or endured'.[61] Among other possibilities, social cohesion is necessary in order to stand up again after the fall, as Jaslyn thinks at the end of the narrative: 'We find in others the ongoing of ourselves. It is enough, almost enough.'[62]

CHAPTER 10

Intertextuality and Intentionality in *TransAtlantic*

Commencing with the title, the motif of connection in McCann's 2013 novel *TransAtlantic* is obvious. Border crossing, a recurrent theme in the whole work, is illustrated here by characters who leap across the ocean from the New World to Ireland or back again. The novel is a series of narratives that span 150 years and two continents. It is divided into three books. The first one is composed of three chapters:

- In 1919 a reporter, Emily Ehrlich, covers an unheard-of event: Jack Alcock and Teddy Brown are ready to set off in a modified bomber to fly the Atlantic, from St John's in Newfoundland all the way to Ireland.
- In 1845 Frederick Douglass, a black American former slave, sets foot in Ireland to give lectures about his personal experience, promote his auto-biography and raise funds for the abolitionist cause. During his tour he meets Daniel O'Connell, the active supporter of Catholic emancipa-tion, and witnesses the approach of the Great Famine. In the house of his publisher, Richard Webb, he gets acquainted with Lily Duggan, a maid he meets again in Cork in the Jennings home, where he stays. Inspired by him, Lily decides to emigrate and try her luck in America. She leaves Cork on foot in the middle of the night to reach the boat, and is given money by Isabelle Jennings on the wharf before embarking.
- In 1998 US Senator George Mitchell, a member of President Clinton's administration, criss-crosses the ocean to negotiate the Good Friday Agreement that brought an end to Northern Ireland's Troubles. His efforts are supported by many politicians, but also by ordinary citizens, such as an old lady in a wheelchair, Lottie Ehrlich.

As the plot oscillates between the Old and New Worlds, the narrative exemplifies a lot of toing and froing between fiction and reality. Indeed, the male protagonists of these first three chapters are historical personages, whereas female characters are fictitious. Nevertheless, the latter play a prominent part in the novel, as they connect different generations.

The second book is focused on Lily's and her children's lives in the US:

- After the deaths of her husband and son during the Civil War, Lily marries an immigrant of Norwegian extraction, Jon Ehrlich, and has six children with him. At the end of her life, once again a widow, she spends her last years with her daughter Emily. Together they read the autobiography of Frederick Douglass, the first American man Lily ever saw, in Dublin forty years before.
- In 1929, on a boat bound for Europe, Emily – a fifty-six-year-old woman accompanied by her own daughter Lottie – remembers her mother who, eight decades before, had crossed the ocean in the opposite direction on a coffin ship.[1] In Wales Emily meets Brown again, the pilot she had interviewed in Newfoundland before he became a hero. Brown returns the letter she had given him then because he had forgotten to send it. This letter was intended for the Jenningses in Cork. During this trip Lottie meets Ambrose, marries him and stays with him in Northern Ireland, where, fifty years later, her grandson Tomas will be killed by paramilitary terrorists.

The plot of the third book is set in Ireland in 2011. Hannah – who is Lottie's daughter and Tomas' mother – is now an old woman. She still has the letter her grandmother had written to the Jenningses one century earlier. She allows a friend of hers – an immigrant academic who takes an interest in her family's history – to unseal and read it for her. In this letter Emily wrote, 'perhaps you will receive this [letter] from two men who have knocked the war from a plane'.[2] And she concluded with these words: 'our stories will most certainly outlast us'.[3]

Over four generations, fictitious or historical characters – whatever their gender or race, the precise points of their departures and arrivals, the means of transport they use – leave one continent to arrive on another. The ocean is thus at the heart of the narrative, inciting people to control not only space but also time; between Lily's voyage and the senator's trip, the duration of the crossing is drastically reduced from eight weeks to six hours. The ocean both separates and connects lands. It is therefore highly symbolic insofar as connections do not only concern the movements and encounters of people from the Old and New Worlds, or the interactions between factual and fictional events, but also the existing relations between the novel and other texts. Transatlantic links can be perceived as metaphors of transtextual relationships. The fact is that *TransAtlantic* cites as many writers from the Americas[4] as from the UK and Ireland.[5] The Dublin-born McCann – who now lives in New York City – draws his quotations and references from both sides of the ocean. In that capacity, intertextual links in the novel can be described as transatlantic. Besides, many characters' journeys mirror the movements of the writers they evoke. For example, Senator Mitchell, who repeatedly crisscrosses the ocean, quotes Robert Frost, an American poet who migrated to England.[6] He is also fond of Seamus Heaney, who, as both a poet based in his native Ireland and a professor at Harvard, regularly leapt across the Atlantic. Senator Mitchell quotes Heaney's line: 'Two buckets were easier carried than one.'[7] This is an extract from the collection *Hailstones*, more precisely from the poem 'Terminus' – Terminus being the god of boundaries – which really makes sense when the following line is also quoted: 'Two buckets were easier carried than one./ I grew up in between.'[8]

This notion of in-betweenness corresponds to the experience of anyone who shares her/his time between two continents, refuses to settle down in one place and values cultural diversity. According to Richard Kearney, transitions from one place to another captivate the poet's imagination. Heaney prefers travel to sojourn. He is more interested in nomadic than sedentary populations. This feature is probably due to his fidelity to the nature of language, as language constantly constructs and deconstructs our *idées reçues* concerning identity. Poetic language as such remains open to opposed viewpoints and looks simultaneously backward to the myths of indigenous culture and forward to the horizons of the future. Kearney thus perceives double-faced Janus as Heaney's literary god.[9] Similarly, is not Janus also McCann's literary god? This writer's personal experience and literary production prove indeed that transitions from one place to another, from one text to another, captivate his imagination as well. Through a transatlantic approach, transtextuality establishes a specific phenomenon of communication, a complex web of connections, which can be compared to the travels of Lily's family members with the passing generations. In her narrative, Hannah remarks that her son wanted to create a mathematical model of where he came from:

Newfoundland, Holland, Norway, Belfast, London, St Louis, Dublin. A zigzag line all the way back to Lily Duggan. I asked him what the diagram might look like and he thought about it for a moment and said that it could be something akin to the nest in a tree … the twigs taken from everywhere, bits and pieces, leaves and branches, crossing and crisscrossing.[10]

The protagonists' individual movements are represented as a 'tangled skein of connections'.[11] These connections, however, are not only limited to the characters' travels and exchanges of letters. Just as a skein gathers many threads that are wound into one long piece of wool, *TransAtlantic* is a text in its etymological sense – that is, a fabric with its tangled web of fibres that are the 'other texts present in it, at varying levels, in more or less recognizable forms'[12] and which make it an intertext. *TransAtlantic* is a particularly rich intertext, for it establishes connections with many other pieces of writing. Among these connections three significant examples will be given here: the first one is obvious, the second one subtler, the third one implicit. These intertextual connections are probably more or less clear according to McCann's consciousness and intention. In the past it was necessary to know what the writer had in mind in order to understand the meaning of the text. Since the 1960s the author's intention has been questioned by many theorists,[13] particularly the supporters of the death of the author, who preferred other interpretive models, such as the intention of the work – that is, what the text means – or the intention of the reader – that is, what can be found by the reader in the text. The death of the author involves the birth of the reader. The author no longer vouches for the meaning of her/his work, which has to be produced by the reader. Umberto Eco therefore establishes the concept of the model reader who perfectly responds to the texts s/he encounters by appealing to collective memory – the 'Encyclopedia' – and by making suggestions that are validated or not by her/his reading:

> A text is a device conceived in order to produce its Model Reader. Such a Model Reader is not the one who makes the only right conjecture. More than one conjecture is possible. The Model Reader reads the text as it must be read, thus arousing many various interpretations.[14]

As producers of the text, we, readers, are invited to identify analogies, establish persuasive connections and wonder whether these connections were deliberately made by the writer in her/his creative process. In spite of the diverging viewpoints on the subject in literary criticism, it appears that intentionality can still be used as an interpretive approach, particularly in its articulation with intertextuality. Indeed, it is worth wondering if the intertextual connections are intentional in McCann's work, if the writer is aware of them, and if the substitutes – the intention of the work and the intention of the reader – are valid and relevant as regards the present textual interpretation.

An instance of recognised intentionality

'Freeman', the second chapter of the novel, narrates Frederick Douglass' stay in Ireland in 1845–46. When this American man is introduced to a score of Dublin notables and tells them about his personal experience, he orally sums up his written autobiography. For, indeed, Frederick Douglass is a historical personage who lived from 1818 to 1895 and published the story of his life in Boston in 1845.[15] This narrative – which was of great use to McCann when he was writing *TransAtlantic* – is also of utmost importance for us, the readers, as it allows us to find clues, complete allusions, confirm the truthfulness of facts evoked in the novel, spot modifications, and, above all, notice undeniable connections between the two texts.

There are some who may consider this text to be much more a source book than an intertext, for McCann did indeed borrow part of his story from this autobiography, and the criticism of sources is slightly different from the intertextual approach.[16] Actually, the present study does not aim to leave out the text and go back to the source books that determined it in order to elucidate its meaning; rather, its purpose is to show how McCann transforms the ideas, plots or stories lifted from another work, then to explore and analyse these modifications within the text itself. In so doing, this study remains in the field of intertextuality.

Born in Maryland from an unknown father and to a mother from whom he was dragged away while still a toddler, Douglass was a slave during his childhood and youth. At the age of twenty, after two vain attempts he managed to escape his wretched condition. As he was literate he wrote his autobiography. The book was greeted with widespread critical acclaim. Douglass then became a publisher and even, at the height of his career, one of President Lincoln's counsellors. A short time after the publication of his book, he set out on a trip to the British Isles on board the *Cambria*, where he was informed that a black man could not be given a first-class cabin but would have to sleep in the steerage. When it was announced that he would give a lecture on slavery in a lounge of the ship, he was nearly thrown overboard by southerners. Captain Judkins had to stand up for the speaker and restore order on his ship. This anecdote – narrated by Douglass himself in a second version of his autobiography, *My Bondage and my Freedom*[17] – is taken up in McCann's novel when he relates Douglass' arrival in Dublin and his encounter with the guests of his Irish publisher, Richard Webb:

> He told them of his long travel from Boston to Dublin, how he was forced into steerage on the steamer *Cambria* even though he had tried to book first class. Six white men had protested his presence on the saloon deck. Threats of blood were urged against him. *Down with the nigger.* They had come within a whisker of blows. The captain stepped in, threatened to throw the white men overboard. Douglass had been allowed to walk the deck, even delivered a speech to the passengers. Still, at night, he had to sleep in the underbelly of the boat.[18]

This passage proves that the author of *TransAtlantic* has carefully read *My Bondage and my Freedom*. McCann's novel contains other clear echoes of Douglass' autobiography, particularly regarding the hardness of his life as a slave on the plantation, the nights he spent on the floor, his experience of corporal punishment, his secret reading and writing lessons, his work on a shipyard in Baltimore, his return on the plantation and his escape. Frederick takes refuge in Massachusetts, changes his name, marries Anna Murray – a free black woman mentioned in the novel[19] – is introduced to the members of the American Anti-slavery Society founded by William Lloyd Garrison – about whom he talks with Daniel O'Connell in the novel[20] – regularly speaks publicly and becomes an activist for abolitionism. In order to raise funds for this just cause but also to escape from the threats that hung over his head in the US, Frederick Douglass stayed for two years in Britain and Ireland. This journey is narrated in the twenty-fourth chapter of *My Bondage and my Freedom*, 'Twenty-one Months in Great-Britain'.[21] In his description his first contact with Ireland is fascinating because it makes him realise his humaneness:

> I am covered with the soft grey fog of the Emerald Isle. I breathe,
> and lo! the chattel becomes a man. I gaze around in vain for one
> who will question my equal humanity, claim me as his slave, or
> offer me an insult.[22]

The word 'chattel' – meaning something that is owned, sold or bought – is significant. Douglass uses it to define himself because he knows that as long as he does not buy his own freedom, he can be returned at any time to his master. No wonder, then, that this symbolic word is taken up by McCann's novel: 'he had made himself free, he said, but remained property. Merchandise. Chattel.'[23]

In his autobiography Douglass praises Irish hospitality and notices no sign of hatred to black people among the locals: 'The truth is, the people here know nothing of the republican negro hate prevalent in our glorious land. They measure and esteem men according to their moral and intellectual worth, and not according to the color of the skin.'[24] In Ireland he has free access to all public places and never hears, as in the US, 'we don't allow niggers in here!'[25] Nevertheless, in the novel Douglass is the subject of racist remarks in a Cork street:

> He heard someone say that a *nigger* had just walked past, a filthy
> *niggerboy*, did he not have a home to go to, he wouldn't find bananas
> in that direction, did he not know there were no trees to swing from
> in Cork, Cromwell had taken them all already, go on now, *nigger*.[26]

A similar distinction is to be seen as far as the context is concerned: the novel insists on Douglass' direct contact with a hungry, poverty-stricken population, whereas the autobiography does not really develop this aspect. As regards his stay in Dublin, Douglass prefers to remember his visit to public buildings with a respectable gentleman who offered to conduct him.[27] Interestingly, the novel makes it possible to identify this gentleman as being Richard Webb, the Irish publisher of Douglass' autobiography: 'In the morning Webb drove him around in a horse and carriage. He wanted to show him the city.'[28] By the same token, Douglass describes an official dinner with the lord mayor of Dublin,[29] which is also mentioned in the novel: 'He was invited to dinner with the Lord Mayor. The chandeliers in the Mansion House sparkled. The ceilings were tall. The paintings majestic. The rooms led into one another like fabulous sentences.'[30]

'Freeman', the second chapter of *TransAtlantic*, is undoubtedly inspired by Douglass' autobiography. McCann's novel takes up, absorbs and freely transforms some episodes of the remarkable destiny of a man whose life story is hardly read nowadays. It thus brings it out of oblivion. McCann's repeated mentions of Douglass' name and narrative in his novel may be so as to incite his readers to turn to this work, to imitate Lily, who, with her daughter Emily, immerses herself in the story of this man who played such a prominent part in her decision to make a new start in America. The first sentence of the auto-biography – 'I was born in Tuckahoe, near Hillsborough, and about twelve miles from Easton, in Talbot county, Maryland' – is quoted on page forty-six, when the author signs a copy of his book for his publisher, but also on page 182, when, forty years later, the publisher's housemaid, Lily, reads the text aloud to her daughter. The repetition of the same words leads the reader to wonder if the copy that mother and daughter have in their hands is not the same as the one signed by Douglass himself; in other words, if Lily Duggan, filled with admiration for the American man, did not spirit away the copy that the author had offered to Richard Webb, which would justify her hasty departure from Cork to Cove in the middle of the night.

Considering the high number of quotations and references to Douglass' autobiography in *TransAtlantic*, it is obvious that McCann intentionally wove this text into his own. Before writing his novel, McCann chose to make an intertextual connection between the two works. Yet it is not always so. Indeed, the connection between two texts can take subtler forms, and be ruled by a relation of dependence or influence that is probably at work when Colum McCann's prose is compared to John Berger's.

An instance of presumed intentionality

It must be borne in mind that Berger is considered by McCann as his mentor, master and model. Indeed, John Berger is repeatedly mentioned in McCann's interviews or dedications. Besides, some quotations from Berger's work can be picked up here and there. For example, Berger's sentence 'Never again will a story be told as if it were the only one' is cited in McCann's interviews with Robert Birnbaum[31] and with Joseph Lennon.[32] This citation so often punctu-ates his discourse that McCann cannot be ignorant of the fact that it is taken from Berger's novel *G.*,[33] and more precisely from the episode considered the central pivot of the novel, the narration of the first flight across the Alps.

Consequently, it is not by pure chance that the motif of a pioneer's aeronautical prowess is also present in *TransAtlantic*.

In reality, as in Berger's novel, Géo Chávez, a twenty-four-year-old Peruvian determined to make the first transalpine flight, takes off from Brig, beneath the Simplon Pass in Switzerland, to land in Domodossola, Piedmont, Italy. The action takes place on 23 September 1910 and arouses the following remark: 'In ten years somebody will fly the Atlantic.'[34] This prediction is confirmed by real facts reported by McCann's novel – that Alcock and Brown achieved the first transatlantic flight in 1919. By the same token Chávez wishes he could take off in June,[35] whereas Alcock and Brown *actually* leave on 13 June.[36] A literary dialogue between both texts goes on as long as these crossings are depicted. These descriptions have a similar structure as they deal first with the preparations and take-off, then with the flight itself, and lastly with the landing on foreign soil.

Preparations and departure

Comparative readings of the two narratives make connections obvious, with identical or similar terms.[37]

	McCann, *TransAtlantic*	Berger, *G.*
The pilots' wait for favourable weather	'they were **waiting for the weather to** turn' (p. 8).	'Chavez has been **waiting for the weather to** improve' (p. 124).
The pilots' worries about the wind	'the **wind blew** bitter blasts off the sea' (p. 9)	'a **wind was blowing** through the valley' (p. 124)
The usual checks	'all the rivets, the split pins, the stitches are **checked** and rechecked' (p. 13)	'everything was **checked**' (p. 126)
The protection from the cold	'their helmets, gloves, **jackets** and knee boots are lined with fur. Underneath they wear Burberry **overalls**' (p. 20)	'Over the paper suit he puts on waterproof working **overalls**, specially quilted with cotton, then some sweaters, and on top a leather shooting **jacket**' (p. 126)
The pilots' decision to take off	'**now** is the time' (p. 17)	'I'm going **now**' (p. 126)

	McCann, *TransAtlantic*	Berger, *G.*
Their resolution not to return	'they know there will be **no** turning **back**' (p. 21)	'he was determined **not** to come **back**' (p. 126)
The loud noise of the engines	'A cough of smoke from the **engines** ... the incredible **roar**' (p. 17)	'the deafening **roar** of the **engine**' (p. 126)
The objective representation of the plane	'the **machine**' (p. 3)	'flying **machine**' (p. 130)
The bird as a metaphorical representation of the plane	'it is an illusion, **a bird** in the foreground' (p. 21)	'the spectators all think of it as **a bird**' (p. 127)
The comparison between the plane and a winged insect	'**it looked as if** it had borrowed its design from a form of dragonfly' (p. 7)	'**it is like** a moth' (p. 127)
The plane's take-off and disappearance from the spectators' view	'**the plane disappearing** into the east' (p. 21).	'they lose sight of **the plane**. It totally **disappears** from view' (p. 127)

In addition to the dominant motif – the achievement of an exploit by aviation pioneers – a parallel reading shows many similarities between the two novels. Nevertheless, there are some who may argue that any narrative about an aeronautical achievement inevitably mentions the weather, the usual checks and more or less stereotypical images to describe the plane. As a result, it is advisable to continue our comparative analysis with the descriptions of the flight itself.

	McCann, *TransAtlantic*	Berger, *G.*
The pilots' positioning from what they see on the soil	'**he could see** the shadow-shift below' (p. 3)	'On his left **he can see** Monte Leone' (p. 138)
The pilots' fear of losing their landmarks	'The terror of a possible whiteout. The prospect of flying blind. Cloud above. Cloud below' (p. 25)	'he can no longer distinguish between rock and silence' (p. 139)
The metaphor of the devouring animal (to describe a big cloud)	'they are swallowed' (p. 29)	'Chavez has the impression that he is about to enter the jaws of an animal' (p. 139)

	McCann, *TransAtlantic*	Berger, *G.*
The strength of the west winds	'the aircraft swings from side to side, fishtailing in the turbulence ... We're a bit **too far** south and **east**' (p. 25)	'Chavez is fighting the wind that is already blowing him **too far** to the **east**' (p. 138)
The loss of height of the plane	'the sudden **loss** of **height**' (p. 25)	'He has **lost height**' (p. 138)
The feeling of emptiness caused by air pockets	'It feels **as if** their seats are falling away from them' (p. 25)	'**as though** the wind had torn holes on its under-side' (p. 138)
The rising of the earth viewed from above	'the sea sprays **upwards** onto the windscreen' (p. 31)	'the lower mountains rise ... he sees rock rising **up** at him' (pp. 138–9)
The necessity to keep high	'**keep** her level' (p. 27)	'**Keep** high! **Keep** high!'(p. 138)
The stillness of the plane in the air	'the Vimy **hangs** motion-less a second, grows heavy' (p. 30)	'the plane **hangs** almost stationary in the air' (p. 138)
The pilots' rapid calculations	'Brown makes **calcula-tions** using the horizon, the seascape and the position of the sun' (p. 22)	'the wind which he once so wrongly underesti-mated. The wrong no longer appears to him a matter of **miscalcula-tion** but of transgression' (p. 138)
Their fear of death	'they sit, silent, rigid with terror' (p. 31)	'he would die in it when his engine stopped' (p. 139)
Their bodies numb with cold	'The cockpit is open to the sky. The cold is fierce. The men hunker behind the windscreen. Even the tip ends of their hair begin to freeze' (p. 12)	'the right side of his face and body are icy' (p. 138)
The feeling of being walled in by the cold	'**the cold** is shrill **around** them ... the small white room of their minds. The blast of noise from **one wall** to the other' (p. 26)	'**the cold surround**s him like the four walls of a cell ... **One wall** presses relentlessly and con-tinually against him ... It is the wall of the wind' (p. 138)

	McCann, *TransAtlantic*	Berger, *G.*
Information about the pilots shaving	'Every morning the men made sure they were carefully **shaved**. A ritual they performed at the far end of the field. They set up a steel washbasin under a canvas tent with a little gas burner to heat the water. A metal hubcap was used as a mirror. They put razor blades in their flight kits for when they landed: they wanted to make sure that if they were to arrive in Ireland, they would be fresh, decently shaved, present-able members of Empire' (p. 9)	'He had not **shaved**, he had got up quickly in the morning and he had just forgotten this detail of his toilet in the dawn of the victorious day' (p. 125)

As we progress in the reading, the specificity of the connection takes shape. True, the pilots' worries about winds and air pockets are details common to other narratives of aviation pioneers' exploits. Yet the use of images such as the devouring animal to refer to a big cloud the plane unwillingly enters, or the walls tightening around the men to describe a colder and colder environment, is unusual. The same is true of the information relating to the pilots shaving: Alcock and Brown make a point of shaving every morning, whereas Chávez neglects to do so. If need be, this small fact is the evidence of an undeniable connection between the two texts; indeed, a novel narrating such a feat has no reason to specify whether the pilot has shaved or not. In any case, the texts relating aeronautical crossings by Antoine de Saint-Exupéry, Pierre Clostermann and Roald Dahl do not mention such details. Therefore if McCann's novel takes up this specificity, it is most probably because a process of imitation is at work here. There is nothing problematic about this word, which has no pejorative undertones in this context; it is not to be regarded as plagiarism. Referring to the faithful reusing of a model, imitation can be understood here in the general sense of mimesis, or literary representation, which can equally be the reproduction of the world as well as the reproduction of the text. As Balzac imitates Walter Scott, McCann imitates Berger. The former is a direct literary descendant of the latter. This affiliation is exemplified by McCann's text, which feeds on Berger's.[38] In the intertextual field, imitation questions the notion of originality. Indeed, it expresses doubts about the creation of a totally innovative work. Writing finally comes down to reproducing what has been read, the previous texts playing a significant role in literary creation. From this angle, *TransAtlantic* is to be perceived as a unique novel, completely created by its author, which, however, contains passages referring to another text, as the imitative practices, as well as the formal, thematic, representational connections testify. This intertextual relationship is confirmed by the end of the flight.

	McCann, *TransAtlantic*	Berger, *G.*
The gathering of the crowd	'a line of people coming from the town, snaking out along the road' (p. 35)	'In the piazza round the cathedral a crowd began to collect' (p. 127)
The wait of the spectators looking up at the sky	'mother and daughter together, **watching, waiting**' (p. 28)	'Everyone **waits**. The factories have stopped work. The workers are **watching** the sky' (p. 140)
Speculations about defeat	'**Perhaps** they fell' (p. 28)	'**Perhaps** he has turned back' (p. 140)
The invasion of hotels by reporters	'In the lobby [of the Cochrane **Hotel** in Newfoundland], the other reporters crowd round the telegraph machine. One by one they link back to their editors. Nothing to report. Fifteen hours gone' (p. 29)	'The **Hotel** Victoria in Brig is full of journalists, flying enthusiasts and friends of competitors' (p. 127)
The brutal landing	'The Vimy sticks out of **the earth** ... **The nose** is buried at least two feet in the bog. The tail in the air ... Brown throws down his walking stick and it hits **like an arrow** in the bog below' (p. 34)	'He flies **like an arrow** towards its target ... One of his wings folded ... This immediately forced **the nose** of the plane down and it dived, engine first, into **the earth**' (pp. 139, 154)
The presence of a priest on the spot	'Look at that. **A priest** in white vestments' (p. 35)	'there's **a priest** over there ... all we need now is a gravedigger' (p. 126)

	McCann, *TransAtlantic*	Berger, *G.*
The pilots' superstitious behaviour	'They have not even allowed the reporters to sit in the plane ... It is a **superstition**' (p. 15)	'Chavez sees the crowd on the terrace below but does not wave back to them. He feels **superstitious**' (p. 130)
The recognition of making possible something thought impossible ...	'anything was **possible** now' (p. 8)	'He has shown that something was **possible** which people thought impossible' (p. 147)
... of knocking down borders	'the unification of the continents ... a great joining of worlds' (pp. 15, 29)	'nation will no longer be separated from nation' (p. 216)
The description of pilots as pioneers ...	'**he is the first man** ever **to fly**' (p. 35)	'**he is the first man to fly** the Alps' (p. 141)
... but also madmen ...	'what form of **madness** is this?' (p. 27)	'I guess we are a little **mad**' (p. 129)
... and idiots	'such glorious **idiocy**' (p. 30)	'he's cursing himself for an **idiot**' (p. 147)

In Berger's novel, as in McCann's, the pioneers do not escape unharmed after their exploits: Chávez is so injured by his crash landing that he dies; Alcock is killed in an air show six months after his transatlantic flight. Brown is the only survivor. These destinies highlight the risks involved by this activity and the passion of these men, who are ready to die not only to achieve an amazing personal feat but also to take an active part in mankind's technological advances. Both texts simply depict reality: these three characters are historical pilots who actually achieved the exploits narrated here. The presence of real personages is common to both novels, which remain works of fiction although they introduce characters who really existed in the past. In addition to this mixing of factual and fictitious elements, both texts also share a particular specificity: they recount an aeronautical achievement that is unfairly neglected today. They pay tribute to pioneers eclipsed by other adventurers, like Blériot and Lindbergh, whose exploits are mentioned in the history books. McCann's approach is thus similar to Berger's: in their respective works, both novelists call into question the great historical narratives about victorious personages and recognise the merits of other, less-known heroes by drawing them from obscurity. They challenge the official historical knowledge, envisage an alternative approach to the past, and are thus perfectly in line with postmodernist fiction. Besides, *G.* and

TransAtlantic are postmodern in several respects: being composed of poetic fragments, philosophical maxims, historical documents or passages of pure narration, they question all kinds of monolithic unity and contest boundaries between fiction and history, but also between men, languages and cultures.

Therefore through the major motif of an aeronautical crossing in similar historical periods, the two extracts from *G.* and *TransAtlantic* show synchronic elements – persistence of a form, presence of a problematic issue, repetition of details – but also diachronic aspects, raising the question of influence. McCann himself repeatedly claims that he is an ardent admirer of Berger. This is probably why his prose looks so much like his predecessor's. Of course, imitation is not limited to plain reproduction. In such hypertextual relationships it is closely linked to transformation. When the imitator gets as close as possible to the admired work, they must adapt and transform it if they do not want to lapse into mechanical reproduction. Thus there is something creative about their work; they are not subordinate to their model but are on an equal footing with it. A phenomenon of emulation (*zèlos*) is at work here: the imitator's contact with a remarkable work stimulates their zeal to imitate, to write a beautiful literary text when their turn comes. Now, are the second authors aware of the imitative nature of their prose? Are the points of similarity between both texts deliberate? In other words, did McCann write the first chapter of *TransAtlantic* with Berger's novel in mind?

When asked by Joseph Lennon if he intentionally built parallels with Joyce's short stories in his own, McCann answered, 'No, there's no intentional parallels. I think the prose would creak if I intentionally set out to mirror such an important book [as *Dubliners*]'.[39] Therefore if this answer is transposed onto our present comparative study, it seems that it is by reading and re-reading Berger that McCann keeps in mind some specific details of the scenes depicted in these novels, without even realising it. Thus the similarity between texts would not correspond to what McCann intends to write but to what the text writes, regardless of its author's intentions. The obvious co-presence would result from the intention of the text, not from the intention of the author. For even if McCann did not want to associate his novel with Berger's, the text does it. The intention of the text is blatant. Therefore is it really necessary to try to know what the author's intention is? 'Between the unattainable intention of the author and the arguable intention of the reader, there is the transparent intention of the text, which disproves an untenable interpretation', writes Eco.[40] There is now sufficient evidence to prove the disconcerting resemblance between McCann's and Berger's novels. As Eco writes again, 'The text is there, and produces its own effects.'[41] Therefore to what extent must the author be taken into account? Is it not enough for us, interpretive readers, to know that we can discover sources of which the writer is totally conscious, others that are completely unknown to her/him, and still others that stem from unconscious mechanisms? We can indeed shed light on influences of readings that the writer has forgotten and that he never thought of when he was writing his novel. Besides, even if the author had an intention, he would not necessarily be aware of all its components. Indeed, as Antoine Compagnon has it, art is an intentional activity, but many intentional activities are neither premeditated nor conscious. The intention of the author does not mean that the author is aware of all the details in writing. Intending to do something is not doing it consciously.[42] Therefore it can be considered that McCann's intention is to write as well as Berger does, but that he is not fully aware of the extent of his model's influence on him. This influence is confirmed by another connection: Berger's same novel – *G.* – narrates a meal during which the guests speak about funfairs:

> At these fairs there is a special kind of roundabout, a combination of a roundabout and a series of swings. The seats are suspended on chains and when they turn –
> A centrifugal force comes into play, said Monsieur Hennequin, and they are thrown outwards. I have seen the kind of which you are speaking. We call them *les petites chaises.*[43]

And it just so happens that an old photograph of people having fun in *petites chaises* illustrates the cover of McCann's novel in its first edition. If, as it is probably the case, the cover was chosen by the novelist himself, is he not here again influenced by Berger? Would he confirm or refute the impact of this influence?

There is no question of it concerning the connection between *TransAtlantic* and a novel by the Polish writer Witold Gombrowicz (1904–69). Indeed, it is a safe bet that, this time, the connection is not intentional and that McCann is even unaware of this relationship insofar as he never quotes, refers or alludes to this work, nor does he ever mention the writer's name. The connection between two texts can be merely accidental. Gombrowicz's novel, published sixty years before McCann's, nevertheless establishes an undeniable connection with it, as it is also titled *Trans-Atlantyk.*[44]

An instance of 'unintentionality'

In this autobiographical novel, the Polish author tells of his unusual experience. After a transatlantic voyage on board a ship between Poland and Argentina, he disembarked in Buenos Aires on 21 August 1939. Two weeks later Poland was invaded by the German army. The man of letters then decided not to go back home but to stay in Argentina, where he spent twenty-five years of his life. Gombrowicz's *Trans-Atlantyk* does not describe a ship, but, as the author reckons, 'something more like "across the Atlantic"; it is a novel directed towards Poland from the Argentine'.[45] This is why he insists that the title of his book should be properly spelled: the distinction between the prefix and the base must be respected. Likewise, the title of McCann's novel is also divided into two parts. This split, revealed by a hyphen and/or a capital letter, shows and claims a transitional intention in both writers, not to say a transgressive intention as far as Gombrowicz is concerned. Indeed, Argentina is the opportunity for the latter to free himself from his chains, be they sexual, social or national taboos. In an archaic oral style, the protagonist, settling in a foreign country, narrates how he meets an Argentinian *puto* who is in love with a young Pole and how he is led by circumstances to be arbiter of the situation and choose between two options: to throw the young man into the homosexual's arms and let him live a debauched life, or make him stay with his father, a very honourable, dignified and old-fashioned Polish major. The protagonist is caught in a dilemma: he is torn between his alienating loyalty to the past and his freedom to create himself as he will. Gombrowicz's writing suggests the destruction of nationalism and the detachment from 'Polishness'.[46] He suggests that fathers' values of order and tradition, which he considers as burdensome and restrictive, should be replaced by sons' principles of freedom, pleasure and subversion. As fatherland is the native land of one's 'fathers', 'filistry' is a concept devised by Gombrowicz to define a nation of sons (in Latin, *filii*). These rejections of extreme nationalism and a preference for liberating internationalism perfectly match McCann's view of the world summarised in an interview: 'I'm Irish. Absolutely Irish. But I am an Irish New Yorker. What I like is the notion of the international bastards of the world, the international mongrels ... I love that there are no boundaries and no borders.'[47] As an Irishman writing in and about other places, he takes an interest in the stories of human beings, whatever their nationalities. Although he holds a passport that makes him the citizen of one nation, he does not aim to represent this nation only, because, beyond the issues of nationality, human nature is what interests him. This specificity is a common feature of these two novels and justifies their identical titles. Written by European expatriates in America, both texts display a culture of mixings and a mixing of cultures. By osmosis, cultures are no longer homogeneous and monolithic but become hybrid as soon as they are exported. As a result, nothing is really foreign anymore. On the contrary, the original culture can become 'other': when in 1876, in Missouri, after a working week in town, Jon Ehrlich offers his wife Lily a painting depicting a bucolic Irish landscape, he does not get a word of thanks. Lily later confesses that the Ireland depicted there is the exact opposite of the one she knew. Besides, aged forty-eight, she has been living twice as long in the States as in Ireland, and now feels a fully fledged citizen of the New World:

> She had been in the country now for more than thirty years. She had become American. At what whirling moment had she halted and turned, unbeknownst to herself, the other way? At what time had her life released its meaning? She couldn't locate it.[48]

Belonging to another world implies that what was nearby becomes distant. This is why the concept of homeland inspires nothing more than a feeling of emptiness and insignificance in her. Irish by birth, American by adoption, Lily is in a state of in-betweenness, like most characters of these identically titled novels and their authors.

Men of two continents, McCann and Gombrowicz are transnational and transcultural writers. No wonder they choose so significant and symbolic a term as 'transatlantic' for the title of their books. In their narratives, which are closely connected with their own emigration, they wonder about the notion of in-betweenness through the movements and encounters of their characters in various places, different times and at any age. In-betweenness is symbolically represented by the ocean, a solvent space where bearings are easily lost, as the pilots fear in the first pages. This loss of bearings is transposed on the psychic stratum: the transatlantic crossing shows the transition between two bodies, two memories, two identities. It is a sign of tension between two poles.[49] Nevertheless, in-betweenness – a notion displayed initially by the title – is also significant of a relationship: it creates hybrid, ambivalent identity that is, here again, characteristic of postmodernism. The multiplicity of characters and the variety of stories told, whether they deal with the Irish in America, Americans in Ireland or Poles in Argentina, prove that the protagonists, like their creators, are moulded by the relationships they establish with other people. The interpersonal link is clearly depicted in both texts as an irreplaceable value.

Furthermore, the war, which played a decisive role in Gombrowicz's life, is also omnipresent, though in varying degrees, in McCann's *TransAtlantic*. Indeed, the text recalls that in the second half of the nineteenth century and the entire twentieth century, wars raged on both sides of the ocean. Between the American Civil War in 1861 and the signing of the peace agreement in Northern Ireland in 1998, Europe and America were involved in two world wars and several local conflicts. Within Lily's family, her son Thaddeus is killed on an American battlefield; five generations later, one of her descendants is murdered on a lake in Ulster. 'If you want peace, prepare for war', the old saying goes. This well-known Roman advice is partly taken up by the title of the chapter 'Para Bellum'.[50] This section narrates the negotiations of the Belfast peace agreement in which Senator Mitchell took part, together with the representatives of the involved communities – nationalists and unionists – and government representatives from the Republic and the UK. At the dawn of the twenty-first century, many people considered that measures had to be taken to put an end to eight decades of conflict in this small nation that remains closely linked to war, as Brown remarks when he lands in Clifden in the early days of the Irish civil war:

> In the pocket of his flight suit, Brown has a small pair of binoculars. The right lens has fogged, but through the good lens he sees figures high-stepping across the bog. Soldiers. Yes, soldiers. They seem for all the world like toy things coming, dark against the complicated Irish sky. As they get closer he can make out the shape of their hats and the slide of rifles across their chests and the bounce of bandolier belts. There's a war going on, he knows. But there's always some sort of war going on in Ireland, isn't there? One never knows quite whom or what to trust. Don't shoot, he thinks. After all this, don't shoot us. *Excuse me. Nein, nein.* But these are his own. British, he is sure of it.[51]

Brown is afraid of being shot by his fellow countrymen, which would be an ironic end to his transatlantic crossing.

Lastly, in addition to these rapprochements, another element common to both texts is their interest in the stories that are narrated. Gombrowicz's comments on his own novel perfectly match McCann's: '*Trans-Atlantyk* has no set themes, except the story it narrates. It is nothing but a narrative; it tells a story which has value if it is bright, colourful, revealing and stimulating, if it is something glowing which reflects a variety of meanings.'[52] What does it matter if men tell their own stories or other people's stories, as all of them are unique, unusual experiences and, thus, worth being narrated? It is regrettable that some stories are lost due to the ones who could tell them no longer being able to do so. 'Nobody should be forgotten', according to McCann, who perceives the novel as a way to 'restore lives which have been devalued by others'.[53] This is why his fiction is anchored in reality: he aims to 'rewrite history as life',[54] because a story created in the 'real world' is so powerful that 'it could become more true than the truth itself'.[55] Narrating one's own story and other people's stories is the actual common denominator of all the texts that are, in varying degrees, present in *TransAtlantic*. Douglass and Gombrowicz relate their own stories, whereas Berger and McCann recount those of Chávez, Alcock, Brown and Mitchell. Their narratives retrieve some events from the shade. They revamp, unearth and resurrect them. This may be why Wendell Berry's poem, significantly titled 'Rising', is used as an epigraph in the second book:

> But this is not the story of a life.
> It is the story of lives, knit together,
> Overlapping in succession, rising
> Again from grave after grave.[56]

These lines echo McCann's motive of sharing with his readers the destinies of personages whose stories are forgotten pages in the history books. So many stories have to be told so that they do not disappear once and for all. This concern justifies the recurrent presence of the words 'story' or 'history' in the quotations borrowed by the novel. Indeed, these words can be noticed in the lines quoted above and also in Berger's sentence previously mentioned and regularly cited by McCann.[57] Likewise, in the epigraph of *TransAtlantic*, Eduardo Galeano insists on the necessity of telling people's stories: 'No history is mute. No matter how much they own it, break it and lie about it, human history refuses to shut its mouth.' Although history speaks for itself, one of the writer's roles is to put it into words, to be a spokesperson, for any story deserves to be narrated, including the one that could be considered insignificant. Perhaps this is the meaning of Seamus Heaney's line quoted in the chapter 'Para Bellum': 'Whatever you say, say nothing.'[58] Though taken from different contexts and cultures, Heaney's and Galeano's quotations share the similar motif of history extracted from silence.[59]

A text is an open world where an endless number of interconnections can be discovered. It is legitimate to emphasise them and make them more visible because they are meaningful. They establish a dialogue between works, and show that texts question and answer one another. They are all the richer as they help texts complement one another. These relationships contribute to a 'stretch[ing]' of 'the parameters, or borders, of the Irish novel', in accordance with McCann's intentions.[60] They can be deliberately established by the writer; they can result from unconscious mechanisms that are at work in him, unless they are merely accidental. Indeed, the *mise en abyme* of Fred Douglass' work in *TransAtlantic* results from the author's obvious intention. McCann mentions the name of Douglass, sets the context of his autobiography, and repeatedly quotes it. The connection between *TransAtlantic* and *G.* is more ambiguous: John Berger's name is not mentioned in McCann's novel, which does not quote or refer to *G.* either. And yet a relationship between the two novels is undeniable, as the pages narrating a feat achieved by aviation pioneers testify. This similarity can be interpreted as no more than presumed intentionality, for who knows if McCann had *G.* in mind when he was writing *TransAtlantic*, if he was aware of these echoes, or if he is so heavily influenced by Berger's fiction that it shows through his own work, whether he likes it or not? The author's intention is a concept that cannot be precisely identified. Intertextual connections are sometimes mysterious: they can stem from the unconscious of the text, if not the unconscious of the writer, which would lead the reader to combine intertextual and psychoanalytical approaches. As far as the connection between McCann's and Gombrowicz's novels is concerned, it is highly likely that McCann did not intentionally choose to take up the title of the Polish novel. True, Gombrowicz's novel is present between the lines of McCann's, but it does not mean that the latter willingly borrowed the former's title. One essential function of a title is to help identify the text, but, as Genette has it, this function is not always strictly performed, as there are many books with the same title.[61] Moreover, this very title is short, rather general, and thus likely to be used and reused.

Thus as the relationship between *TransAtlantic* and Douglass' autobiography results from the author's intention, the connections between McCann's novel and Berger's or Gombrowicz's would tend to leave the writer offside and prove that what the text writes is more important than what the writer meant.[62] Yet the intention of the text is not a completely satisfying concept insofar as the text has no intention as such. Antoine Compagnon even perceives a solecism there: as the text has no mind, speaking about its intention is surreptitiously reintroducing the intention of the author as a safeguard of interpretation.[63] Therefore it may be better to consider an intertextual relationship that does not correspond to the author's will as the evidence of the authority of the text rather than its intention. Indeed, the text asserts its rights when it establishes irrefutable connections.

As for the intention of the reader, no one can deny that what has been discovered here corresponds to what the text offers, and not to what we wanted to find in it. Of course, the reader can legitimately wonder if her/his own cultural background does not incite her/him to make spontaneous connections between texts, and if these connections do not result from her/his own intention, when the author is unaware of them. But does not the problem arise concerning any interpretive critical work inasmuch as any metatextual approach can give the text a meaning that the writer did not intend to give? It is obvious that a text read by a wide variety of people is not interpreted according to the intention of the author. The latter is conscious of this. The main thing is that the reader's interpretation is valid, justified, soundly argued and that it deals with something that has been discovered somewhere.[64] The concept of intentionality is far from being an essential decisive criterion for interpretive analysis. However, it is not devoid of interest, particularly when it illustrates that the text produces its own effects and writes on its own, regardless of the intention of its author. Intentionality thus proves that the text is a living, independent body that leads its own life and keeps on providing readers with a whole range of meanings.

CHAPTER 11

Mirrors and Collages in
Thirteen Ways of Looking

Thirteen Ways of Looking (2015) is not only the title of Colum McCann's latest book of short stories but is also the name of the longest story of the collection. Divided into thirteen sections, this 140–page novella narrates the dying day of Peter J. Quinn Mendelssohn. The eighty-two-year-old widower is weakened; as it is difficult for him to move, he needs a home helper, Sally, to stay in his Manhattan apartment on Eighty-sixth Street. The man, of Jewish denomination, is haunted by many memories: his childhood in Lithuania; his family's migration to Ireland, then to the US; his marriage to Eileen, a girl he had met in Dublin; the births of their children Elliot and Katya; and his career as a judge in Brooklyn Supreme Court. The narrative alternates between the past and present, the latter being limited to the old man's very last hours. It first describes how he wakes up, gets up, and feels humiliated for needing an 'incontinence pad'. After getting ready, he goes out with Sally, who leaves him at Chialli's restaurant, where he meets Elliot. Their lunch is spoiled by his son's selfishness, coarseness and unavailability. Peter Mendelssohn is desperately sorry that there is no real communication between them: not only do they make small talk, they are continuously interrupted by repeated calls on Elliot's cell phone. The disappointed father finds small comfort in bantering with the African waitress. When he leaves the restaurant alone, the old man is caught in a snowstorm. He protects himself as best as he can and is managing to somehow walk with his stick and doggy bag when a stranger calls him and violently punches him in the face. The story is the chronicle of a death foretold, as the end of the old man's life is conjured up in advance right from the third section. In addition, the mention of detectives implies that the protagonist was intentionally killed, which is confirmed later on in the story. In the fifth and seventh sections the investigators view the footage recorded by the cameras. In the last sections they question the main suspect, whose guilt is established; then the verdict of the trial is delivered.

The 'thirteen ways of looking' refer to the visual world of the narrative, the different viewpoints, the angles of shot and all of these devices recording images: Mendelssohn's building is equipped with eight video cameras, the spatial distribution of which is specified.[1] The restaurant is equipped with twelve of these objects.[2] Likewise, cameras are set up in the protagonist's apartment, in his street, but also in the interrogation room, the courtroom, the subway, along the boardwalk in Coney Island, and even in the funeral home – hence the ironic conclusion, in which it is stated that our civilisation is so much obsessed with surveillance that it encroaches upon nature, as there are 'more cameras in the city than birds in the sky'.[3]

A scissors-and-paste man

This reference to birds, but also and above all the title common to the novella and the collection, clearly echo Wallace Stevens' poem 'Thirteen Ways of Looking at a Blackbird'.[4] The thirteen sections of the story are modelled on the thirteen stanzas of the poem. Besides, at the start of each section there appears an epigraph that turns out to be a stanza of the poem. All stanzas are thus quoted in the original structural order. As a result, Stevens' poem is fully present in McCann's story. The quotation is the prevailing intertextual practice here. It reproduces a phrase or a short piece of writing taken from an original work of literature to introduce it into another one and to give it a new value. Writing thus amounts to rewriting: it arranges links and transitions between different parts and makes up a coherent whole from various elements. This is why, as Antoine Compagnon's study of quotation puts it, any writing is collage, gloss, quote and comment.[5]

Viewing intertextuality as collage is putting the stress on the traces of a borrowing, on a transfer of external material. Heterogeneousness is particularly emphasised when the absorption is not complete and shows the joints, as is the case here with the epigraphs. In his rewriting, Colum McCann can be envisaged as a DIY enthusiast whose activity responds to a modern aesthetic sense of fragmentation, which prevails throughout intertextual relationships. For, indeed, the process of rewriting which is at work in 'Thirteen Ways of Looking' has certain similarities to a DIY activity, the stanzas of Stevens' poem coming in like strips of paper stuck between the sections of the short story. The technique can be interpreted as the expression of nostalgia for child's play. It is also part of Joycean tradition, the works of McCann's famous predecessor making great use of quotations and making the process of collage clearly apparent. Like Joyce, McCann is 'a scissors and paste man',[6] whose work contains not only a mixture of references and quotations but also words or expressions borrowed from foreign languages, such as Irish, Spanish and Hebrew.

The juxtaposition of various pieces of writing in the narrative is coupled with pictorial collage.[7] Indeed, the collection of short stories includes five black-and-white photographs showing one or several blackbirds on a tree. The first photo forms the frontispiece to the book; it faces the page listing the title, the name of the author and the publisher. The four other pictures illustrate the title page of each story. Intertextuality is thus backed up by these visual aids, the recurrence of photos of blackbirds inciting McCann's reader not to forget the link with Stevens' poem. This piece of writing is borrowed by McCann, who gives it a new environment and, in return, establishes a connection with his own text. In this interactive communication, echoes and reflections are created by the introduction of an already expressed thought or an explicit image: the narrative structure clearly shows a mirror effect between both texts. Just like the video camera, the mirror is omnipresent in the collection. It can be found in various places, including the bedroom and bathroom of the protagonist, who cannot stand looking at himself, fearing to see confirmation of his body's sorry state. Moreover, the mirror fixes him in alienating genealogy: 'how in tarnation did I acquire the face of my father's father?'[8] Mendelssohn only catches glimpses of himself in the mirror because it makes him realise that his life is not moving in the right direction.

Another specular object has pride of place in the protagonist's living room: 'There is a large painting on the wall above the table, a portrait of Mendelssohn, wearing suit and tie, large rimmed glasses, a serious gaze.'[9] This pictorial representation of the master of the house can be compared to an anachronistic mirror: 'Mendelssohn at the table, sipping his coffee and reading his paper, looking down upon himself from his own portrait, the older self looking considerably more wan.'[10] The latter is 'looked down upon' but is never described peering at the representation of himself. He always seems to be looking away. Conversely, Elliot is a narcissist: 'He always was a boy vain for the mirror, especially in his college days, glancing at himself sideways every chance he got, that long blond hair on him.'[11] As the mirror duplicates reversed images, father and son are clearly depicted as symmetrically different. The father's paleness, previously mentioned, contrasts with the 'red and veiny'[12] face of his son, a carnivore who eats 'a porterhouse steak, medium rare'.[13] Elliot is described as 'a full-bodied fellow'[14] who has 'a large stomach, as if he has swallowed a bag of rocks',[15] whereas his father is depicted as weak and skinny.[16] The son's body refers to flesh used for food, as 'his big, meaty hands'[17] show. Besides, his father sees a bovine in him when he starts eating: 'Kill the fatted calf. Elliot parks his large carcass in the seat opposite, his face engine-red.'[18] In the Gospel, the fatted calf is killed on the orders of the father to greet his son who has been away for a long time.[19] Here, ironically, there is no special celebration: the father has no reason to be delighted about his son's behaviour; quite the opposite. At the end of a meal that is not really shared, he feels betrayed, 'jilted by (his) own son',[20] and even disowns him: 'He's not mine, I promise you, he's an alien … To hell or high water with Elliot.'[21]

Another ironic contrast is about the son's sexuality: as the prodigal son – after spending his money on women – thinks about his disorderly life and is reconciled with his father, Elliot remains a confirmed fornicator whose liaison with Maria Casillias is the cause of his father's murder. The colour of blood conspicuously displayed by his body infers evocations of manly brute strength. Blood not only circulates in his veins but is also visible from the outside, as if it overflowed his physical structure, as if, by transfusion, the son had drunk all the liquid from the body of his father, whose paleness would be the result of a haemorrhage. By a rhetoric of filling and emptying, the text implies that the son, by a process of 'vampirisation',[22] sucks the blood from his father,[23] deprives him of his energy, and leaves him literally bloodless – a symbolic castration, the red colour of which is a metaphor. As a result, both of them make up two antithetical types of characters, the son being nothing else than the father's negative. Nevertheless, Peter cannot deny his fatherhood: 'Elliot most certainly is not his mother, and maybe I have to face it: he is more me.'[24] Besides, is Pedro[25] Jimenez's terrible mistake not due to the resemblance between father and son? Indeed, the restaurant's dishwasher confuses the two men, and, by mistake, kills the father.

Mirror images permeate the narrative, not only thematically[26] but also intertextually. On several occasions some words used by Stevens in a stanza of his poem are taken up by the section immediately following the epigraph. For instance, the eleventh section of the story – narrating Pedro Jimenez's inter-rogation – and its epigraph – which is thus the eleventh stanza of the poem – both mention the word 'Connecticut', the state where Elliot lives.[27] This section and stanza also hinge on the verb 'mistake',[28] which heralds Jimenez's action and its unwanted result. Furthermore, the words of McCann's story – 'the terror on his face'[29] – echo the line of Stevens' poem about fear. Similarly, in the sixth section the snow-covered environment in Manhattan mirrors the description icicles in the poem. Lastly, it is also worth noting that the phrase 'the shadow of death crossing to and fro' takes up Stevens' lines quoted in the epigraph.[30] This connection, with its paradigmatic substitution, vouches for the fact that McCann sees a symbol of death in the blackbird. Traditionally, this bird with black feathers appears sinister, as it speaks in riddles and brings bad tidings. Its association with number thirteen in the poem's title confirms fatal evolution, this number being always considered an ill-omen. Yet, there are several ways of interpreting the blackbird: for some critics it is an allegory of imagination; for others it symbolises the world's reality, unless it represents the unknown, which gives meaning to a particular context.

Mentioned in each stanza, the blackbird brings an element of mystery: faced with his son that he fails to understand, Mendelssohn is confronted with an 'indecipherable' enigma.[31] His 'way of looking' at his child has so far been erroneous, distorted by the young man's respectable façade. But Mendelssohn sees his son in his true colours at the restaurant in an epiphanic moment of intense perception, which is also characteristic of the poem. His eyes are opened: as with the bird's piercing gaze, the father shows clear-sightedness and sees what his son is really like. As a result, the blackbird is not only a harbinger of death but also hints at the mystery inherent in any human relationship, as implied by the short story, as well as by the poem.

In the poem, the shifty usages of 'to be' are legion and many include *A* is *B*. As a link between the subject and predicate, the copula is the basic link for constructing images. It connects and relates – Elliot *is* Peter's son – although there can be interference in the relation: 'I is, I am, I was, I will be.'[32] In the poem, as in the story, there are variations in register, in ways of looking as well as ways of telling. These ways are more verbal than visual, as can be seen from the different perspectives, focalisations and voices.[33] 'Ways of looking' have more in common with rhetorical riddles than with geometric angles of vision. Yet for police investigators who collect testimonies and watch videos recorded by cameras, the purpose is to solve a mystery in order to discover the truth, in the tradition of the whodunnit detective novel. Their careful examination is often compared by the narrator to the task of the poets, who are always in search of the right random word that suddenly makes sense of everything.[34] Yet the murder is solved once and for all, whereas the poem cannot be interpreted on a permanent basis.[35]

Imagined by McCann, the mirror effect between literary texts also establishes a reflection between artistic disciplines: in addition to the previously mentioned link with photography, the texts also refer to the pictorial world. Indeed, as they are made of assembled fragments, these pieces of writing may be justified by the conceptual drive of cubism, especially its concern with structure and multiplicity. The components gain autonomy and work as points of reference that combine with other parts to form a homogeneous composition.

Similarly, the world of music is conjured up by both texts: on the one hand, Stevens' poem is initially published in a collection the title of which is musical, as it refers to an instrument, *Harmonium*; on the other, the last name of McCann's protagonist makes him the namesake of Felix Mendelssohn, the nineteenth-century German composer. In this respect, the latter's symphony no. 4 is the background music in Chialli's restaurant, which arouses the old man's comment: 'Three Mendelssohns in one movement, father, son, symphony.'[36] This remark creates unity from three distinct entities, a tripartite association that can also be seen in the poem's fourth stanza: 'A man and a woman and a blackbird/ Are one'. Moreover, the text repeatedly echoes another story by Colum McCann (published in *Fishing the Sloe-black River*), 'Step We Gaily, On We Go', the title of which turns out to be an excerpt from a traditional Scottish song, 'Marie's Wedding', and which the text partly quotes: 'Step we gaily, on we go, heel for heel and toe for toe; arm in arm and row in row, off for Marie's wedding.'[37] Indeed, the protagonist of this story, Flaherty, is reminiscent of Mendelssohn when he goes out of his apartment and starts walking in the street. The two characters are elderly men who once lived in Ireland and are now settled in the US. Both of them are dressed in overcoats and wear hats. They wonder about unimportant cultural issues,[38] and offer personal opinions on the pieces of graffiti they observe on the walls of their neighbourhood.[39] The two of them also call up memories of their dead wives with tenderness and nostalgia,[40] and comment upon the way they step out: the original phrase 'Step we gaily, on we go' is taken up by 'Here we go … one step two steps three steps'[41] or 'on we go',[42] the two characters referring to themselves by a plural personal pronoun, as if they needed a motivating imaginary presence to start out. These old gentlemen's jesting tone contrasts with the sad fate that awaits them: Flaherty is insulted and punched forcefully, and Mendelssohn is fatally wounded.

The chain of causes and effects makes Elliot Mendelssohn responsible for his father's death: it is because he commits adultery with his secretary Maria, a married woman and a mother, then fires her without any valid reason, that Maria's father decides to avenge his daughter's honour and teach a lesson to the troublemaker. But Pedro makes a mistake: he violently punches Elliot's father, who falls to the ground and fails to get back on his feet. Wrapped up in his coat and scarf to protect himself from the storm, the father is mistaken for the son. The biblical tradition of the Torah by which sons are punished for the iniquity of their fathers[43] is here ironically reversed: in this instance the father pays for the erring ways of his son. The latter brings destruction, like the Black Death to which he is compared by his own father.[44] Besides, just like Cain, the first murderer of the Bible, the dark mark he has on his forehead is the sign of his sin.[45] The short story echoes legends of tragic heroes as the narrative acknowledges: '… when Mendelssohn steps out into the snowstorm: there is something of the greek epic about it'.[46] Focused on a police investigation, which discloses unconscious parricide, the story has certain similarities to Sophocles' tragedy *Oedipus the King*, a detective play structured as an enigma. Like the Greek hero, Elliot is blamed for his father's death. Both of them want to manage things efficiently, follow their ideas through, but finally find their true selves: they are just playthings in the hands of gods, authors of their own ruins – in other words the opposites of what they thought they were. They picture themselves as dispensers of justice but actually are culprits. In the tragedy, as in the short story, the son from whom the stain comes has only got himself to blame and never recovers from the shock.[47] When he realises he is a criminal and the cause of his father's death, Elliot can make the words of Oedipus his own:

> 'the worse for me! I may have set myself
> under a dreadful curse without my knowledge!
> […]
> I did not want to be my father's killer'.[48]

Approached by a man who mistakes him for his son, Peter Mendelssohn, numbed by the cold, does not immediately react, but wonders, 'Am I my son? … Am I the son of my son?'[49] If it is the case, symbolically, Elliot would be responsible for his 'son's' death, which, this time, would ally him to Cuchulainn, the hero of Irish mythology who happens to kill his son without knowing it.[50] This episode is staged in Yeats' play *On Baile's Strand*, in which Cuchulainn exclaims:

I have that clean hawk out of the air
That, as men say, begot this body of mine
Upon a mortal woman.[51]

The threefold association man–woman–bird is reminiscent of the fourth stanza in Wallace Stevens' poem, 'A man and a woman and a blackbird/ Are one'. In biblical tradition, man and woman 'become one flesh'.[52] In Irish mythology, woman and bird are one. Indeed, the Irish war goddess, the Morrigan, appears in the form of three women; they often change into blackbirds, harbingers of death and destruction. Badb – sometimes known as Badb Catha, 'battle raven' – assists Cuchulainn, but makes herself seen in the form of a bird on his shoulder, making his enemies bold enough to move forward and behead him.

These allusions to the Bible and to Greek and Irish myths may be as many 'ways of looking' at the text, of interpreting it according to different perspectives, and particularly as establishing connections to works known as parts of the canon. They also contribute to an intensifying of the dramatic content of the narrative and accentuate the recounted disaster. In addition to the numerous literary references in the text,[53] it is obviously the connection with Wallace Stevens' poem that is most worked here by McCann. As a result, the technique of collage and the parallels created by mirror images allow him to emphasise the depth of his text, but also its polyphony and mystery.

The three other texts of the collection thematically run counter to the title novella. Indeed, as the latter is a meditation on the relationship between father and son, they depict three symbolic relationships between mother and son. In this respect, these short stories could comfortably find a place in Colm Tóibín's collection – eloquently titled *Mothers and Sons*[54] – which focuses on this elemental relationship.

In 'What Time Is it Now, Where You Are?', a writer is constructing a short story about Sandi, an American woman serving in the US armed forces in Afghanistan, from where she is about to phone her 'son' in the US on New Year's Eve. This fourteen-year-old teenager, Joel, is not her biological son, as Sandi is only twenty-six years of age. The configuration of the family causes questioning in the reader's mind. It is highly likely that Sandi has been living for four years with Kimberlee, Joel's mother, and that Joel thus has two mothers, as he reckons himself.[55]

'Sh'khol' is located in a seaside village of County Galway, where Rebecca, a translator, brings up Tomas, a child she adopted in Russia seven years before. There is very little communication between mother and son because the latter is in his early teens, but also and mostly because he is deaf. Thus when he goes missing the day after Christmas, Rebecca is panic-stricken.

Lastly, 'Treaty' concerns Beverly, an elderly nun perturbed to recognise the man who once kidnapped and brutalised her in a South American jail thirty-seven years before. The difference in age between them – she was then forty, he was twenty-three – has certain similarities to a relationship between mother and son, a link that is contemplated by the protagonist herself.[56] Besides, the image of a mother breastfeeding her child is here perverted by the sadistic behaviour of the corrupt symbolic 'son': 'he bit her breast until it bled'.[57]

Throughout the collection, the relations between generations are associated with the motifs of loss, destitution and ending, as can be seen from the recurrence of freezing winter scenes. Genuine relationships between people – providing human touch and comfort – are supplanted or interfered with by so-called communication devices that actually impose coldness and detachment, whether they are video cameras, telephones, or computer and television screens. These machines are as many 'ways of looking' at the other with disappointment, anxiety and fright.

The shadows of Irish writers

Like the first story of the book, the second one is composed of thirteen sections, the last of which is duplicated ('13 redux'). Composed of nine words, this ultimate section focuses on the phone that 'rings and rings and rings',[58] implying that guardswoman Sandi has just been killed, betrayed by the light she used in order to dial her home number. In this story again, the number of sections is of ill omen, as the final death confirms. Sandi, her partner and their son are diegetic characters created by a fictitious writer who shares a common address with Mendelssohn, the protagonist of 'Thirteen Ways of Looking'. Indeed, the characters in these two stories are neighbours, as can be seen in the reference to the writer's 'apartment on Eighty-sixth Street in New York'.[59] Likewise, the features of this fictitious writer seem to correspond to the actual one: like McCann, he is from Dublin, lives in New York, promotes his books in France and writes short stories for magazines. To the three traditional entities – author, narrator, character – can be added an extra one: that of the writing character. The story is thus a metatextual reflection on the creative process. The writer shares with the reader his doubts and questionings, his search for verisimilitude and the reconsideration of his choices. Many opportunities are presented to him.[60] He has to choose the most plausible situations, to gather information on specific details, so that he can write a realistic work: 'Are there any female engagement teams in the Kerengal Valley? Is there even such a thing as a Browning M-57?'[61] With this fictitious, anonymous writer, McCann holds out a mirror to his readers to show them his own experience and creative art. The work of fiction comes first and foremost from his imagination, as illustrated by the word 'say', which is repeated seven times: 'He could find himself, *say*, in a barracks on New Year's Eve in Afghanistan, the simple notion of a Marine – let's *say* a young woman …'[62] His plot is initially constructed from 'the beginning of an idea': 'All the *beginnings* he attempted – scribbled down in notebooks – wrote themselves into the dark. In early summer he landed on *the idea* that …'[63] Interestingly, 'The Beginning of an Idea' is a short story by John McGahern, published in 1978, that itself focuses on creative writing. There is a lot of similarity between the two works. Both of them are *mise en abyme* – of a story within the story.[64] As in McCann's text, McGahern's relates the creative process of a work of fiction: 'she decided to face the solitary white page. She had an end … and a beginning … What she had to do was to imagine the life in between.'[65] Some periods are more or less productive. It occasionally happens that inspiration is lacking,[66] that an excuse is given to justify the writer's procrastination.[67]

In both cases – whether it is a woman writing about a man (McGahern's story) or a man writing about a woman (McCann's story) – the artists are depicted as solitary beings who let their imagination carry them away to the other side of the world. For, indeed, there is a great distance between the place of writing and the place of fiction: in Andalusia, McGahern's protagonist is imagining a work about Russia; from France, McCann's character focuses on the US and Afghanistan. The last day of the year is also common to both plots.[68] It symbolises the end of life, death closing up each story: with McGahern, Chekhov's corpse is the last image of Eva's story; with McCann, the ultimate sentence alludes to Sandi's death. On the seaside, McGahern's protagonist – obsessed by the vision of Chekhov's body carried to Moscow for burial in an oyster wagon because of the fierce heat of July – realises that the sea 'would still yield up its oyster shells long after all the living had become the dead'.[69] This contrast is mirrored by the phrase that McCann's fictitious writer cannot get out of his mind: '*The living and the dead*.'[70] These words in italics, haunting the writer from Dublin, do not bear the mark of a borrowing. And yet they are precisely the last words of James Joyce's story 'The Dead', which also closed the collection *Dubliners*. Indeed, the narrative, dealing with Gabriel, the protagonist, ends with the following sentence: 'His soul swooned slowly as he heard the snow falling faintly through the universe and faintly falling, like the descent of their last end, upon all the living and the dead.'[71] Once more, death has the last word.

The borrowing of a phrase taken from a pre-existing text and introduced into another one shows different worlds. Yet, here again, there are many points of similarity between the two texts. Joyce's and McCann's stories both narrate a dramatic change from the joy of Christmas and New Year celebrations to the melancholy of memories and the experience of death foreshadowed by a cold, dark night.[72] Michael Furey, the young man Gretta sadly remembers (Joyce), but also Sandi, who suffers from being far from home (McCann), are both cut down in their prime. Nostalgia is a feeling shared by the fictitious author of the story: 'And what about his own childhood New Year's Eves in Dublin? … What was that song his father used to sing?'[73] These questions echo the songs heard during the Christmas party at Gabriel's aunts' home. Some tunes are also commented upon, and one of these songs – '*Let Me Like a Soldier Fall*' – recalls McCann's text.[74] Besides, the specific shape of the protagonists' family in 'What Time Is it Now, Where You Are?' is clearly reminiscent of Joyce's story: a male character is surrounded by three female characters – a girlfriend and two women from the previous generation. Joel and Tracey (McCann) recall Gabriel and Gretta (Joyce), as the two mothers, Kimberlee and Sandi, bring back to mind the two aunts, Kate and Julia. By the same token, as McCann in his fiction introduces a character who seems to be very close to himself – that is, a writer of short stories for magazines – Joyce makes his own protagonist the writer of literary columns in newspapers. Likewise, these two characters often leave Ireland to travel abroad.

Doubtless Irish literature is at the heart of the intertextual connections established by the short story 'What Time Is it Now, Where You Are?'.

Intratextual mirror effects

'Sh'khol' is rather characterised by some kind of *intra*textuality within McCann's fiction. Indeed, its plot refers to another story by the same author, 'Hunger Strike', published in 2000 in *Everything in this Country Must*. That story relates the powerlessness of Kevin, a teenager who follows the evolution of the hunger strike started by his father's brother in prison. From the west coast of the Republic, he witnesses the tragic Troubles that tear the Northern Irish nation apart. As he feels helpless and cannot stand the geographic distance that separates him from his uncle imprisoned in Long Kesh, he decides to run away and take the bus that enables him to go from Galway to Northern Ireland. Thirty minutes after the departure, the journey comes to a sudden end:

> He slid down in the rear seat, but a policeman touched his shoulder, leaned down and said his name aloud. He began to cry. Your Mammy's worried sick, they said. They were gentle as they guided him down along the seats, other passengers staring at him.[75]

The mother's anxiety is mentioned by the policeman but is not described by the narrative. As it spreads out over long hours, it is only reported by the by: a short phrase – 'Your Mammy's worried sick' – covers these hours, without further detail. This is what Gerard Genette calls a 'basic narrative', in which the time of telling is much shorter than the duration of the story told. The mother's anxiety is a low point of the plot in 'Hunger Strike', as it is mentioned only incidentally by a secondary character. Conversely, it becomes one of the high points in 'Sh'khol', as it is the very subject of the story. The narrative regime shows different rhythms and scopes from one story to another: an accelerated scene summed up in one sentence in the 2000 text becomes a scene described in detail over thirty-six pages in the 2015 text. The speed ratio between the duration of the event and that of the narrative is thus transformed. 'Sh'khol' can thus be envisaged as the development of a summarised scene in a previous story ('Hunger Strike').

Here, again, a parallel reading of the two texts shows a mirror image with many common points. On both sides the plots stage a mother and her son who have recently settled on the west coast of Ireland in order to live in peace and quiet, near Galway, a territory unknown to the young man. The two stories are set against tragic backdrops: on the one hand, the hunger strikes of Bobby Sands and his companions in Northern Ireland in 1981; on the other, the devastation caused by the explosion of the power station in Chernobyl in 1986. As if they needed to 'wash themselves' of these sad events, mother and son regularly go swimming in the sea: 'He was a quicker swimmer than she and soon he caught up with her and swam past. She treaded water and splashed him. He began splashing back and soon they were both laughing.'[76] The scenes match each other in both texts: 'Stop it, please, said Rebecca softly. You're soaking me. He splashed her again …'[77] The yellow kayak mentioned in this description[78] may be the one used by the old Lithuanian couple in 'Hunger Strike'.[79] Besides, the diegetic place, the western fringe of Europe, is a counterpoint to the Eastern countries such as Lithuania or Russia, from where Tomas, the child in 'Sh'khol', was adopted .

The two texts describe the mother as a beautiful woman with dark hair[80] who raises her thirteen-year-old son on her own.[81] The latter is long-haired.[82] His body develops, like his libido – as his masturbatory practices show – and he makes efforts to hide his erections.[83] His rapid growth prepares him for his identity as a man. In anticipation, he already wears men's clothes, but they are still too big for him.[84] This change of status from child to adult, which is proper to adolescence, fuels the young man's thoughts of independence: Tomas and Kevin take advantage of the fact that their mothers are sleeping to go out early in the morning; they physically move away from them, thus confirming their rejections of maternal embraces. The lexical recurrence of the structure 'she … but he … away' is significant: '*she* moved to hug him *but he* stepped *away* … *She* came across and took his shoulders *but he* curved himself *away* from her grip.'[85] Words are arranged in the same particular order in 'Sh'khol': '*She* reached for him, *but he* slapped her hand *away* … *She* reached to help, *but he* stepped *away*.'[86] The repetition of the adverb 'away' is also reminiscent of the recurrent injunction in another story by McCann, 'Stolen Child': 'come away, stolen child'.[87] Born in Russia, from where he is taken in order to live in Ireland, Tomas can be seen as one of the children stolen by fairies in Irish mythological legends.[88] Moreover, his disappearance on St Stephen's Day is puzzling: could he be under the sea, held hostage by selkies, these seals of Scottish folklore that can shed their skins and transform into human beings?[89] Faced with her son's unexplained absence, the mother's anxiety is fuelled by lost hopes: something is moving in the waves, but it is only a marine animal. Many people take part in the search and call the teenager, but Tomas cannot hear them: 'the search parties were spread out along the cliffs, their hopeless whistles in the air, her son's name blown back by the wind'.[90] The cries of despair vanish in the wind, and the mother seems to abandon hope, thus reflecting her bedside book: 'she cracked the spine on an old blue hardcover. Nadia Mandelstam.'[91] Further down, the narrative specifies that this book is a record by the famous Russian writer's wife of their lives and experiences together: 'Mandelstam's memoir lay open, a quarter of the way through.'[92] Nadia Mandelstam's autobiographical book, relating the poet's arrest, exile and death in a camp, is titled *Hope Abandoned*.[93] It evokes the dictatorial policies of the Stalinist regime that reduced a whole generation of intellectuals to silence in the Soviet Union during the 1920s and 1930s. *Hope Abandoned* is a book about the suffocation of culture in a totalitarian system where a wind of liberty is blowing in spite of everything. Its motifs – silence, anxiety, destruction and hope alternating with despair in public and private spheres – are also developed in 'Sh'khol'.

Once Tomas is back home, a smell of smoke comes off his clothing, which could be the result of Kevin's initiative: 'In the rocks near the pier he lit a fire with the rest of the newspaper. He warmed his hands as the pages burned and curled. The smoke made his eyes water.'[94] The two runaways are brought back to their mothers in the presence of policemen described as interchangeable, as the analogies between the texts confirm: 'The policemen came and went as if they had learned from long practice. They seemed to ghost into one another. It was almost as if they could slip into one another's faces.'[95] In response to the son's disappearance, the mother's anxiety, briefly evoked in the first story and described in detail in the second one, attests to the difficulty of raising a child by oneself. In this respect, it is significant that these women open a bottle of wine and drink on their own.[96]

Mother and son are two hurt beings, as their fingers show: in 'Sh'khol', the mother's forefinger is injured and her scar mirrors the one the son in 'Hunger Strike' bears on the same finger.[97] It is not by chance that this very finger – which is supposed to be the finger of life and a symbol of the command of speech – is marked, considering the context of death and the difficulty of communication between mother and son in both texts. The forefinger also symbolises 'self-control', a virtue the characters seem to lack. Indeed, mother and son harm each other: she slaps him on the cheek,[98] and he hits her: 'His arm shot out. His elbow caught the side of her chin. She felt for blood.'[99] From the closed space of the protagonist's mouth, the blood metaphorically spreads on the immensity of the sky, above the western coast at the end of the day: 'The sun went very fast when it touched the horizon. The colours in the sky *bled* away. It became shadowy.'[100] This quotation from the first story is echoed by a sentence taken from the second: 'The sky was shot through with red.'[101] Bloodshed is potentially a portent of death:[102] that of Kevin's uncle, on the one hand, and Tomas' death, on the other. Obsessed with the untranslatable word 'Sh'khol', which denotes a parent who has lost a child, Rebecca dreads being characterised by this term. Similarly, when Kevin's mother hears that her brother-in-law will not put an end to his hunger strike, she shows compassion for her mother-in-law – 'Oh your poor grandmother … your poor poor grandmother'[103] – because she knows that, at short notice, the latter is bound to become 'sh'khol'.

The way these scenes are superposed highlights an identity or similarity of spatio-temporal, thematic and family configurations. Besides, it makes it possible to disclose a common structure: both stories work as a diptych and can be read like variations on the same theme. McCann gives magnitude to what was undeveloped, focuses on a teenager running away – which was only quickly mentioned in the first text – to concentrate on the anxious mother who straightaway imagines herself as mourning for her son. He pursues and develops an idea that had first been dealt with superficially. What was potential is finally achieved. By doing so, McCann shows that creative writing amounts to choosing from a set of possibilities, as the fictitious writer of 'What Time Is it Now, Where You Are?' points out: '*He could* stay with Kimberlee, or *he could* return to Afghanistan, or *he could* slide into the past, or *he could* follow Joel down to the bleachers …'[104] Such conformity between two texts of the same author also confirms that writers continue to tell the same stories and to take up the same characters again and again. Besides, it shows that the memory of the literary work is displayed when writing proves to be rewriting.

Rebecca, the protagonist of 'Sh'khol', is an independent divorcee who runs her own life and does not like to be given orders. There is a marked contrast between her and her biblical namesake, a submissive woman who draws water to give it to men and their animals, then obediently walks behind Abraham's servant to become Isaac's wife.[105] McCann's Rebecca is also the exact opposite of the stereotyped images of Ireland, Kathleen Ni Houlihan or the *Sean Bhean Bhocht* – mothers who call their fine strong sons to self-sacrifice so that a new nation might be created. Such clichés of Mother Ireland persist with Catholic mother figures – virtuous women who excel in obedience and abnegation. Silent, pious and charitable, this fulcrum of the family is a model of fortitude that was placed at the heart of the Irish Constitution devised by the government led by Eamon de Valera. The mother remained confined within her traditional role as carer and consoler, keeper of the home and the peace, and loving and smiling in spite of her fatigues, humiliations and frustrations. Although she haunts twentieth-century Irish literature, this popular ideological representation is interrogated and even rejected by many writers: James Joyce, like his character Stephen Dedalus, felt compelled to flee into exile from Mother Ireland, Mother Church, a mother tongue – Gaelic struggling to reassert itself – and, ultimately, his own mother.

In the tradition of these predecessors, Colum McCann in 'Sh'khol' or 'What Time Is it Now, Where You Are?' stages mothers who are not religious persons, who are not in the kitchen all the time, but characters assuming their independence, even if they obviously suffer from guilt and loneliness, and find it difficult to communicate with their sons, whose autonomous personalities assert themselves. Alcohol, to which these mothers resort, not only alleviates their anxiety but also gives them the illusion of personal space, together with a sense of freedom and selfhood. The evolution of women's position in society, which can be observed in Ireland as in the whole Western world, is mirrored by the literary text. Even if the latter is highly intertextual, as is the case here, the text is not a closed system and does not exist in isolation. Indeed, McCann's work is deeply rooted in contextual reality and does not try to hide social issues or the harsh events of the world. *Thirteen Ways of Looking* refers to the explosion of the nuclear reactor in Chernobyl, the 9/11 attacks in New York City, the conflict in Afghanistan, and also the scandals in the Catholic Church – the Magdalene laundries in Ireland, the fights between pro- and anti-abortion campaigners in the US – and the rapes and torture committed against their hostages by the Revolutionary Armed Forces of Colombia. So much violence and injustice can be interpreted as the common denominator of the four texts of the collection.

Death and the old maid

In 'Treaty', the last story of the book, Beverly, a seventy-six-year-old nun, watches a TV newsflash in a convalescent home in Long Island, and recognises the man who held and brutalised her in Colombia thirty-seven years before. The latter is masquerading as an agent of peace in a London summit. The sight of his hypocritical face arouses a flood of painful memories and sordid details in Beverly, who decides to go to London in order to meet with her former kidnapper.

Once again, Ireland is inseparable from the intertextuality implicit in the short story insofar as the protagonists and motifs do not fail to recall the diegetic world of Edna O'Brien's work. Indeed, the Irish writer's fiction is peppered with characters living in convents or Catholic schools, with women mutilated by men's cruel deeds. The recurrent motifs of its terse vignettes and narratives are the alienation of flesh, together with the destruction of the female body; characters are wounded souls who bear the indelible scars of a barbarian past. Edna O'Brien's fiction is a world of sadism, sexual violence, obsession with the past, and difficulty in reconstructing, forgetting and forgiving, in spite of the overwhelming presence of religion. Besides, the location linked to Beverly's painful memories – a torture place in the middle of a huge dark forest where a woman's blood is spilt by a ruthless tyrant – spontaneously evokes the macabre atmosphere of Gothic novels. This gruesome environment is also hinted at in the nuns' convalescent home where Beverly stays. Indeed, ghostly virgins bump into one another at night in the passages and stairways of a large, dark house:

> There is a flick of shadow at the top of the stairs. A creak. Flecks of light ordering and reordering themselves. She moves through the darkened living room, grabs ahold of the banisters. Sister Anne is sitting in the middle of the stairs …
> – Can't sleep?
> – I'm just fidgety.
> … Her face is lean and spectral, her neck striated.[106]

The ghosts of Irish Gothic literature are fleetingly perceptible here, whether they come from the works of Stoker, Maturin or Le Fanu.

Moreover, considering the duration of her captivity,[107] Beverly is reminiscent of Persephone, or Proserpina, a young woman kidnapped by Hades and confined against her will in the underworld, where she stays for six months before being sent back to her family. Furthermore, her detention in Amazonia and the mutilation of her breast also make her similar to the Amazons, those forceful women whose right breast was cut so that they could handle the bow more conveniently. Besides, the Amazons are descended from Artemis, the goddess of virginity, a state that characterises Beverly's way of life. This integrity of the female body is harmed by male perversity: an innocent virgin is handed over to a wild demon, as in a dance of death. The theme of the *danse macabre* – staging a girl dancing with a single personification of death – was especially popular in the sixteenth century onwards. The motif appealed particularly to artists, painters, musicians and poets,[108] and this influence has continued to our own time.

An outstanding modern variation on this traditional idea was achieved in *Death and the Maiden*, a play in three acts written by Chilean playwright Ariel Dorfman in 1991. The plot unfolds in an unnamed Latin American country that has given itself a democratic government just after a long period of military dictatorship. One evening, in an isolated house by the seaside, Paulina, a former political prisoner who had been raped and tortured by her captors in the past, recognises one of them in the man who drives her husband home and introduces himself as Dr Miranda. Beverly's experience is like Paulina's: both of them, victims of the junta, had a hellish life for months. Rape, torture and mutilation obviously had devastating effects on them. By chance, they happen to see again their torturers, who so much lack humanity that they cannot even call them by their names. Beverly's confession to her brother:

– He came back, you know.
– Who came back, Bev?[109]

recalls Paulina's laconic dialogue with her husband:

PAULINA: It's him.
GERARDO: Him? Who?
PAULINA: The doctor.
GERARDO: What doctor?
PAULINA: The doctor who put on Schubert.
GERARDO: How do you know?[110]

Because they were often blindfolded, they can recognise their kidnappers from their voices. In 'Treaty', the narrative mentions 'the sound of his voice, quiet and controlled'.[111] As for Paulina, she tells her husband:

All right, then I am ill. But I can be ill and recognize a voice. What's more, when you lose one of your senses, the other ones make up for it and become sharper … It's his voice. I recognized it as soon as he arrived last night. The way he laughed. Certain phrases he used …[112]

In both texts, the victim is determined to confound her torturer and let him know she is aware of his true identity hidden behind a masquerade of respectable appearance. He should know she has survived, in spite of the ugly scars he left in her flesh and mind. The encounter between them stages a relative reversal of roles: the victim now takes control of the situation suffered by the former torturer, who, upset, claims that his interlocutor is mistaken. Identified behind the mask of Euclides, Carlos repeats, 'I think you've mistaken me',[113] but finally calls Beverly a *puta*,[114] as he used to do so many years before. Likewise, Roberto Miranda tells Paulina: 'I don't know you, Madam. I have never seen you before in my life',[115] but betrays his guilt when he gets caught out by her. The confrontation introduces notions of honour, justice and identification: as the culprit is not prosecuted but granted an absurd amnesty, the victim makes it a point of honour to resort to 'some kind of moral sanction',[116] and organises a 'private trial',[117] the purpose of which is to drag a snatch of confession out of the criminal. As the female victim could have given vent to her desire for revenge – an option chosen by Pedro in the first story of the collection – she does not lapse into crime here but holds out the mirror of his perversity to her kidnapper in the hope of being able 'to get rid of her ghosts'.[118] Although the trauma aroused a deep sense of injustice in her, she refuses to avenge. Yet, as Beverly admits in the confessional,[119] forgiveness is not so easily granted, in spite of her being a nun. The motif of forgiveness is crucial in the text, as the original title of the story – initially published in a magazine – emphasises: 'Treaty, Torture and Forgiveness'.[120] It does not mean oblivion, as remarked by a character in *Death and the Maiden*,[121] but forgiveness distinguishes the person from the action. In other words, some acts remain inexcusable, whereas anyone can be forgiven. The act of forgiving is a process of liberation, of reconciliation with oneself, then with the other, as Beverly hears in her therapy sessions: 'Forgiveness for herself first, they told her. In order, then, to forgive him.'[122] The nun shows great moral fibre. Looking into her torturer's eyes, she closes the door of the past, not so as to forget it but to free herself from it. In spite of her sufferings, Beverly is willing to do things that benefit other people. In her convent in Houston she welcomes the young patients of the adjacent private hospital where abortions are performed. She listens to these women, advises them, and invites them to stay with her, without paying attention to the indignation her behaviour arouses among local conservative extremists. She is motivated to help others because of the painful experience she went through herself.[123]

This tendency to altruism, cooperation and empathy is felt everywhere in McCann's work, whose 'ways of looking' at human beings are tinged with optimism. Working on the principle that all individuals have potentialities for love and altruism but also hatred and violence, it is advisable to favour situations that are likely to fuel what is best in everyone. It must not be overlooked that no society can change individuals completely. As a result, everyone has their own responsibilities. Unlike the media, which focuses on the dark side of humanity, the writer's texts are invitations to consider one's fellow creatures positively, to develop a proclivity for empathy among readers, and to express it through benevolent actions. Essential values and attitudes such as trust, respect or cooperation have an impact on relationships among people but also on social life as a whole, as Narrative 4 illustrates. This collective initiated and chaired by Colum McCann, in which everyone is invited to fully and truly tell another's tales, levers up concrete actions. Whether they are narratives for peace, social justice or the environment, they foster 'radical empathy'.[124] Empathy is sharing someone else's feelings or experiences. In the field of literature, this ability can translate into intertextuality that attaches great value to others. Otherness is a key notion of intertextuality. By its connections, whether they are collages or mirror images, McCann's work, which so often refers to other texts, shows that nothing can be done without others. The latter are inevitably present in the life as well as in the text of any human being. Persons form themselves in relation to others. Likewise, texts do not exist on their own. They are composed of words and thoughts, original fragments or memories, references or borrowings. Similarly, human beings are made of snatches of identification, mixed images and traits of character; all of these component parts make a unique fiction that is called the self.

Conclusion

McCann's work has repeatedly been described here as postmodern. The use of this qualifying adjective is justified by the numerous transgressions, such as the development of excentric voices, the opposition to authority and signification, or the multiplicity of local stories that problematise history. And as postmodernism suggests a dialogue with the past in the light of the present, intertextuality is also one of its essential components. As a result, in McCann's work readers are often invited to discover a text they do not know, to reread a classic author or a forgotten book, to direct their attention towards a stimulating association.

The preceding chapters are focused on this work in its articulation with other writers' literary texts that it absorbs and transforms. As its name indicates, the intertext essentially concentrates on the text itself and precisely on the connections it establishes with other texts. Composed of various, heterogeneous elements, it is not an isolated phenomenon: it is made up of a mosaic, a patchwork or a kaleidoscope. The intertext is varied, multiple and fragmentary – hence its recurrent presence in postmodern fiction.

Mentioning other texts in a direct or indirect way aims to maintain, protect and remember them. McCann shows respect and admiration for the texts he refers to, even if he regularly challenges and disrupts them. When he borrows a sentence, an idea or a situation from another work, he not only rewrites the past in a new context but also attacks and subverts the canon, which is, according to Declan Kiberd, the best way to protect a tradition.[1] The questioning of authority suggests transformation, transposition and transgression, and is involved in making the intertextual process a parodic entertainment. McCann acknowledges the authority of his famous predecessors, but contests and distorts it by establishing ironic distance through the form, style and themes he uses. He emulates these models and simultaneously emancipates himself from their literary authority. No one can deny that values have changed, that myths are no longer credible, that life itself is ironic. The postmodern intertext is a response to this statement of fact. It is a way of contemplating traditional

186

values and myths with critical distance, of joking over them, which may be the evidence of a vestige of confidence in them.[2]

As it brings the past and present together, the intertext also bridges the gap between fiction and reality when it introduces historical personages into the diegesis, between literary genres when it absorbs extracts of poems or plays into novels and short stories, or between nationalities when it refers to Irish or American writers, but also artists from continental Europe, Africa or South America.

Perhaps the intertext is also conceivable as a process that aims to bridge any other kind of gap. It can be a way for McCann to heighten his readers' awareness of all kinds of disparities and inequalities among men. Knocking down boundaries makes it possible to participate in the construction of a mixed, hybrid universe that is enhanced by the other's presence. Intertextuality, one of the characteristic features of McCann's work, contributes to identifying the author's world as the exact opposite of nationalistic narrow-mindedness. By connecting texts of all languages and nationalities, it generates transnational articulations and gives full meaning to the concept of world literature.

Appendix:
The Fate of the Children of Lir

[Lady Augusta Gregory, 'The Fate of the Children of Lir' [1904], in idem, *Gods and Fighting Men* (London: Forgotten Books, 2007), pp. 76–80]

After the battle of Tailltin, the Tuatha de Danaan chose a king for themselves. The kingship was given to Bodb Dearg, which did not please Lir, son of Manannan, god of the sea, for he thought he had a right to be made king. He refused to give obedience to the king and went away. Later, a great misfortune came on him, for his wife died. That came very hard on Lir, and there was heaviness on his mind after her.

And Bodb said: 'If Lir had a mind for it, my help and my friendship would be good for him now, since his wife is not living to him. For I have here with me the three young girls of the best shape in all Ireland.' Lir chose Bodb's eldest daughter, Aobh, and made a great wedding feast. In the course of time Aobh brought forth two children, a daughter and a son, Fionnuala and Aodh their names were. And after a while she was brought to bed again, and this time she gave birth to two sons, and they called them Fiachra and Conn. And she herself died at their birth. And that weighed very heavy on Lir, and only for the way his mind was set on his four children he would have gone near to die of grief. Bodb Dearg said: 'Our friendship with one another will not be broken, for I will give him for a wife her sister Aoife.' When Lir heard that, he came for the girl and married her, and brought her home to his house.

A fire of jealousy was kindled in Aoife, and she got to have a dislike and a hatred of her sister's children. Then she let on to have a sickness. And one day she got her chariot yoked, and she took the four children in it, and they went forward towards the house of Bodb Dearg.

When they were on their way Aoife said to her people: 'Let you kill now the four children of Lir, for whose sake their father has given up my love.' 'We will not do that indeed,' they said. When they would not do as she bade them, she took out a sword herself to put an end to the children with; but she was not able to do it.

They went on then west to Loch Dairbhreach, the Lake of the Oaks, and the horses were stopped there, and Aoife bade the children of Lir to go out and bathe in the lake, and they did as she bade them. And as soon as Aoife saw them out in the lake she struck them with a Druid rod, and put on them the shape of four swans, white and beautiful. They said: 'Witch! It is a bad deed you have done; put some bounds now to the time this enchantment is to stop on us.' 'I will do that,' said Aoife. 'The bounds set to your time are this, till the Woman from the South and the Man from the North will come together. And since you ask to hear it of me,' she said, 'no friends and no power that you have will be able to bring you out of these shapes you are in through the length of your lives, until you have been three hundred years on Loch Dairbhreach, and three hundred years on Sruth na Maoile between Ireland and Alban, and three hundred years at Irrus Domnann and Inis Gluaire; and these are to be your journeys from this out,' she said.

But then repentance came on Aoife, and she said: 'Since there is no other help for me to give you now, you may keep your own speech; and you will be singing sweet music of the Sidhe, that would put the men of the earth to sleep, and there will be no music in the world equal to it. And go away out of my sight now, children of Lir.'

Aoife went on to the palace of Bodb Dearg. The chief asked her why she did not bring the children of Lir with her. She said: 'It is because Lir has no liking for you, and he will not trust you with his children, for fear you might keep them from him altogether.' Bodb Dearg thought in his own mind it was deceit the woman was doing on him; he sent messengers to Lir. Lir was downhearted and sorrowful at the news, for he understood well it was Aoife had destroyed or made an end of his children.

Bodb struck Aoife with a Druid wand, and she was turned into a witch of the air there and then, and she went away on the wind in that shape, and she is in it yet, and will be in it to the end of life and time.

Bodb Dearg and Lir came to the shore of Loch Dairbhreach, and they made their camp there.

Men came from every part of Ireland to be listening to the music of the swans, for there was never any delight to compare with that music. Swans used to be telling stories, and to be talking with men every day. And every night, they used to sing very sweet music of the Sidhe; and every one that heard that music would sleep sound and quiet whatever trouble or long sickness might be on him.

After three hundred years, Fionnula said: 'The time is come, as I think, for us to part from you, O pleasant company. From this day out, it is on the tormented course of the Maoil we will be, without the voice of any person near us.' After that complaint they took to flight, lightly, airily, till they came to Sruth na Maoile between Ireland and Alban. And that was a grief to the men of Ireland, and they gave out an order no swan was to be killed from that out, whatever chance might be of killing one, all through Ireland.

It was a bad dwelling place for the children of Lir they to be on Sruth na Maoile. When they saw the wide coast about them, they were filled with cold and with sorrow.

A rough storm came sweeping down, the way the children of Lir were scattered over the great sea, and the wideness of it set them astray, so that no one of them could know what way the others went. They stayed there a long time after that, suffering cold and misery on the Maoil.

The children of Lir went to the Inis Gluaire, and all the birds of the country gathered near them on Loch na-n Ean, the Lake of the Birds … St Mochaomhog came to Inis Gluaire after the faith of Christ and blessed Patrick came into Ireland. And the first night he came to the island, the children of Lir heard the voice of his bell, ringing near them. And the brothers started up with fright when they heard it. 'We do not know,' they said, 'what is that weak, unpleasing voice we hear.' 'That is the voice of the bell of Mochaomhog,' said Fionnuala; 'and it is through that bell you will be set free from pain and from misery' … They put trust in Mochaomhog, and they used to be hearing Mass with him … No danger and no distress that was on the swans before put any trouble on them now.

Now the king of Connacht at that time was Lairgren, son of Colman, son of Cobthach, and Deoch, daughter of Finghin, was his wife. And that was the coming together of the Man from the North and the Woman from the South, that Aoife had spoken of. And the woman heard talk of the birds, and a great desire came on her to get them, and she bade Lairgren to bring them to her.

Lairgren sent messengers to ask the birds of Mochaomhog, and he did not get them. There was great anger on him then: Lairgren rose up, and he took hold of the swans, and pulled them off the altar, two birds in each hand, to bring them away to Deoch. But no sooner had he laid his hand on them than their skins fell off, and what was in their place was three lean, withered old men and a thin withered old woman, without blood or flesh.

Fionnuala said to Mochaomhog: 'Come and baptise us now, for it is short till our death comes.' The children of Lir were baptised then, and they died and were buried, and Heaven was gained for their souls.

Notes and References

Abbreviations (Colum McCann's short-story collections)

EITCM Colum McCann, *Everything in this Country Must* (London: Phoenix, 2000)

FTSBR Colum McCann, *Fishing the Sloe-black River* (London: Phoenix, 1994)

TWOL Colum McCann, *Thirteen Ways of Looking* (London, Oxford, New York, New Delhi and Sydney: Bloomsbury, 2015)

Introduction

1 Joseph Lennon, '"The First Man to Whistle": two interviews with Colum McCann', in Susan Cahill and Eoin Flannery (eds), *This Side of Brightness: essays on the fiction of Colum McCann* (Bern: Peter Lang, 2012), p. 157.

2 'Books of poetry talk to one another on the floor': McCann, 'Step We Gaily, On We Go', *FTSBR*, p. 71.

3 Some novels such as *Zoli* or *This Side of Brightness*, for example, incite their readers to look differently at Roma, the homeless and, generally speaking, the outcasts of Western societies.

4 For instance, the motif of a dark, polluted river is common to *Fishing the Sloe-black River*, *Songdogs* and *Zoli*.

5 Gérard Genette, *Palimpsests: literature in the second degree* (Lincoln, NE: University of Nebraska Press, 1997), p. 8, my emphasis.

6 Roland Barthes, 'Theory of the Text', in *Encyclopaedia Universalis* (Paris: Claude Grégory, 1973), p. 575, my translation and emphasis.

7 Genette, *Palimpsests*, p. 8.

Chapter 1

1 Dave Welch, 'There Goes Colum McCann, Telling His Bonfire Stories Again: an interview with Colum McCann', http://www.powells.com/post/interviews/there-goes-colum-mccann-telling-his-bonfire-stories-again (accessed 6 April 2016).

2 Vivian Mercier, *The Irish Comic Tradition* (Oxford: Oxford University Press, 1962), see chapter 8, 'Joyce and the Irish Tradition of Parody'.

3 'la transformation ludique d'un texte singulier': Gérard Genette, *Palimpsestes: la littérature au second degré* (Paris: Seuil, 1982), p. 164.

4 Linda Hutcheon, *A Theory of Parody: the teachings of twentieth-century art forms* (Chicago, IL: University of Illinois Press, 1985), introduction, p. 6.

5   'The Irish mind is innately destructive … Even the philosophic systems of Berkeley contain an undeniable element of nihilism': Mercier, *Irish Comic Tradition,* p. 233.

6   Linda Hutcheon, *A Poetics of Postmodernism: history, theory, fiction* (New York, NY & London: Routledge, 1988), p. 35.

7   Neil Corcoran's book, eloquently titled *After Yeats and Joyce* (Oxford & New York. NY: Oxford University Press, 1997), suggests the immense influence of these two writers on the styles, stances and preoccupations of those who have succeeded them. Harold Bloom maintains that the anxiety of influence is so powerful that the young author may despair of being able to write anything at all; Bloom, *The Anxiety of Influence: a theory of poetry* (Oxford: Oxford University Press, 1973).

8   Joseph O'Connor, *True Believers* (London: Flamingo, 1992).

9   Jamie O'Neill, *At Swim, Two Boys* (London: Scribner, 2001). Regarding this novel, see Bertrand Cardin's online article 'Intertextual Re-creation in Jamie O'Neill's *At Swim, Two Boys*', *Estudios Irlandeses/Journal of Irish Studies,* no. 1 (2006), http://www.estudiosirlandeses.org/2006/03/intertextual-re-creation-in-jamie-oneills-at-swim-two-boys/ (accessed 6 April 2016).

10   Flann O'Brien, *At Swim-Two-Birds* (Harmondsworth: Penguin, 1939).

11   Colum McCann, *Fishing the Sloe-black River* (London: Phoenix, 1994).

12   Ibid., p. 56.

13   Ibid.

14   Even if the word 'melancholy' cannot be found in the story, the feeling is perceptible in Mrs Conheeny's sigh: 'She looked out to the sloe-black river as they drove off, then sighed': ibid., p. 56.

15   Interviewed by Anna Metcalfe on his literary influences, Colum McCann quoted Dylan Thomas: 'My earliest literary influence was Dylan Thomas. His books were strewn all around our house'; Anna Metcalfe, 'Small Talk: Colum McCann', *Financial Times,* 29 Aug. 2009.

16   Dylan Thomas, *Under Milk Wood: a play for voices* (London: J.M. Dent & Sons, 1954), p. 1.

17   McCann, *Fishing the Sloe-black River,* p. 53.

18   Ibid., p. 55.

19   'Una Harrison's parents left her a box of Milk Tray after six o'clock visit and Maggie the Moaner ate them up. All because the lady loves Milk Tray, I suppose': Colum McCann, 'Around the Bend and Back Again', *FTSBR,* p. 129. It is worth mentioning that 'All because the lady loves Milk Tray' was the slogan of Milk Tray advertisements. This chocolate brand was very popular in the 1970s; therefore the ad is also parodied here.

20   Hutcheon, *Theory of Parody,* introduction, p. 6.

21   Mikhail Bakhtin, *The Dialogic Imagination* (Austin, TX: University of Texas Press, 1984), p. 119.

22   'as if she were communing with the past': James Joyce, 'Sisters', in idem, *Dubliners* [1914], in *The Portable James Joyce,* ed. Harry Levin (Harmondsworth: Penguin, 1983), p. 27.

23   From the Greek *ódè* (song) and *para* (along, close by).

24 Umberto Eco, *The Name of the Rose* (London: Harcourt, 1984), postscript, p. 77.

25 W.B. Yeats, 'The Stolen Child', in idem, *Crossways* [1889], in *Collected Poems* (London: Papermac, 1989), pp. 20–2.

26 Ibid., p. 20.

27 Colum McCann, 'Stolen Child', *FTSBR,* p. 100.

28 Ibid., p. 102, italics in original text.

29 'on ne peut percevoir et apprécier la fonction de l'un sans avoir l'autre à l'esprit ou sous la main': Gérard Genette, *Palimpsests: literature in the second degree* (Lincoln, NE: University of Nebraska Press, 1997), p. 31.

30 'Sometimes a new-wed bride or a new-born baby goes with the unearthly troop into their mountains; the door swings-to behind, and the new-born or the new-wed moves henceforth in the bloodless land of Fairy': W.B. Yeats, 'Kidnappers' from the *Scots Observer* [1889], in W.B. Yeats, *Writings on Irish Folklore, Legend and Myth* [1933] (London: Penguin, 1993), p. 39.

31 McCann, 'Stolen Child', *FTSBR,* p. 105.

32 Ibid., p. 105.

33 Ibid., p. 106.

34 'Make up is smudged around her eyes': ibid., p. 106.

35 Ibid.

36 Ibid., p. 107.

37 Hutcheon, *Theory of Parody,* p. 6.

38 McCann, 'Stolen Child', *FTSBR,* p. 106.

39 'conformisme ironique', as Vladimir Jankélévitch puts it in *L'Ironie* (Paris: Flammarion, 1964), p. 110.

40 'le contraste entre une forme grammaticalement conforme au propos de l'autre et une intention qu'on devine subversive': ibid., p. 114.

41 Colum McCann, 'As Kingfishers Catch Fire', in David Marcus (ed.), *Phoenix Irish Short Stories* (London: Phoenix, 1997), pp. 75–86. This short story is commented upon in Bertrand Cardin's essay, *Lectures d'un texte étoilé. 'Corée' de John McGahern* (Paris: L'Harmattan, 2009), pp. 137–45.

42 Gérard Genette in *Palimpsests: literature in the second degree* (Lincoln, NE: University of Nebraska Press, 1997) defines the hypertext as a text that takes another text (the hypotext) and transforms it without simply being a commentary on the original. Apart from its title, McCann's story 'As Kingfishers Catch Fire' does not quote any other line from Hopkins. Nevertheless, it is worth noting that Hopkins' poem is also quoted in McCann's story 'Sisters' without any precise reference to the source of the quotation or the poet's name: 'The words of a poet who should have known: "What I do is me. For that I came"': Colum McCann, 'Sisters', *FTSBR,* p. 16.

43 Michelle Hannoosh, *Parody and Decadence: Laforgue's* Moralités Légendaires (Columbus, OH: Ohio State University Press, 1989), p. 29.

44 Hutcheon, *Theory of Parody,* p. 33.

Chapter 2

1 Colum McCann, 'Cathal's Lake', *FTSBR*, pp. 182–3.

2 Mircea Eliade, *Myth and Reality* (New York: Harper & Row, 1963), p. 6.

3 John Cusatis, *Understanding Colum McCann* (Columbia, SC: University of South Carolina Press, 2011), p. 52.

4 See appendix.

5 Thomas Moore, *Irish Melodies*, II, 9. 'Silent O Moyle, Be The Roar Of Thy Water' (The Song of Fionnuala) (1808).

6 Lady Augusta Gregory, *Gods and Fighting Men* [1904] (Gerrards Cross: Colin Smythe, 1987).

7 Marie Heaney, *Over Nine Waves: a book of Irish legends* (London: Faber & Faber, 1995).

8 Greg Delanty, 'The Children of Lir', in idem, *American Wake* (Belfast: Blackstaff Press, 1996).

9 Vladimir Propp, *Morphology of the Folktale* [1928] (Austin, TX: University of Texas Press, 1968), p. 25 ff.

10 McCann, 'Cathal's Lake', *FTSBR*, p. 174.

11 Bruno Bettelheim, *The Uses of Enchantment: the meaning and importance of fairy tales* (New York: A.A. Knopf, 1976), introduction, p. 11.

12 McCann, 'Cathal's Lake', *FTSBR*, p. 174.

13 Ibid., p. 176.

14 'And maybe the soldier who fired the riot gun was just a boy himself ... Maybe all he wanted ... was to be home ... perhaps all the soldier thought of was ... Perhaps he was wishing that ... Maybe his eyes were as deep and green as bottles in a cellar. Perhaps a Wilfred Owen book was tucked under his pillow ... Perhaps a picture of the soldier's girlfriend hangs on the wall ... Or maybe not. Maybe him with a face like a rat': ibid., pp. 175–6.

15 McCann, 'Cathal's Lake', *FTSBR*, p. 173. This sadness is enhanced by the alliteration 'sad Sunday'.

16 The terms 'sad' and 'rain' can be picked up in the first and last pages of the story.

17 McCann, 'Cathal's Lake', *FTSBR*, p. 173.

18 Ibid., p. 178.

19 'A young mother, her face hysterical with mascara stains, flailing at the air with soapy fists, remembering a page of unfinished homework left on the kitchen table beside a vase of wilting marigolds': ibid., p. 174.

20 Cathal is etymologically the one who battles against authority. This Celtic name comes from *cath* (battle) and *val* (the rule).

21 McCann, 'Cathal's Lake', *FTSBR*, p. 184.

22 Ibid., p. 178.

23 'Christ, the things a man could be doing now if he wasn't cursed to dig. Could be fixing the distributor cap on the tractor. Or binding up the northern fence. Putting some paraffin down that foxhole to make sure that little red-tailed bastard doesn't come hunting chickens anymore. Or down there in the southernmost field, making sure the cattle have enough cubes to last them through the cold. Or simply just

sitting by the fire having a smoke and watching television, like any decent man fifty-six-years-old would want to do': ibid.

24 About this curse, McCann has commented on the influence of the Jewish legend of the Lamed Vav Tzadikim. According to this story, the existence of the world depends on thirty-six just men in each generation. These righteous men are privileged to be in touch with the Divine Presence, and their prayers are always answered. Yet they live in secret, disguised as humble and poor ordinary people. One of these hidden saints is considered to be the Messiah, but one of them is forgotten by God and has no communication with him. For McCann, Cathal is that forgotten saint: 'Cathal was just cursed, cursed to do this thing, cursed to bear the sorrows of what was happening in the North': Cusatis, *Understanding Colum McCann*, p. 53. Interestingly, this legend is mentioned by Corrigan in *Let the Great World Spin*: 'I recalled the myth that I had once heard as a university student – thirty-six hidden saints in the world, all of them doing the work of humble men, carpenters, cobblers, shepherds. They bore the sorrows of the earth and they had a line of communication with God, all except one, the hidden saint, who was forgotten. The forgotten one was left to struggle on his own, with no line of communication to that which he so hugely needed. Corrigan had lost his line with God: he bore the sorrows on his own, the story of stories': Colum McCann, *Let the Great World Spin* (New York: Random House, 2009), p. 45.

25 Genesis 3:17.

26 'So the Lord God drove him out of the garden of Eden to till the ground from which he had been taken': Genesis 3:23. The motifs of Paradise, the original sin and the fall are also noticeable in other details: after eating the forbidden fruit, Adam and Eve realise that they are naked and hide to cover their nakedness, just as Cathal, first naked, dresses before going out. Besides, Adam and Eve's disobedience introduces sin among humans. This is testified to by their children, as Cain murders Abel, but also, in the diegetic present, by the killings in the Northern Irish conflict.

27 McCann, 'Cathal's Lake', *FTSBR*, p. 179.

28 Reparation is made once the evil spell is lifted: the Children of Lir resume their human form and are transfigured by baptism before they die in peace.

29 McCann, 'Cathal's Lake', *FTSBR*, p. 184.

30 Ibid.

31 Traditional breakfast – tea, bacon, eggs – Bushmills whiskey, allusions to emigration and religious interjections ('Sweet Jesus, Christ').

32 'plastic bullet': ibid., p. 173; 'Saracen, armalite': ibid., p. 181.

33 'his daughter in a dress of tar and chicken feathers': ibid., p. 181.

34 'And last week, just before Christmas, the old man found on the roadside with his kneecaps missing, beside his blue bicycle': ibid.

35 Ian Reid, *The Short Story* (London: Methuen, 1977), p. 32.

36 In an interview with Cécile Maudet, Colum McCann says: 'I don't see a massive difference between the literary forms, between short stories and novels. I also don't even see a huge difference between novels and journalism, nor poems and

playwriting. I believe that the well-chosen word properly put down upon the page can be as influential in no matter what form it happens to be': Cécile Maudet, 'Deux entretiens avec Colum McCann', *Transatlantica* (American Studies Journal), no. 1 (2014), 'Expatriation and Exile', http://transatlantica.revues.org/6940 (accessed 6 April 2016).

37   Edward W. Said, 'An Ideology of Difference', *Critical Inquiry*, vol. 12, no. 1 (1985), p. 43.

38   As Linda Hutcheon remarks, 'Borders between literary genres have become fluid': Hutcheon, *A Poetics of Postmodernism* (London: Routledge, 1988), p. 9.

39   Matthew Arnold, *The Study of Celtic Literature* [1867] (Charleston: Bibliobazaar Publishing, 2009), p. 41.

40   'la race celtique possède un amour de la nature pour elle-même, l'impression de sa magie, accompagnée du mouvement de tristesse que l'homme éprouve quand, face à face avec elle, il croit l'entendre lui parler de son origine et de sa destinée': Ernest Renan, *La Poésie des races celtiques* in *Oeuvres complètes de Ernest Renan*, ed. Henriette Psichari (Paris: Calmann-Lévy, 1947–61), pp. 268–9.

41   Miranda Jane Green, *Celtic Myths* (Austin, TX: University of Texas Press, 1993), p. 142.

42   McCann, 'Cathal's Lake', *FTSBR*, p. 176.

43   Ibid., p. 174.

44   Lady Gregory, *Visions and Beliefs in the West of Ireland* [1920] (Whitefish, MT: Kessinger Publishing, 2010).

45   W.B. Yeats, *The Collected Works of W.B. Yeats: a vision* [1925], vol. xiii, eds Catherine E. Paul and Margaret Mills Harper (New York: Scribner Book Company, 2008).

46   W.B. Yeats, 'The Wild Swans at Coole', in idem, *Collected Poems* (London: Papermac, 1989), p. 147.

47   Ibid.

48   W.B. Yeats, 'Leda and the Swan', in *Collected Poems of W.B. Yeats*, p. 241.

49   'Les mythes de l'ancienne Grèce, comme ceux de l'Irlande et ceux, plus personnels, du poète sont l'approche poétique d'une interrogation sur les rapports du naturel et du surnaturel': Jacqueline Genet, *William Butler Yeats* (Paris: Aden, 2003), p. 74.

50   W.B. Yeats, 'Nineteen Hundred and Nineteen', in idem, *The Tower* [1928], in *Collected Poems of W.B. Yeats*, p. 234.

51   Ibid., p. 236.

52   Seamus Deane, *A Short History of Irish Literature* (London: Hutchinson, 1986), p. 226.

53   McCann, 'Cathal's Lake', *FTSBR*, p. 173.

54   Ibid., p. 176.

55   Ibid., p. 178.

56   'ces cas de troubles réactionnels, ces psychotisations où l'ensemble de la personnalité est définitivement disloqué' writes Frantz Fanon in *Les Damnés de la terre* (Paris: François Maspéro, 1961), p. 303.

57   Neil Corcoran, *After Yeats and Joyce: reading modern Irish literature* (Oxford: Oxford University Press, 1997), p. vi.

Chapter 3

1   Declan Kiberd, 'Storytelling: the Gaelic tradition', in idem, *The Irish Writer and the World* (Cambridge University Press, Cambridge, 2005), p. 48.

2   Edgar Allan Poe, 'Twice-told Tales', in idem, *Selected Writings* (London: Penguin, 1967), p. 447.

3   Ben Forkner, introduction, in idem (ed.), *Modern Irish Short Stories* (London: Penguin, 1980), p. 23.

4   Fiction can be a way to express identity: 'Stories become the method colonized people use to assert their own identity and the existence of their own history', remarks Edward Said, who observes a connection between literary genres and the way the land is approached. He considers that 'nations themselves are narrations': Edward W. Said, *Culture and Imperialism* (London: Vintage, 1993), p. xiii. Edward Said and Homi K. Bhabha – in a work significantly titled *Nation and Narration* (Abingdon: Routledge, 1990) – exemplify their theories with the uninterrupted tradition of the novel in France and Britain, whereas a shorter art form – the short story – flourished in Ireland, which was subject to sovereign authority.

5   McCann, 'Wood', *EITCM*, pp. 27–8.

6   'Stolen Child' and 'Along the Riverwall'.

7   McCann, 'Along the Riverwall', *FTSBR*, p. 149.

8   Ibid.

9   Ibid., p. 150.

10   In the two stories that give the collections their titles – 'Fishing the Sloe-black River' and 'Everything in this Country Must' – the river is somewhat the main character. And yet the cliché of a fertile water stream is subverted here, as the river residents get little satisfaction from the river, which is not nourishing – people 'cast in vain' (McCann, 'Fishing the Sloe-black River', *FTSBR*, p. 56) – and even lethal (McCann, 'Everything in this Country Must', *EITCM*). Death is omnipresent in the collection *Everything in this Country Must*. Commencing with the elliptic title, death hangs over the collection. The implicit is clarified by the female narrator of the story, who nearly drowned as she was trying to rescue the mare: 'I was wearing Stevie's jacket but I was shivering and wet and cold and scared because Stevie and the draft horse were going to die, since everything in this country must' (McCann, 'Everything in this Country Must', *EITCM*, p. 10). This sentence solves the riddle of the mysterious title. Death is close, potential or effective in most of the stories. This motif does not necessarily establish a gloomy, ominous universe; on the contrary, most of the short stories translate energy and vitality, as the youth and constant movements of the protagonists testify. By the same token, the verb 'stand', which is opposed to the passive lying position, is utilised twice in the key location of the last sentence of a story: 'I stood at the window' (McCann, 'Everything in this Country Must', *EITCM*, p. 15); 'the couple standing together' (McCann, 'Hunger Strike', *EITCM*, p. 143). These texts – 'Everything in this Country Must' and 'Hunger Strike' – end with characters who are standing: their vertical state shows their capacity to act and move; they are recognised in their human dignity.

11   McCann, 'Along the Riverwall', *FTSBR*, p. 155.

12   McCann, 'Cathal's Lake', *FTSBR*, p. 181.

13   McCann, 'Hunger Strike', *EITCM*, pp. 77–8.

14   Frank O'Connor, *The Lonely Voice* (London: Penguin, 1962), p. 16.

15   'She kissed the top of his eye where he'd been cut' (McCann, 'Step We Gaily, On We Go', *FTSBR*, p. 65).

16   McCann, 'A Basket Full of Wallpaper', *FTSBR*, p. 37.

17   McCann, 'Breakfast with Enrique', *FTSBR*, p. 32.

18   McCann, 'Wood', *EITCM*, p. 20.

19   Stevie 'had a head full of blood pouring down from where the draft horse kicked him above his eye': McCann, 'Everything in this Country Must', *EITCM*, p. 10.

20   Colum McCann, 'Hunger Strike', *EITCM*, p. 55.

21   As Declan Kiberd puts it in *Inventing Ireland* (London: Jonathan Cape, 1995), p. 494, 'The short story is the form which renders the lives of the marginal and the isolated'.

22   'Ce qui m'intéresse, ce n'est pas d'imposer à mes lecteurs un message ou une idéologie, mais de dépeindre le monde tel que je le perçois, à la manière de mon maître John Berger, qui invente des histoires en s'inspirant de personnages auxquels on ne donne jamais la parole parce qu'ils sont des exclus, des parias ou des humbles reclus dans l'ombre': 'Colum McCann sur le fil', interview with Colum McCann, *L'Express*, 20 August 2009, http://www.lexpress.fr/culture/livre/colum-mccann-sur-le-fil_823679.html (accessed 6 April 2016).

23   McCann, 'Hunger Strike', *EITCM*, and 'Around the Bend and Back Again' and 'Stolen Child', *FTSBR*.

24   McCann, 'Breakfast for Enrique' and 'Fishing the Sloe-black River' *FTSBR*.

25   Colm Tóibín, preface, in idem (ed.), *The Penguin Book of Irish Fiction* (London: Penguin, 2001), p. xxiii.

26   McCann, 'Fishing the Sloe-black River', *FTSBR*, p. 56.

27   Ibid., p. 53.

28   McCann, 'Hunger Strike', *EITCM*, p. 128.

29   McCann, 'A Basket Full of Wallpaper', *FTSBR*, p. 44.

30   Ibid., p. 48.

31   In an interview with Robert Birnbaum, McCann says: 'I don't write about myself as such, though ultimately all we do is write about ourselves': Robert Birnbaum, 'Colum McCann', *Morning News*, 3 May 2007, http://www.themorningnews.org/article/colum-mccann (accessed 6 April 2016). As he was born in Ireland and is now living in New York City, is not McCann writing about his own migratory experience, as exemplified by his stories, which are set either in Ireland or in the US? There is a fair proportion: out of the twelve stories of the collection *Fishing the Sloe-black River*, six are set in the author's country of origin, and six in his host country.

32   In the story, the adjective is used right from the first word and is repeated several times.

33   McCann, 'Sisters', *FTSBR*.

34   McCann, 'Step We Gaily, On We Go', *FTSBR*.

35   McCann, 'Through the Field', *FTSBR*.

36   It must be noticed that these transgressions do not generate feelings of guilt among characters. McCann's narratives are definitely anchored in our postmodern world, and thus reflect contemporary Western mentality.

37   McCann, 'Sisters', *FTSBR*, p. 10.

38   McCann, 'Breakfast for Enrique', *FTSBR*, p. 34.

39   McCann, 'Stolen Child', *FTSBR*, p. 110.

40   McCann, 'Step We Gaily, On We Go', *FTSBR*, p. 69.

41   McCann, 'Sisters', *FTSBR*, p. 1.

42   McCann, 'Through the Field', *FTSBR*, p. 82.

43   Ibid., p. 83.

44   McCann, 'Sisters', *FTSBR*, p. 2.

45   McCann, 'Step We Gaily, On We Go', *FTSBR*, p. 66.

46   McCann, 'Sisters', *FTSBR*, p. 9.

47   McCann, 'Stolen Child', *FTSBR*, p. 96.

48   McCann, 'Along the Riverwall', *FTSBR*, p. 150.

49   McCann, 'Step We Gaily, On We Go', *FTSBR*, p. 65.

50   McCann, 'Breakfast for Enrique', *FTSBR*.

51   By the same token, is not reading also a kind of travelling? As readers, are we not carried away by a gripping text?

52   Birnbaum, 'McCann'.

53   Gérard Genette defines transtextuality as anything that establishes an obvious or hidden connection between the text and other texts: idem, *Palimpsests* (Lincoln, NE: University of Nebraska Press, 1997), p. 7.

54   Ibid., p. 8.

55   'any text is constructed as a mosaic of quotations; *any text* is the absorption and transformation of another' writes Julia Kristeva in *Desire in Language: a semiotic approach to literature and art* (New York: Columbia University Press, 1980), p. 66.

56   See Chapter 1: Parodic Transgression in the First Short Stories.

57   Colum McCann, 'Sisters', *FTSBR*, p. 16.

58   Published in 1997, McCann's short story 'As Kingfishers Catch Fire' relates the story of Rhianon, an Irish girl who leaves Roscommon for New York City in 1950. It takes up the motif of emigration of Irish girls to the US, which is also present in 'Sisters'.

59   Gerard Manley Hopkins, *The Collected Works of Gerard Manley Hopkins,* vol. vii: The Dublin Notebook (Oxford: Oxford University Press, 2014), p. 65.

60   In addition to the epigraph, another quotation is to be noticed in the book. As Kevin, the protagonist of 'Hunger Strike', is thinking about his uncle's imminent death, he remembers the line of a poem: 'the boy began to think that death was a thing that only the living carried with them. He remembered a poem from school. *Death once dead there's no more dying then.* The line shot around in his mouth, as he slumped through town': McCann, 'Hunger Strike', *EITCM*, p. 126. The text gives no precise reference concerning the original line, which is actually the conclusion of Sonnet 146 by Shakespeare, in which the poet calls 'poor souls' to remind them of the mortal nature of beauty and the corruption of the flesh, and to incite them to

become clear-sighted and aware of profound realities. As long as death is not dead, it will have the last word, as the end of the sonnet emphasises: 'So shalt thou feed on Death, that feeds on men,/And, Death once dead, there's no more dying then.' The intertextual allusion is significant insofar as a semantic field about food can be observed in the poem, with three occurrences of the verb 'feed', which echo the verb 'eat'. The sonnet also mentions antithetical words – 'within/without', 'poor/ rich' and 'live/die' – death being a major motif both in the poem and the story, as exemplified by the lines quoted above.

61   Antoine Compagnon, *La Seconde Main ou le travail de la citation* (Paris: Seuil, 1979), p. 30.

62   Paul Muldoon, 'Dancers at the Moy', in *New Weather* [1973] (London: Faber & Faber, 1994).

63   McCann, 'Everything in this Country Must', *EITCM*, p. 20.

64   Ibid., p. 10.

65   Muldoon, 'Dancers at the Moy'.

66   McCann, 'Everything in this Country Must', *EITCM*, pp. 3–4.

67   McCann, 'Wood', *EITCM*, pp. 23–4.

68   Ibid., p. 23.

69   As mentioned earlier, McCann's story 'Sisters' implicitly refers to Joyce's 'The Sisters'; cf. Chapter 1: Parodic Transgression in the First Short Stories.

70   McCann, 'Cathal's Lake', *FTSBR*, p. 176.

71   McCann, 'Stolen Child', *FTSBR*, p. 97.

72   McCann, 'Hunger Strike', *EITCM*, p. 91.

73   McCann, 'Sisters', *FTSBR*, p. 6.

74   Ibid., p. 14.

75   Ibid., p. 7.

76   Another allusion to Patrick Kavanagh's poetry is perceptible in the words of Flaherty, the protagonist of the story 'Step We Gaily, On We Go': 'In a great poem …, there was a man who tripped lightly along the ledge of a deep ravine where passions were pledged' (p. 61). The poem referred to here is Kavanagh's 'On Raglan Road', in which he writes: 'On Grafton Street in November we tripped lightly along the ledge/Of the deep ravine where can be seen the worth of passion's pledge … O I loved too much and by such and such is happiness thrown away … On a quiet street where old ghosts meet I see her walking now/Away from me so hurriedly my reason must allow/That I had wooed not as I should a creature made of clay …' Like the poet, Flaherty is walking in a quiet street and remembering a love story that he knew was bound to fail.

77   McCann, 'Step We Gaily, On We Go', *FTSBR*, p. 63. The original text differs slightly from this quotation; indeed, Thoreau writes: 'We should go forth on the shortest walk perchance, in the spirit of undying adventure, never to return, – prepared to send back our embalmed hearts only as relics to our desolate kingdoms': Henry David Thoreau, *Walking* (1862).

78   McCann, 'Step We Gaily, On We Go', *FTSBR*, p. 73.

79   McCann, 'Around the Bend and Back Again', *FTSBR*, p. 117.

80 Ibid.

81 McCann, 'Stolen Child', *FTSBR*, p. 107.

82 Eileen seems to have only vague memories of her school days. As a result, her evocation is more a reference than an allusion, all the more so as the word 'urn' is mentioned: 'A poet one time wrote about a vase, or an urn, and something about beauty and truth. A damnsight we were away from truth those nights, hai?': McCann, 'A Word in Edgewise', *FTSBR*, p. 157. The reader – or 'narratee' – is encouraged to identify the poet as John Keats, whose poem 'Ode on a Grecian Urn', written in 1820, ends with these lines: 'Beauty is truth, truth beauty, – that is all/Ye know on earth, and all ye need to know'.

83 McCann, 'A Word in Edgewise', *FTSBR*, pp. 158–60.

84 James Joyce, *Ulysses* [1922] (London: Penguin, 1973), p. 435.

85 McCann, 'A Word in Edgewise', *FTSBR*, p. 160.

86 Molly Bloom is Spanish and lived in Gibraltar.

87 McCann, 'Breakfast for Enrique', *FTSBR*, p. 25.

88 Ibid.

89 Ibid., p. 27.

90 Ibid., p. 24.

91 John Steinbeck, *Cannery Row* [1945] (Harmondsworth: Penguin, 1970), p. 91.

92 McCann, 'Breakfast for Enrique', *FTSBR*, p. 24.

93 Ibid., p. 32.

94 Steinbeck, *Cannery Row*, p. 102.

95 Cf. Steinbeck, *Cannery Row*, chapter 14.

96 McCann, 'Breakfast for Enrique', *FTSBR*, p. 23.

97 Ibid., pp. 27–9.

98 Steinbeck, *Cannery Row*, pp. 93–4.

99 McCann, 'Breakfast for Enrique', *FTSBR*, p. 28.

100 Steinbeck, *Cannery Row*, p. 91.

101 Cf. Steinbeck, *Cannery Row*, chapter 28.

102 McCann, 'Breakfast for Enrique', *FTSBR*, p. 24. This description recalls the room in which Steinbeck's characters live: see Steinbeck, *Cannery Row*, chapter 20.

103 Steinbeck, *Cannery Row*, p. 111.

104 Ibid., p. 109.

105 'frantic, globalized, dislocated Ireland': Fintan O'Toole, 'Writing the Boom', *Irish Times*, 25 January 2001.

Chapter 4

1 Colum McCann, *Songdogs* (London: Phoenix, 1995), p. 4.

2 Ibid., p. 143.

3 'The filiative scheme belongs to the realms of nature and of 'life' whereas affiliation belongs exclusively to culture and society' writes Edward Said in *The World, the Text and the Critic* (Cambridge, MA: Harvard University Press, 1983), p. 20.

4 A son's narrative focused on the father is a recurrent situation in contemporary

Irish literature. Indeed, a good many Irish writers are frequently engaged in obsessive encounters with the past, which are metaphorically reduced to an emotional relationship between father and son. For further on this, see Bertrand Cardin, *Miroirs de la filiation: parcours dans huit romans irlandais contemporains* (Caen: Presses Universitaires de Caen, 2005).

5   McCann, *Songdogs*, p. 5.

6   Ibid., p. 9.

7   The analepsis and the mainstream narrative are linked up by the father, as the taking up of the personal pronoun that refers to him emphasises. Indeed, the analepsis ends with 'he might still believe' (ibid., p. 23) and the mainstream narrative starts with 'he fell asleep' (ibid., p. 24).

8   'I noticed how much bigger his hands were than mine': ibid., p. 150.

9   'He bent down to try to pick the cigarette up from the ground but his fingers couldn't quite get it. I reached for it but his boot crunched it first, ploughed it into the ground': ibid., pp. 43–4.

10   Ibid., p. 175.

11   Ibid., pp. 163–4.

12   In an interview, McCann was asked: 'Could you comment on some of the deeper reasons why you wrote your earlier books?' His reply: 'One of the things about *Songdogs* was I didn't realize why I wrote it, whatsoever, until years afterwards. I finally understood that I was examining what would happen if an artist gave himself over to his or her art so much so that he destroyed everything around him. And I realize now that I was unconsciously wondering whether I was going to be the sort of person who dedicates everything to his art to the detriment of my family. It's a hidden theme, if you will. One that comes along and blindsides you with a personal truth. Books, or fiction, or stories become a way of examining these different priorities that, at other times, we might just let slide by': Joseph Lennon, 'Colum McCann on Rudolf Nureyev and Writing Toward the Unknown', *Poets and Writers*, 14 March 2003. Of course, McCann is referring here to the father in *Songdogs*, who, out of selfishness, destroys his family without even realising it, and ends his life alone.

13   McCann, *Songdogs*, p. 182.

14   See Mircea Eliade, *The Sacred and the Profane: the nature of religion* [1957] (Wilmington, MA: Mariner Books, 1968), pp. 159ff, and idem, *Rites and Symbols of Initiation: the mysteries of birth and rebirth* (New York: Spring Publications, 1994).

15   McCann, *Songdogs*, p. 26.

16   'Eliza put her brown wrinkled hand on my upper arm and squeezed tight until we drew away safely, in the dark': McCann, *Songdogs*, p. 134.

17   Ibid., p. 125.

18   Luke 15:11–32.

19   Luke 15:14.

20   'So he went and attached himself to one of the local landowners, who sent him on to his farm to mind the pigs' (Luke 15:15).

21 McCann, *Songdogs*, p. 26.

22 Ibid.

23 Ibid., p. 205.

24 Luke 15:20.

25 McCann, *Songdogs*, p. 25.

26 Luke 15:32.

27 Luke 15:23.

28 McCann, *Songdogs*, p. 16.

29 Ibid., pp. 125–6.

30 Harold Bloom, *The Anxiety of Influence: a theory of poetry* [1973] (Oxford & New York: Oxford University Press, 1997, 2nd edn).

31 During his short stay in his father's house, Conor remarks: 'Enough of the old man's disease … This contagion of days': McCann, *Songdogs*, p. 101. The word 'contagion' is significant and reminiscent of Bloom's theory.

32 A correct reading is impossible for it would merely repeat the text.

33 McCann, *Songdogs*, p. 166. The son keeps on experiencing ambivalent feelings for his father, as he remarks before his departure – 'even when I hated him I loved him' (ibid., p. 173) – and after his return: 'I felt a foul revulsion and love for him' (ibid., p. 183).

34 Ibid., p. 205.

35 'I stood': ibid., p. 205.

36 'He hunched himself up': ibid., p. 206.

37 Ibid.

38 Ibid., p. 192.

39 Umberto Eco, 'Borges and My Anxiety of Influence', in idem, *On Literature* (London: Vintage, 2006), p. 120.

40 Ibid., p. 132.

41 McCann, *Songdogs*, p. 14.

42 Ibid., p. 99.

43 Ibid., p. 109.

44 Ibid., p. 123.

45 Ibid., p. 152.

46 The ban on eating something appetising makes the story a Gaelic version of the Hebrew myth of the forbidden tree in the Garden of Eden.

47 Charles Squire, *Celtic Myth and Legend* (Mineola: Dover Publications, 2003), pp. 53–64.

48 Michael's father is an Irishman who fought in a British army uniform and was 'fed to the guns of the Great War': McCann, *Songdogs*, p. 6. Deserted by his mother – 'a madwoman' – Michael was found and raised by two Protestant women.

49 Ibid., p. 16.

50 Ibid., p. 211, my emphasis.

51 Cf. ibid., pp. 5–6.

52 Exodus 2:5.

53 McCann, *Songdogs*, p. 6.

54 'He called each of them "Mammy"': ibid., p. 6.

55 Exodus 2:10.

56 McCann, *Songdogs*, p. 5.

57 Exodus 2:16.

58 McCann, *Songdogs*, p. 17.

59 Exodus 2:10.

60 McCann, *Songdogs*, p. 38.

61 Ibid., p. 196.

62 Harold Bloom, *Agon: towards a theory of revisionism* (New York: Oxford University Press, 1982).

63 McCann, *Songdogs*, p. 157.

64 Ibid., p. 115. Founded in 1953 by Peter D. Martin and the poet Lawrence Ferlinghetti, City Lights is one of the few truly great independent bookstores in the US, a place where book-lovers go to browse, read and just soak in the ambiance of alternative culture's only 'literary landmark'. Although it has been more than fifty years since tour buses with passengers eager to sight 'beatniks' began pulling up in front of City Lights, the beats' legacy of anti-authoritarian politics and insurgent thinking continues to be a strong influence in the store, most evident in the selection of titles.

65 'The fact is that every writer creates his precursors': Jorge Luis Borges, 'Kafka and his Precursors' [1951], in idem, *Other Inquisitions, 1937–1952* (Austin, TX: University of Texas Press, 1975), p. 147.

66 Harold Bloom, *The Anatomy of Influence* (New Haven, CT & London: Yale University Press, 2011) introduction, p. 5.

67 Colum McCann, 'Ben Kiely: let us hear him', in *The Collected Stories of Benedict Kiely* (London: Methuen, 2001), p. ix.

68 Jack Kerouac, *The Dharma Bums* [1959] (London: Penguin Books, 2007), p. 100.

69 McCann, *Songdogs*, p. 122.

70 Ibid., p. 79.

71 Ibid., p. 132.

72 Ibid., p. 145.

73 Ibid., p. 140.

74 Ibid., p. 132.

75 Ibid., p. 156.

76 Allen Ginsberg, *Howl and Other Poems* [1956] (San Francisco, CA: City Lights Pocket Poets, 2001).

77 McCann, *Songdogs*, p. 120, my emphasis. Likewise, as an allusion to Ginsberg's collection, the word is also used in Kerouac's *The Dharma Bums*: 'the whole gang of howling poets': Kerouac, *Dharma Bums*, p. 15. Similarly, in the first pages of McCann's novel *Let the Great World Spin*, Ciaran Corrigan 'came through John F. Kennedy airport … carrying a torn copy of *Howl*' that he clutches to his chest in the cab: Colum McCann, *Let the Great World Spin* (New York: Random House, 2009), pp. 22–3.

78 McCann, *Songdogs*, p. 175.

79 Ibid., p. 140.

80 'Letters to Cici are returned unopened': ibid., p. 149.

81 Ibid.

82 Ibid., p. 111.

83 Ibid., p. 115.

84 Ibid., p. 110.

85 Like Kerouac's characters, Cici practises free love, likes Oriental religions and proves to be completely detached from material goods.

86 Ibid., p. 107.

87 The alternation of the diegetic present, which brings Conor and his old father together in Ireland, and the analepses, which relate past experiences, show a contrasting image of the narrator's father. The latter, Michael, is alternately depicted as a young man brimming with energy and an old man whose body fails him to such an extent that he can take up the Yeatsian character's words: 'My arms are like the twisted thorn.' This line is taken from the poem 'A Man Young and Old', in the collection titled *The Tower* (1928). Conor's narrative indeed depicts his father as 'a man young and old': even if he describes him as a young man, he nevertheless refers to him as 'the old man': McCann, *Songdogs,* p. 104.

88 'I suggest that when you feel that you could almost have written the book yourself – that's the moment when it's influencing you. You are not influenced when you say, "How marvellous! What a revelation! How monumental. Oh!" You are being extended. You are being influenced when you say "I might have written that myself if I hadn't been so busy"': E.M. Forster, 'A Book that Influenced Me' [1944], in idem, *Two Cheers for Democracy* (London: Edward Arnold & Co., 1951), p. 227.

89 This assumption could be confirmed by the analogies between *Songdogs* and *The Dharma Bums*: like Conor, Ray Smith, the narrator of the American novel, comes back home, watches his father who is unaware of being watched, then 'strides out in the moonlight' (Kerouac, *Dharma Bums,* p. 113), walks down to the river and has a swim in a night of ecstasy: 'I let out a big Hoo … I felt like yelling it to the stars. I clasped my hands and prayed, "O wise and serene spirit of Awakenhood, everything's all right forever and forever and forever and thank you thank you thank you amen"': ibid., p. 117. As for Conor, he narrates: 'I went on swimming, saying hallelujah to the stars … roaring stupidities at the night': McCann, *Songdogs,* pp. 125–6. With this initiation baptism, the two boys become men: one of them feels that 'another skin had developed over … [his] body' (ibid., p. 169), the other feels 'like a new man' (Kerouac, *Dharma Bums,* p. 92). Considering McCann as the potential writer of Kerouac's novels implies that the reader revises and rewrites the text to such an extent that he really becomes the producer of the text, as Roland Barthes wants him to be. Jorge Luis Borges also makes the most of this idea in his short story 'Pierre Menard, Author of the Quixote', in idem, *Fictions* (London: Penguin, 1998).

90 In her essay 'In the Absence of Mentors/Monsters: notes on writerly influences', Joyce Carol Oates deplores rivalries among her contemporaries, particularly male writers; Oates, *In Rough Country: essays and reviews* (New York: Harper Collins Publishers, 2010), pp. 357ff.

91   Bertrand Cardin, *Miroirs de la filiation: parcours dans huit romans irlandais contemporains* (Caen: Presses Universitaires de Caen, 2005).

92   Neil Jordan directed *The Butcher Boy* (1997), a film adapted from Patrick McCabe's novel of the same title. The two men wrote the screenplay together.

Chapter 5

1   Paul Ricœur in *Penser la Bible* (Paris: Seuil, 1998), p. 235, writes: 'Le mythe est reprise créatrice de sens, reprise, et donc mémoire, et comme tel, tournée vers la ou les paroles antérieures, mais aussi créatrice et donc tournée vers l'avenir, parole inventive.'

2   'l'intertextualité est même, en bien des cas, l'un des processus fondamentaux de l'édification, voire de la pérennité du mythe': Danièle Chauvin, André Siganos and Philippe Walter, *Questions de mythocritique: dictionnaire* (Paris: Éditions Imago, 2005), p. 175.

3   Colum McCann, *This Side of Brightness* (London: Phoenix, 1998), p. 155.

4   Pierre Brunel in *Mythocritique: théorie et parcours* (Paris: PUF, 1992), p. 39, writes: 'La mythocritique vise à dévoiler un système pertinent de dynamismes imaginaires.'

5   2 Samuel 7.

6   2 Samuel 12.

7   2 Samuel 12–13.

8   Tamar's rape brings about Amnon's death by Absalom, whose revolt is his ruin.

9   This is the content of René Girard's first book, *Deceit, Desire and the Novel* (Baltimore, MD: Johns Hopkins University Press, 1976): 'we borrow our desires from others. Far from being autonomous, our desire for a certain object is always provoked by the desire of another person – the model – for this same object. This means that the relationship between the subject and the object is not direct: there is always a triangular relationship of subject, model, and object' (p. 32).

10   René Girard, *The Scapegoat* (Baltimore, MD: Johns Hopkins University Press, 1989).

11   McCann, *This Side of Brightness*, p. 151.

12   Ibid., pp. 150–1.

13   1 Kings 17:3.

14   1 Kings 19:5–8. Lastly, unequivocal is the analogy between the prophet announcing the end of the drought – 'I hear the sound of coming rain' (1 Kings 18:41) – and *This Side of Brightness*, whose protagonist 'can predict a rainy day by the pain in his fingertips': McCann, *This Side of Brightness*, p. 76.

15   McCann, *This Side of Brightness*, p. 190.

16   Angela is a battered woman and a rape victim. Traumatised, she gets drunk, takes drugs, has casual sex, and incites Treefrog to kill Elijah: ibid., p. 199.

17   2 Kings 1:8.

18   1 Kings 19:13.

19   McCann, *This Side of Brightness*, p. 27.

20   Ibid., p. 27.

21   Ibid., p. 236.

22   2 Kings 2:8.

23   1 Kings 17:17.

24   Luke 7:11. Besides, Elijah and Moses are present when Jesus is transfigured, which illustrates the close links among these three biblical figures: Matthew 17:1.

25   McCann, *This Side of Brightness*, p. 143.

26   Ibid., p. 144, my emphasis.

27   Ibid., p. 149.

28   An instrument of torture and redemption, the cross is an ambivalent symbol of life and death. Metaphorically, the tree of the cross is the tree of Jesse depicted by Isaiah: 'Then a shoot shall grow from the stock of Jesse, and a branch shall spring from his roots': Isaiah 11:1. The tree of Jesse establishes a genealogical connection between David and Jesus. Besides, the tree of the cross also matches the tree of life in the Garden of Eden.

29   McCann, *This Side of Brightness*, p. 2.

30   Ibid., p. 2.

31   Ibid., p. 247.

32   'Its neck was tucked under its wingpit and the head was submerged in the river': ibid., p. 1. The first scene of the novel depicting a man setting a bird in motion is reminiscent of the beginning of 'Cathal's Lake'.

33   Ibid., p. 233.

34   Matthew 5:39. By these numerous allusions, references and citations, the crushed, humiliated men who are reduced to living in a black tunnel stand comparison to Jesus, whose bruised body is abandoned to the dark tomb. The tunnel is also an isolated place comparable to catacombs, the rooms below ground where the dead were buried by the first Christians.

35   McCann, *This Side of Brightness*, p. 290.

36   'Stand up, take your bed, and go home': Matthew 9:6.

37   Matthew 9:25.

38   McCann, *This Side of Brightness*, p. 222.

39   Ibid., p. 139.

40   'une telle irradiation se fait, le plus souvent, à partir du mot': Brunel, *Mythocritique*, p. 83.

41   McCann, *This Side of Brightness*, p. 15.

42   Denis de Rougemont, *Love in the Western World* (New York: Harper Collins Publishers, 1974), p. 254.

43   McCann, *This Side of Brightness*, pp. 239, 244, 247. Likewise, facts narrated in the Bible are questioned in sentences such as 'It doesn't come to him like a burning bush or a pillar of light': ibid., p. 244. These are references to the Book of Exodus: as Moses is minding the flock, the angel of the Lord appears to him in the flame in a burning bush and asks him to take his people out of Egypt: Exodus 3. In this exodus from Egypt, God goes before his people all the time, by day as a pillar of cloud to guide them on their journey, by night as a pillar of fire to give them light, so that they could travel night and day: Exodus 13. Interestingly, a character of

Let the Great World Spin also says: 'There aint no burning bushes and there aint no pillars of light': Colum McCann, *Let the Great World Spin* (New York: Random House, 2009), p. 246.

44   McCann, *This Side of Brightness*, p. 15.

45   Luke 24:46, my emphasis.

46   Acts 1:9.

47   McCann, *This Side of Brightness*, p. 16, my emphasis.

48   2 Kings 2:11–13.

49   McCann, *This Side of Brightness*, p. 97.

50   Ibid., p. 107.

51   Ibid., pp. 16–17, my emphasis. The word 'ascension' refers to the way Jesus is described at the end of the Gospels as being taken up into Heaven.

52   Cf. ibid., pp. 17, 74.

53   Cf. ibid., chapter 14.

54   Ibid., p. 87.

55   'La structure archétypale du mythe est un système de forces antagonistes', according to Gilbert Durand in *Le Décor mythique de* La Chartreuse de Parme (Paris: José Corti, 1961), p. 5.

56   McCann, *This Side of Brightness*, p. 33. These memories are recurrent in the words of the protagonists, who are haunted by ghosts and images of the past. Once again, this typical feature contributes to making them the exact opposites of the prophets, whose main mission is to predict future events and disclose hidden truths in advance.

57   This is why Jesus is considered by Paul as the new Adam: 'As in Adam all men die, so in Christ all will be brought to life': 1 Corinthians 15:22.

58   'Resurrection' is indeed the very last word of the novel: McCann, *This Side of Brightness* p. 248.

59   John Cusatis, *Understanding Colum McCann* (Columbia, SC: University of South Carolina Press, 2011), p. 17.

60   'Colum McCann grew up in the suburb of Deansgrange, where he attended Catholic elementary and secondary schools': ibid., p. 1.

61   Northrop Frye, *The Great Code: the Bible and literature* (Fort Washington, PA: Harvest Books, 1981).

62   McCann, *This Side of Brightness*, p. 241.

63   Cusatis, *Understanding Colum McCann*, p. 78. In a Christian context, writing about resurrection amounts to writing about Jesus who said: 'I am the resurrection': John 11:25.

64   Colum McCann, '"I Am Here to Live Out Loud". In defense of the social novel: an essay on Emile Zola', http://www.colummccann.com/zola.htm (accessed 26 October 2011).

65   'He was completing research for a novel set entirely in New York City, work that involved McCann's spending many months among the homeless beneath the subway systems': Cusatis, *Understanding Colum McCann*, p. 8.

Chapter 6

1   'Le texte de fiction ne conduit à aucune réalité extratextuelle, chaque emprunt qu'il fait à la réalité se transforme en élément de fiction, comme Napoléon dans *Guerre et Paix*', writes Gérard Genette in *Fiction et diction* [1991] (Paris: Seuil, 2004), p. 115.

2   Colum McCann, *Dancer* (London: Weidenfeld & Nicolson, 2003), p. 341.

3   Diane Solway, *Nureyev: his life* (London: Weidenfeld & Nicolson, 1998), p. 37.

4   Ibid., pp. 25, 29.

5   Ibid., p. 35. The first names of Rudolf's parents are not changed in the novel: Hamet and Farida.

6   Ibid., pp. 29–30.

7   Ibid., p. 32.

8   Ibid., p. 31.

9   McCann, *Dancer,* p. 341.

10   Ibid.

11   'The only sadness: Father never once saw me dance': ibid., p. 187.

12   Solway, *Nureyev*, p. 116.

13   McCann, *Dancer*, acknowledgements, p. 341.

14   'le discours de fiction est en fait un patchwork ou un amalgame plus ou moins homogénéisé d'éléments hétéroclites empruntés pour la plupart à la réalité', according to Gérard Genette in *Fiction et diction*, p. 58.

15   'La présence d'un livre dans la fiction semble inviter le lecteur à le mettre en relation avec ce roman qu'il est en train de lire. Un livre représenté porte en lui un programme narratif potentiel … mais aussi un texte et un contenu sémantique qui peuvent, actualisés, interférer avec des éléments du livre représentant', as Joëlle Gleize puts it in *Le Double Miroir: le livre dans les livres de Stendhal à Proust* (Paris: Hachette, 1992), p. 18.

16   McCann, *Dancer*, p. 43.

17   Boris Pasternak, 'Winter Sky', in idem, *Selected Poems,* trans. Jon Stallworthy and Peter France (London: Allen Lane, 1983), p. 53.

18   Ibid.

19   Ibid.

20   McCann, *Dancer*, p. 94.

21   Ibid., p. 149.

22   Ibid.

23   Ibid., p. 77.

24   Maxim Gorky, *My Childhood* [1921] (Harmondsworth: Penguin, 1974), p. 46.

25   Ibid., p. 25.

26   Ibid., p. 48.

27   Ibid.

28   Henri Mitterand mentions 'livres-miroirs' in *Le Roman à l'œuvre: Genèse et valeurs* (Paris: PUF, 1998), p. 54.

29   McCann, *Dancer*, p. 85.

30   Ibid., p. 91.

31   Nureyev's biographers, Diane Solway and Julie Kavanagh, mention the dancer's complete adoration of the Russian writer of the nineteenth century – 'he revered Dostoyevsky' (Solway, *Nureyev*, p. 201), 'his fervor for Dostoyevsky' (Julie Kavanagh, *Nureyev: the life* (New York: Pantheon Books, 2007), p. 59) – and his capacity to speak for hours about the novel *The Brothers Karamazov* (ibid., p. 636). Moreover, in 1980, at the Met, Nureyev was starring in *The Idiot,* based on the Dostoyevsky novel (Solway, *Nureyev,* p. 449). Lastly, that same year his bedside book was Dostoyevsky's diary, according to his friend Nigel Gosling: 'he had been gripped that holiday by Dostoyevsky's *Diary of a Writer'* (Kavanagh, *Nureyev,* p. 535).

32   Fedor Dostoyevsky, *Notes from the Underground* [1864] (Oxford: Oxford Paperbacks, 2008), p. 174.

33   McCann, *Dancer,* p. 187.

34   Nureyev's father mentions 'my son the traitor' (ibid., p. 137), Yulia speaks about 'Rudi's defection' (ibid. p. 144). A report of the Ufa Committee on State Security, in February 1962, officially sentences Rudolf Nureyev to seven years' hard labour because he 'betrayed his Motherland in Paris' (ibid., p. 143).

35   Ibid., pp. 137, 143.

36   Ibid., p. 98.

37   Ibid., p. 156.

38   In the late 1980s, in Verona, Nureyev appeared in *The Overcoat,* a ballet based on Gogol's tale.

39   McCann, *Dancer,* p. 75.

40   Nikolay Gogol, 'Nevsky Prospect' [1843], in idem, *Diary of a Madman, the Government Inspector and Selected Stories* (London: Penguin, 2005), p. 111.

41   Ibid., pp. 111–12.

42   William Maxwell, *So Long, See You Tomorrow* (London: Vintage Books, 2012), p. 36.

43   McCann, *Dancer,* p. 85.

44   Ibid., p. 32.

45   James Joyce, *A Portrait of the Artist as a Young Man* [1904], in idem, *The Portable James Joyce,* ed. Harry Levin (Harmondsworth: Penguin, 1983), p. 519.

46   McCann, *Dancer,* p. 246.

47   Samuel Beckett, *Molloy: the Beckett trilogy* (London: Picador/Pan Books, 1979), p. 26.

48   McCann, *Dancer,* p. 247.

49   Ibid., p. 246.

50   Beckett, *Molloy,* p. 73.

51   Ibid., p. 9.

52   Ibid., p. 60.

53   Ibid., p. 51.

54   Ibid., p. 157.

55   McCann, *Dancer,* p. 100.

56   Lord Byron, *The Corsair* [1814], canto iii (Paris: Truchy, 1830), pp. 134–5.

57   'To Harold Hobson of the *Christian Science Monitor* … Nureyev is the saddest and

most romantic figure seen in Europe since the days of Byron … a grieved figure who sought freedom and has found no home …': Diane Solway, *Nureyev*, p. 216.

58 McCann, *Dancer*, p. 197.

59 'By June [1981] the general public was beginning to talk about a new "plague" afflicting American homosexuals, although the disease did not yet have a name … Articles about "gay cancer" were now appearing in mainstream newspapers and magazines … Rudolf had no intention of changing his sexual habits. It was the summer he had been "inseparable" from Flaubert's travel notes and letters from Egypt, an account of the young writer's 1849 tour – a period saturated with immense vices … Rudolf had been tremendously excited by Flaubert's frankness. "Those letters are fantastic – huh? Aren't they *great*?" he exclaimed during an interview with Elizabeth Kaye. It was not only the discovery of Flaubert's "how you call it? – bawdy" side that delighted him, but the fact that the novelist's journey anticipated almost exactly the trip up the Nile that he had recently made with Douce … "Sex was very liberating for Flaubert. Well, for me, too, it's liberation … liberation", he told a journalist in 1981, and, as if equating Flaubert's "venereal souvenirs" with the current perilous sexual climate, his voice had faded "ruefully" as he repeated the last word': Kavanagh, *Nureyev*, pp. 539–40.

60 Gustave Flaubert, *Flaubert in Egypt: a sensibility on tour* [1972], Flaubert to Louis Bouilhet, Cairo, 1 December 1849 (London: Penguin, 1996), pp. 43–4.

61 Ibid., Flaubert to Louis Bouilhet, Cairo, 15 January 1850, pp. 84–5.

62 McCann, *Dancer*, p. 196.

63 'He was interested in literature': Solway, *Nureyev*, p. 70; 'he loved books and reading': ibid. p. 78.

Chapter 7

1 Isabel Fonseca, *Bury Me Standing: the Gypsies and their journey* (London: Vintage, 1996).

2 Ibid., p. 304.

3 'There are no words in Romani proper for 'to write' or 'to read'. Gypsies borrow from other languages to describe these activities' (ibid., p. 11).

4 Ibid., p. 4.

5 Ibid., p. 5.

6 Ibid., p. 7.

7 Dave Welch, 'There Goes Colum McCann, Telling His Bonfire Stories Again: an interview with Colum McCann', http://www.powells.com/post/interviews/there-goes-colum-mccann-telling-his-bonfire-stories-again (accessed 6 April 2016).

8 'I simply found this photograph of this woman. And she haunted me. They are simple beginnings that turn toward complicated endings': Robert Birnbaum, 'Colum McCann', *Morning News*, 3 May 2007, http://www.themorningnews.org/article/colum-mccann (accessed 6 April 2016).

9 Cf. Fonseca, *Bury Me Standing*, p. 10.

10 Colum McCann, *Zoli* (London: Phoenix, 2007), acknowledgements/author's note, p. 356.

11   'I was completely ignorant of what had happened with the Roma in Europe': Welch, 'There Goes Colum McCann'.

12   Ibid.

13   Among the books about the Roma community, Jan Yoors' *The Gypsies* (Long Grove, IL: Waveland Press, 1987) is particularly interesting. It narrates the adventure of the author himself who, when he was twelve years of age, made friends with the children of a camp of nomads and left Antwerp, his family's town, with a Gypsy caravan. His parents did not see him for six months. Many analogies between *Zoli* and *The Gypsies* are noticeable. The notion of membership is a central theme in the two texts. Both of them make the most of the contrast inside/outside. One text relates a foreigner's integration, the other the expulsion of a full member of the group. Nevertheless, in the end both protagonists are outsiders, as Jan, like Zoli, is finally 'torn away from the kumpania': Yoors, *Gypsies*, p. 239.

14   'I carted the same sort of prejudices that the journalist in the novel's beginning section brings': Welch, 'There Goes Colum McCann'.

15   This practice is alluded to in *Zoli*: 'You can hear stories about the badges that were sewn on the sleeves, and the Z that split the length of our people's arms': McCann, *Zoli*, p. 51.

16   Cf. Frantz Fanon, *The Wretched of the Earth* [1961] (New York: Grove Press, 2004). The original work is titled *Les Damnés de la terre* (Paris: Editions François Maspéro, 1961).

17   'It was interesting to write in a woman's voice. I've written in a woman's voice in short stories, but this was the first time I'd done it in a novel. I enjoyed it. I enjoyed the leap out of gender, the leap out of time, the leap out of cultural background. That's what interests me as a writer, very much': Welch, 'There Goes Colum McCann'.

18   Gérard Genette, *Palimpsests: literature in the second degree* (Lincoln, NE: University of Nebraska Press, 1997), p. 87.

19   McCann, *Zoli*, p. 177, my emphasis.

20   Isabel Fonseca, *Bury Me Standing*, p. 5, my emphasis. According to Jan Yoors, Gypsies attach great value to running water: Yoors, *Gypsies*, p. 86.

21   McCann, *Zoli*, p. 301, and Fonseca, *Bury Me Standing*, p. 4.

22   McCann, *Zoli*, p. 302.

23   Fonseca, *Bury Me Standing*, p. 4.

24   Ibid., pp. 4–5.

25   McCann, *Zoli*, p. 301.

26   Ibid., p. 302.

27   Fonseca, *Bury Me Standing*, p. 4.

28   Ibid., p. 8.

29   McCann, *Zoli*, p. 304.

30   Ibid., p. 301.

31   Fonseca, *Bury Me Standing*, p. 4. Yoors quotes a saying used by Gypsies when they speak about their complexion: 'the darkest cherry is the best one': Yoors, *Gypsies*, p. 69.

32 Fonseca, *Bury Me Standing*, p. 7.

33 McCann, *Zoli*, pp. 301–4. The last lines of the poem refer to the genocide against Gypsies: 25,000 Romas lost their lives in Auschwitz.

34 McCann, *Zoli*, pp. 255–6.

35 *Gadjo* (or *gadji* in the plural form) is the Romani word for non-Romani people.

36 *Zoli*, p. 88. On the contrary, Jan Yoors writes: 'One day I caught myself saying "we, Gypsies", which shows I had become one of them': Yoors, *Gypsies*, p. 22.

37 Edward W. Said, *Culture and Imperialism* (London: Vintage, 1993), introduction, p. xxviii.

38 Initially the term 'intertextuality' was coined by Julia Kristeva in her study of Bakhtin's work on dialogue.

39 Julia Kristeva, *Desire in Language: a semiotic approach to literature and art* (New York: Columbia University Press, 1980), p. 66, my emphasis.

40 Matthew Arnold, *Culture and Anarchy and other Writings* [1869] (Cambridge: Cambridge University Press, 1994), p. 50.

41 Said, *Culture and Imperialism,* introduction, p. xiii.

42 John Wilson Foster, *Colonial Consequences: essays in Irish literature and culture* (Dublin: Lilliput Press, 1991), p. 267.

43 In a novel by Maeve Binchy, a father dissuades his son from fighting alongside the English. As an Irishman, he clearly considers the Englishman as 'the other'. In his speech, the personal pronoun 'they' refers to the emblematic figures of the empire, the metropolitan centre, the imperial power: 'Tell me boy, why we should lift one finger to help them, let alone lose our young men for them in their fight? Yes, it's their fight. What ever did they do for us except bring us torture and humiliation for eight hundred years … Yes, and leave our country when they had to leave it … leave it in the state it's in … half the land still bitter about the Civil War and a good quarter of it they're still hanging on to … When they give us back the North, which belongs to us by right, when they make some compensation for all they did, then I'd consider fighting in their wars …': Maeve Binchy, *Light a Penny Candle* (New York: Dell, 1982), p. 42. The same ethnocentric speech can be seen in Timothy O'Grady's novel *Motherland,* in which an English character consolidates the gap between the Anglo-Saxon and the Celt. This extract takes up the British imperial discourse, in which the 'other' is identified by his difference, by the fact that he does not belong to the metropolitan centre of culture: 'The experiment is essentially an attempt to strike a harmonious balance between the characteristics of our race and those of our hosts, which I perceive at present to be diametrically opposed. We are town-builders; they are pastoral. We can generalise; they see everything in particular. We tend to be even-handed and restrained, they celebrate the final realisation of the passions. Likewise, while we are sanguine they are fatalistic. They are strongly bonded culturally but politically disparate, we are the inverse – we do not care about racial memory, but we thrive on the building of societies. I could go on': Timothy O'Grady, *Motherland* (London: Vintage, 1995), p. 77.

44 'Dans une telle situation, il est très utile d'être irlandais, car cela signifie qu'on n'appartient pas à la culture dominante, à une culture d'oppression': Colum McCann

interviewed by Gilles Anquetil and François Armanet, 'Le roman des Rom', *Le Nouvel Observateur*, 13 September 2007, http://bibliobs.nouvelobs.com/actualites/20070913. BIB0057/le-roman-des-rom.html (accessed 6 April 2016).

45   'He had a precious book I did not know the name of and in truth I did not care ... It was his only book ... I found out years later that it was *Das Kapital*': McCann, *Zoli*, p. 23.

46   Ibid., pp. 327–8.

47   The term 'other' is analysed by Michel Foucault, who sees the outcasts who are kept at a distance from society as *ethnically, culturally* or *sexually* others. Whoever the other is, his culture is always perceived as being the exact opposite of ours. This idea is emphasised by Jan Yoors, who tackles the hostility between Gypsies and *gadji* with resignation: 'Once it was clear to me that Gypsies and gadje had so many opposed views of life that they would never get on well, I bowed to the inevitable. I stopped feeling I was being got at each time the word gadje was used in a rude way, which was almost always the case. Our civilization does not make any sense for Gypsies who just see its dirtiness, its injustice, its extravagance and vice': Yoors, *Gypsies*, p. 63.

48   McCann, *Zoli*, pp. 88–9.

49   Said, *Culture and Imperialism*, p. xxi.

50   As John Wilson Foster remarks, 'The fate of the infantilized is to be ignored or condescended to, at best contemptuously regarded': Foster, *Colonial Consequences* p. 272.

51   McCann, *Zoli*, p. 242. Likewise, although he always feels very well disposed towards the Gypsy community, Jan Yoors mentions their 'wild children' (Yoors, *Gypsies*, p. 140) or 'the savage beauty of girls' (ibid., p. 141).

52   Cf. Robert Hughes, *The Fatal Shore* (London: Pan Books, 1988).

53   McCann, *Zoli*, p. 240.

54   Ibid., p. 33.

55   Albert Memmi, *The Colonizer and the Colonized* [1957] (Boston, MA: Beacon Press, 1967), p. 85.

56   'She hears some dogs in the anonymous distance ... A high chorus, getting closer. Trained bloodhounds maybe. The sound of men's voices, their rifles pointed at the sky ... She crouches down into the grass ... The dogs only a short distance away now ... Over her shoulder the soldiers follow, shouting. She races forward and through a low ditch. Water sprays upwards ... She punches her way through a brake of long grass. The thorns of a single bush rip her hands. She hears another dog's barking and then a yelp': McCann, *Zoli*, pp. 217–18. To illustrate that Gypsies have always suffered *gadji* persecutions, Yoors writes: 'Old Roma remember the time when they were chased like wild beasts by tyrannical governments. They used to hide in forests and feed on acorns': Yoors, *Gypsies*, p. 135. 'They shouted savagely and bared their teeth': ibid., p. 248.

57   McCann, *Zoli*, p. 90.

58   L.P. Curtis, *Apes and Angels: the Irishman in Victorian caricature* (Washington, DC: Smithsonian Institution Press, 1971).

59   Joseph O'Connor, *Star of the Sea* (London: Vintage, 2003), pp. 173, 287.

60 This common interest is confirmed by McCann himself, who in an interview stated how he understands and shares his fellow-countryman's feelings: 'I identify with Joe O'Connor': Joseph Lennon, '"The First Man to Whistle": two interviews with Colum McCann', in Susan Cahill and Eoin Flannery (eds), *This Side of Brightness: essays on the fiction of Colum McCann* (Bern: Peter Lang, 2012), p. 152.

61 A 'subaltern' is in a lower rank, in an inferior position, etymologically below another one: *sub-alter(nus)*.

62 Cf. T. Eagleton, F. Jameson and E. Said, *Nationalism, Colonialism and Literature* (Minneapolis, MN: University of Minnesota Press, 1990), introduction.

63 'if anybody comes out of it at the end a little bit changed': Welch, 'There Goes Colum McCann'.

64 McCann, *Zoli*, p. 288.

65 Of course, the harp is also recognised as the emblem of Ireland.

66 Nebuchadnezzar captured Jerusalem, destroyed both the city and the temple, and deported many of the prominent citizens along with a sizeable portion of the Jewish population of Judea to Babylon in 587 BC.

67 Psalm 137.

68 In her poems Zoli brings the two communities together: 'Look at our fallen homes/ And all the Jews and Gypsies broken!': McCann, *Zoli*, p. 304.

69 The adjective 'Irish' is mentioned twice in the novel, about Stephen Swann, whose mother is Irish and whose father is Slovak. Raised in Liverpool, Swann is often considered as an Englishman, but feels, as he himself admits, 'too Irish to be fully English': ibid., p. 97.

70 'le concept d'absence est un concept clé dans le discours théorique sur les rapports entre texte et idéologie', according to Philippe Hamon in *Texte et idéologie* [1984] (Paris: Quadrige PUF, 1997), p. 11.

71 McCann, *Zoli*, p. 107.

72 Ibid. Jaroslav Seifert (1901–86) and Dominik Tatarka (1913–89) were considered as dissidents during the revolt of Czech intellectuals who responded to the communists' takeover in Prague in 1948. Banned, they were forced to leave their country.

73 McCann, *Zoli*, p. 157.

74 Pablo Neruda, *Memoirs* [1974] (London: Rupa & Co., 2005), p. 470.

75 McCann, *Zoli*, p. 96.

76 Neruda, *Memoirs*, p. 297.

77 Ibid., p. 430.

78 Ibid., p. 455.

79 McCann, *Zoli*, p. 112.

80 In *Zoli*, the cited author is sometimes more important than the text, which is not quoted verbatim. Some quotations are just indirectly and approximately evoked, as if the narrator did not know or did not remember the exact words. For example, Swann relates about Zoli: 'She quoted a line from Neruda about falling out of a tree he had not climbed' (ibid., p. 120). Similarly, Zoli recounts that Swann took her to the library to show her a photograph of Anna Akhmatova: 'Swann read to her a line about standing as witness to the common lot' (ibid., p. 157).

81   Neruda, *Memoirs*, p. 480.

82   See Julia Carlson, *Banned in Ireland: censorship and the Irish writer* (London: Routledge, 1990).

83   Julia Kristeva, *Strangers to Ourselves* (New York: Columbia University Press, 1991), p. 95.

84   *Reading the Future: Irish writers in conversation with Mike Murphy*, ed. Clíodhna Ní Anluain (Dublin: Lilliput Press, 2000), p. 224.

85   Seamus Deane, *A Short History of Irish Literature* (London: Hutchinson, 1986), p. 216.

86   Lennon, "'The First Man to Whistle'", p. 169.

87   My translation. 'Je me considère comme un romancier social. Ce n'est plus guère à la mode, comme cela a pu l'être jusqu'aux années 1930 ou 1940, dans une tradition qui va de Zola à Steinbeck en passant par Dreiser. Ces auteurs tentaient par leurs écrits de faire évoluer la conscience collective, d'agir sur la société': McCann interviewed by Anquetil and Armanet, 'Le roman des Rom'.

88   See McCann, *Zoli*, pp. 76, 105, 112.

89   Birnbaum, 'Colum McCann'.

90   See Jean-Paul Sartre, *What is Literature and Other Essays* [1948] (Harvard, MA: Harvard University Press, 1989), pp. 28ff.

91   Colum McCann, "'I Am Here to Live Out Loud". In defense of the social novel: an essay on Emile Zola', http://www.colummccann.com/zola.htm (accessed 26 October 2011).

92   Likewise, as Terry Eagleton contends in *Literary Theory: an introduction* (Oxford: Blackwell, 1983), 'pure' literary theory does not exist: 'The idea that there are non-political forms of criticism is simply a myth' (p. 170).

Chapter 8

1   Alfred Lord Tennyson, 'Locksley Hall' [1842], in idem, *The Works of Alfred Lord Tennyson* (London: Wordsworth Editions, 2008).

2   Aleksandar Hemon, *The Lazarus Project* (New York: Riverhead Books, 2008).

3   Gérard Genette in *Palimpsests: literature in the second degree* (Lincoln, NE: University of Nebraska Press, 1997) defines intertextuality as 'copresence between two or several texts' (p. 8).

4   Antoine Compagnon, *Literature, Theory and Common Sense* (Princeton, NJ: Princeton University Press, 2004), p. 56.

5   Roland Barthes, 'The Death of the Author' [1968], in idem, *The Rustle of Language* (Oakland, CA: University of California Press, 1989), p. 66. For Barthes, a figure like an 'author-God' is no longer viable. In place of the author, the modern world presents us with a figure Barthes calls the 'scriptor', whose only power is to combine pre-existing texts in new ways. 'Author' and 'scriptor' are terms Barthes uses to describe different ways of thinking about the creators of texts. Barthes believes that all writing draws on previous texts, norms and conventions, and that these are the things to which we must turn to understand a text.

6   Ibid., p. 65.

7   All books by Colum McCann, except the first, *Fishing the Sloe-black River*, begin with an epigraph. *Dancer* is the only one dedicated to a writer. Apart from *Let the Great World Spin*, no other titles of his novels are quotations. Yet,McCann's 2015 book of short stories, *Thirteen Ways of Looking*, is also a quotation.

8   Kelly Oliver, *The Portable Kristeva* (Columbia: Columbia University Press, 2002, 2nd edn), p. 85.

9   Colum McCann, *Let the Great World Spin* (New York: Random House, 2009), author's note, p. 365.

10   Harold Bloom, *The Anxiety of Influence: a theory of poetry* (New York: Oxford University Press, 1973).

11   Michael Riffaterre, *Text Production* (Columbia: Columbia University Press, 1985).

12   Aleksandar Hemon, *The Lazarus Project* (New York: Riverhead Books, 2008), p. 12.

13   Bloom, *Anxiety of Influence*.

14   Gérard Genette, *Paratexts: thresholds of interpretation* (Cambridge: Cambridge University Press, 1997), p. 160.

15   This word is used by Neil Corcoran in *After Yeats and Joyce: reading modern Irish literature* (Oxford & New York: Oxford University Press, 1997), preface, p. ix.

16   'mon maître, John Berger': 'Colum McCann sur le fil', interview with Colum McCann, *L'Express*, 20 August 2009, http://www.lexpress.fr/culture/livre/colum-mccann-sur-le-fil_823679.html (accessed 6 April 2016).

17   Genette, *Paratexts*, p. 160.

18   It must be borne in mind that the name of John Berger is repeatedly mentioned in the paratexts of McCann's books. For example, at the start of *Zoli* there appears an epigraph taken from Berger's book, *And our Faces, My Heart, Brief as Photos*. Besides, McCann frequently refers to the English writer in his interviews: 'I read books because people like John Berger create stories that call the world into silence': 'Conversation with Sasha Hemon', http://colummccann.com/interviews/conversation-with-sasha-hemon/ (accessed 6 April 2016). He quotes him as well: Berger's sentence 'Never again will a story be told as if it were the only one' is cited in McCann's interviews with Robert Birnbaum (John Cusatis, *Understanding Colum McCann* (Columbia, SC: University of South Carolina Press, 2011), p. 20) and with Joseph Lennon (Joseph Lennon, '"The First Man to Whistle": two interviews with Colum McCann', in Susan Cahill and Eoin Flannery (eds), *This Side of Brightness: essays on the fiction of Colum McCann* (Bern: Peter Lang, 2012), p. 170). This citation so often punctuates his discourse that McCann sometimes forgets to mention the source. Nevertheless, he cannot be ignorant of the fact that it is taken from Berger's novel *G.* (London: Bloomsbury, 1972), p. 133.

19   Corcoran, *After Yeats and Joyce*, preface, p. viii.

20   André Clavel considers John Berger to be 'un reporter qui sait voir et écouter': André Clavel, 'John Berger, l'Anglais volant', *L'Express*, 1 February 2009, http://www.lexpress.fr/culture/livre/john-berger-l-anglais-volant_815592.html (accessed 6 April 2016).

21   Genette, *Palimpsests*, p. 453.

22   Jorge Luis Borges, *The Total Library: non-fiction 1922–1986* (London: Penguin, 2007), p. 244.

23   Michel Foucault, 'What is an Author?' [1969], in idem, *Power: Essential Works of Foucault, 1954–1984,* vol. 3, ed. James D. Faubion (New York: New Press, 2001), p. 293.

Chapter 9

1   Colum McCann, *Let the Great World Spin* (New York: Random House, 2009), p. 6.

2   Ibid., p. 199. This character, who never feels dizzy and has a good head for heights, is reminiscent of Clarence Nathan (Treefrog) in *This Side of Brightness.*

3   Sheila Hones, *Literary Geographies: narrative space in* Let the Great World Spin (New York: Palgrave Macmillan, 2014), p. 119ff.

4   Ibid., p. 131.

5   Ibid., p. 120.

6   Ibid., p. 123.

7   Ibid., p. 121.

8   Lara Liveman, the narrator of the chapter, offers to drive Ciaran Corrigan back home after Jazzlyn's funeral. When Ciaran sees Lara's car, with its smashed headlight and dented fender, he realises Lara's connection with the crash:

> – This is the car, isn't it?
> […]
> – Were you driving it or not?
> – I suppose I was.
> It was the only lie I've ever told that has made any sense to me.
> […]
> – You should have stopped. (McCann, *Let the Great World Spin,*
> pp. 157–8)

At the end of the chapter, Lara admits:

> – I wasn't driving, I said.
> Ciaran folded his body all the way across the table, kissed me.
> – I figured that. (McCann, *Let the Great World Spin,* pp. 162–3)

This dialogue is reminiscent of the conversation after the car crash between Gatsby and Nick Carraway, the narrator of the novel:

> Suddenly I guessed at the truth.
> Was Daisy driving?
> Yes, he said after a moment, but of course I'll say I was. (Francis
> Scott Fitzgerald, *The Great Gatsby* [1926] (Harmondsworth:
> Penguin, 1973), p. 150)

9   Lara narrates: 'Blaine was thirty-two. I was twenty-eight': McCann, *Let the Great World Spin,* p. 121. Like his friends, *Gatsby's* narrator, Nick, is exactly thirty years old: '"I just remembered that to-day's my birthday". I was thirty': Fitzgerald, *Great Gatsby,* p. 142.

10   McCann, *Let the Great World Spin,* p. 131.

11   Fitzgerald, *Great Gatsby,* p. 29.

12   McCann, *Let the Great World Spin,* p. 248.

13   Jaslyn is Jazzlyn's daughter.

14   McCann, *Let the Great World Spin,* p. 339.

15   Ibid., p. 257.

16   Ibid., p. 302. In John Updike's novel *Terrorist* (London: Penguin, 2006), a character remarks about the morning of 9/11 in New York City: 'the fabled blue sky that has become mythic, a Heavenly irony, part of American legend' (p. 265).

17   McCann, *Let the Great World Spin,* p. 171.

18   'at night there are whole colonies of birds that fly into the World Trade Center buildings, their glass reflection. The bash and fall': McCann, *Let the Great World Spin,* p. 109.

19   Ibid., pp. 8–9.

20   Don DeLillo, *Falling Man* [2007] (London: Picador, 2011), p. 4.

21   Ibid., p. 4.

22   Jay McInerney, *The Good Life* (London: Bloomsbury, 2006), p. 71.

23   Updike, *Terrorist,* p. 187.

24   Joseph O'Neill, *Netherland* (New York: Pantheon Books, 2008), p. 182.

25   McCann, *Let the Great World Spin,* p. 151.

26   'the pretend fall … the slowest sort of falling … Don't fall backwards … Nobody falls halfway … He had only fallen once … the fall had smashed several ribs': McCann, *Let the Great World Spin,* pp. 166–9.

27   DeLillo, *Falling Man,* p. 221.

28   Genesis 3:19.

29   In Updike's novel *Terrorist,* Charlie tells Ahmad, the young protagonist: 'You must think of it as a war. War isn't tidy. There is collateral damage': Updike, *Terrorist,* p. 187.

30   'Je ne supporte plus la machine à entretenir le chagrin': Colum McCann, 'Littérature et traumatisme', *Assises du roman,* 'Roman et réalité', *Le Monde*–Villa Gillet, no. 64 (Paris: Christian Bourgois, 2007), p. 305.

31   Dramatic irony arises when readers know in advance what is about to happen when the characters do not.

32   McCann, *Let the Great World Spin,* p. 339.

33   Ibid., p. 297.

34   This tribute is mentioned by John Cusatis in *Understanding Colum McCann,* (Columbia, SC: University of South Carolina Press, 2011), p. 173.

35   W.B. Yeats, *Collected Poems* (London: Papermac, 1989), p. 210.

36   'The Second Coming', composed by Yeats in 1919, was first published in *The Dial* in 1920, and was included in his 1921 collection of verse, *Michael Robartes and the Dancer.*

37   The Beast supports Babylon, the Great Whore, the symbol of the Roman Empire, which persecuted Christians. It is given power by the Dragon, which is routed by Michael and his army of angels.

38   McInerney, *Good Life,* p. 154.

39   Ibid., p. 70. The word 'apocalypse' can also be noticed in O'Neill's *Netherland*, the narrator of which remarks: 'our situation was merely near-apocalyptic' (p. 24).

40   DeLillo, *Falling Man*, p. 100; McInerney, *Good Life*, p. 181.

41   McInerney, *Good Life*, pp. 114–15. In DeLillo's novel a character notes: 'People read poems. People I know, they read poetry to ease the shock and pain, give them a kind of space, something beautiful in language … to bring comfort or composure': DeLillo, *Falling Man*, p. 42.

42   McCann, *Let the Great World Spin*, p. 17.

43   Ibid., p. 106. 'Devils do good imitation of angels' can be read in Updike's novel *Terrorist* (p. 109). The novel also mentions 'the armies of Satan versus those of God': ibid. p. 201.

44   DeLillo, *Falling Man*, p. 222.

45   McInerney, *Good Life*, p. 254.

46   Ibid., p. 162. By the same token, in DeLillo's novel the narrator mentions a blind man and his guide dog roaming the streets, lost in the smoke, the running frenzy and the debris, and notes: 'it was like something out of the Bible': DeLillo, *Falling Man*, p. 57.

47   Ibid., p. 69.

48   McCann, *Let the Great World Spin*, p. 257.

49   Genesis 19:26.

50   McCann, *Let the Great World Spin*, p. 330.

51   1 Kings 3:16–28.

52   McCann, *Let the Great World Spin*, p. 116.

53   Ibid., p. 84.

54   Luke 2:14.

55   McCann, *Let the Great World Spin*, p. 79.

56   Linda Hutcheon, *A Poetics of Postmodernism: history, theory, fiction* (New York, NY & London: Routledge, 1988), p. 35.

57   McCann, *Let the Great World Spin*, p. 65.

58   Ibid., p. 246. Interestingly, these references to the Old Testament are present, too, in *This Side of Brightness* – 'It doesn't come to him like a burning bush or a pillar of light' (Colum McCann, *This Side of Brightness* (London: Phoenix, 1998), p. 244) – and in 'Treaty': 'No burning bush, no pillar of light' (McCann, 'Treaty', *TWOL*, p. 207). These words imply that no miracles are to be expected for Beverly, who must live in guilt and suffering after the rapes and tortures she went through. They refer to a biblical episode of the Book of Exodus: as Moses is minding the flock, the angel of the Lord appears to him in the flame of a burning bush and asks him to take his people out of Egypt (Exodus 3). In this exodus from Egypt, God goes before his people all the time, by day as a pillar of cloud to guide them on their journey, by night as a pillar of fire to give them light, so that they could travel night and day (Exodus 13). Interestingly, these very episodes are mentioned by the priest in the second chapter of John Updike's novel *Terrorist*: 'The voice from the burning bush had been a clear sign. The pillars of cloud by day and of fire by night had been signs': Updike, *Terrorist*, p. 56.

59   Eoin Flannery, *Colum McCann and the Aesthetics of Redemption* (Dublin and Portland, OR: Irish Academic Press, 2011), p. 216.

60   Ibid., p. 207.

61   Ibid.

62   McCann, *Let the Great World Spin*, p. 364.

Chapter 10

1   Colum McCann, *TransAtlantic* (London, New Delhi, New York, Sydney: Bloomsbury, 2013), p. 193.

2   Ibid., p. 291.

3   Ibid.

4   Frost, Douglass, Galeano.

5   Woolf, Berry, Beckett, Heaney.

6   In his quest for peace in Northern Ireland, Mitchell remembers a poem which is well known to many American schoolchildren: 'There is a Frost poem from school days. *Whose woods these are I think I know.* He hears it again, distantly, brokenly. *Miles to go before I sleep.* There are times he wishes he could knock an absolute simplicity into the process. Take it or leave it': McCann, *TransAtlantic*, p. 135. These lines are taken from a poem titled 'Stopping by Woods on a Snowy Evening' in the collection *New Hampshire* (Baltimore, MD: Henry Holt, 1923).

7   McCann, *TransAtlantic*, p. 108.

8   Seamus Heaney, *Hailstones* (Dublin: Gallery Books, 1984).

9   In his introduction to Seamus Heaney's *Poèmes, 1966–1984* (Paris: Gallimard, 1988), Richard Kearney writes: 'Ce sont les transitions d'un lieu à un autre qui captivent l'imagination du poète. Heaney préfère le thème du voyage à celui du séjour, s'intéresse plus aux nomades qu'aux sédentaires par fidélité à la nature du langage lui-même car ... le langage construit et déconstruit perpétuellement nos notions reçues d'identité. En tant que tel, le langage poétique reste ouvert à des points de vue opposés, portant le regard vers au moins deux côtés à la fois. Le Janus à deux visages est le dieu littéraire de Heaney' (pp. 7–8).

10   McCann, *TransAtlantic*, p. 257.

11   Ibid., p. 256.

12   Roland Barthes, 'Texte (theorie du)', *Encyclopaedia Universalis* (Paris: Encyclopaedia Britannica, 1973).

13   For many critics, the author's intended meaning is not to be confused with the actual meaning of the text. Wimsatt and Beardsley describe this 'intentional fallacy': they argue that the author's design or intention is neither available for study nor desirable as a standard for judging the success of a work of literary art. According to them, the intentional fallacy is a Romantic illusion that confuses the poem with its origins, attempts to derive a standard of criticism from the psychological cause, and ends in either biography or relativism.

14   Umberto Eco, *Interpretation and Overinterpretation* (Cambridge: Cambridge University Press, 1992), p. 64.

15   Frederick Douglass, *Narrative of the Life of Frederick Douglass, an American Slave. Written by himself* [1845] (San Francisco: City Lights Books, 2010).

16   As the text chooses its sources, a parallel reading of the text and the source book makes it easier to understand it. The same statement of fact can be made with intertextual references. As a result, it is not so easy to make a clear distinction between intertextuality and the criticism of sources. Both of them deal with the same phenomenon but describe it differently, according to Massimo Fusillo, an Italian Hellenist who studies intertextuality in the ancient novel. For him, the point of view is different, but the object is not. In 'Modern Critical Theories and the Ancient World' in Gareth Schmeling (ed.), *The Novel in the Ancient World* (Leiden: E.J. Brill, 1996), Fusillo shows that the criticism of sources is a preliminary condition for the intertextual approach, and that intertextuality is the corollary of the study of sources (pp. 277–305). For, indeed, it is necessary to identify the source book before analysing its transformations.

17   Frederick Douglass, *My Bondage and my Freedom* [1855] (Chicago, IL: University of Illinois Press, 1987), p. 224.

18   McCann, *TransAtlantic*, pp. 37–8.

19   'He crawled out of bed to write Anna a note. He needed to be judicious. She could not read nor write, so it would be spoken aloud to her by their friend Harriet': ibid., p. 45.

20   '[Douglass and O'Connell] talked gravely about the situation in America, about Garrison … the prospect of secession': ibid., pp. 61–2.

21   'Twenty-one Months in Great Britain'. In 1800, with the Act of Union, the two kingdoms of Great Britain and Ireland were united into one.

22   Douglass, *My Bondage and my Freedom*, p. 226.

23   McCann, *TransAtlantic*, p. 39.

24   Douglass, *My Bondage and my Freedom*, p. 227.

25   Ibid., p. 227.

26   McCann, *TransAtlantic*, p. 83.

27   'I had been in Dublin but a few days, when a gentleman of great respectability kindly offered to conduct me through all the public buildings of that beautiful city': Douglass, *My Bondage and my Freedom*, p. 227.

28   McCann, *TransAtlantic*, p. 40.

29   'And a little afterward, I found myself dining with the lord mayor of Dublin': Douglass, *My Bondage and my Freedom*, p. 227.

30   McCann, *TransAtlantic*, p. 54.

31   John Cusatis, *Understanding Colum McCann* (Columbia, SC: University of South Carolina Press, 2011), p. 20.

32   'Hear me tout it one more time, the great John Berger: "Never again will a single story be told as if it were the only one"': Joseph Lennon, '"The First Man to Whistle": two interviews with Colum McCann', in Susan Cahill and Eoin Flannery (eds), *This Side of Brightness: essays on the fiction of Colum McCann* (Bern: Peter Lang, 2012), p. 170.

33   John Berger, *G.* (London: Bloomsbury, 1972), p. 133.

34 Ibid., p. 157.

35 See Berger, *G.,* p. 124.

36 See McCann, *TransAtlantic*, p. 13.

37 It is also worth noticing that Colum McCann and John Berger share the same publishing house, Bloomsbury.

38 In the sixteenth century, the notion of imitation combined with the notion of innutrition.

39 'Joseph Lennon: "Lastly, in *Everything in this Country Must* did you intentionally build parallels to *Dubliners* (using adolescent protagonists; weaving in themes of paralysis; representing fractured families; creating alienated characters)?" Colum McCann: "No, there's no intentional parallels. I think the prose would creak if I intentionally set out to mirror such an important book"': Lennon, "'The First Man to Whistle"', pp. 158–9.

40 Eco, *Interpretation and Overinterpretation*, p. 78.

41 Ibid., p. 7.

42 'L'art est une activité intentionnelle mais il existe de nombreuses activités intention- nelles qui ne sont ni préméditées ni conscientes ... L'intention d'auteur n'implique pas une conscience de tous les détails que l'écriture accomplit, ni ne constitue un événement séparé qui précéderait ou accompagnerait la performance. Avoir l'intention de faire quelque chose, ce n'est pas faire avec conscience ni projeter', according to Antoine Compagnon in *Le Démon de la théorie* (Paris: Seuil, 1998), p. 105.

43 Berger, *G.,* pp. 165–6.

44 Witold Gombrowicz, *Trans-Atlantyk* [1957] (Yale: Yale University Press, 1995).

45 Ibid., p. 20.

46 'Stand up! Let's be free from politics. Let's be something greater than the Pole, something superior to the Pole': ibid., p. 9.

47 Robert Birnbaum, 'Colum McCann', *Morning News*, 3 May 2007, http://www. themorningnews.org/article/colum-mccann (accessed 6 April 2016).

48 McCann, *TransAtlantic*, p. 173.

49 Death and (re)birth, youth and old age, Old and New Worlds, etc.

50 *Si vis pacem, para bellum.* The third chapter of the novel is titled '1998. Para bellum': McCann, *TransAtlantic*, p. 96.

51 McCann, *TransAtlantic*, p. 34.

52 Gombrowicz, *Trans-Atlantyk,* introduction, p. 9.

53 Colum McCann, "'I Am Here to Live Out Loud". In defense of the social novel: an essay on Emile Zola', http://www.colummccann.com/zola.htm (accessed 26 October 2011).

54 Ibid.

55 Ibid.

56 McCann, *TransAtlantic,* p. 149.

57 'Never again will a story be told as if it were the only one.'

58 McCann, *TransAtlantic*, p. 108.

59 By the same token, during their transatlantic journey in 1929, Emily Ehrlich and

her daughter read a novel by Virginia Woolf. The title of this book is not given but the extract makes it possible to recognise the novel they read as being *Jacob's Room*, the plot of which narrates the destiny of a young man from his childhood to his death. Both readers have a consuming passion for this book and the specific style of Virginia Woolf: 'They read the Woolf novel in tandem, matched each other almost page for page. The voice had an extraordinary sadness. Pure from all body, pure from all passion, going out into the world, solitary, unanswered, breaking against rocks – so it sounded. What Emily liked most of all was the appearance of ease that Woolf brought. The words slid so easily into one another. There was a sense of a full life being translated. It was, in Woolf's hands, a display of humility': McCann, *TransAtlantic*, p. 191. As fiction is able to recount a whole life, 'there's always another story to tell', according to McCann, who perceives there 'the true value of literature': McCann, '"I Am Here to Live Out Loud"'.

60   'It's certainly my intention to try to stretch the parameters, or borders, of the Irish novel': Joseph Lennon, '"The First Man to Whistle"', p. 151.

61   'cette fonction n'est pas toujours rigoureusement remplie, car bien des livres partagent le même titre homonyme: Gérard Genette, *Seuils* (Paris: Seuil, 1987), p. 80.

62   'Ce que dit le texte importe davantage que ce que l'auteur a voulu dire', writes Paul Ricœur in *Du Texte à l'action: essais d'herméneutique II* (Paris: Seuil, 1986), p. 187.

63   Comme le texte est sans conscience, parler d'intention du texte ou d'*intentio operis*, c'est réintroduire subrepticement l'intention d'auteur comme garde-fou de l'interprétation, sous un terme moins suspect ou provocateur': Compagnon, *Le Démon de la théorie,* p. 96.

64   Eco, *Interpretation and Overinterpretation*, p. 39.

Chapter 11

1   McCann, 'Thirteen Ways of Looking', *TWOL*, pp. 42–3.

2   Ibid., p. 66.

3   Ibid., p. 143.

4   Wallace Stevens, *Collected Poems* (London and Boston: Faber & Faber, 1984), p. 92.

5   Antoine Compagnon, *La Seconde Main ou le travail de la citation* (Paris: Seuil, 1979), p. 52.

6   In his 'Letter to George Antheil' (3 January 1931), James Joyce writes: 'I am quite content to go down to posterity as a scissors and paste man for that seems to me a harsh but not unjust description': Richard Ellmann (ed.), *Selected Letters of James Joyce* (London: Faber & Faber, 1975), p. 243.

7   Once again, the influence of John Berger on Colum McCann can be detected; indeed, the British writer is the author of books made of texts and photographs, the titles of which – *Ways of Seeing* (London: Penguin, 1972) and *Another Way of Telling* (New York: Vintage, 1982) – echo McCann's 2015 novel, *Thirteen Ways of Looking*.

8   McCann, 'Thirteen Ways of Looking', *TWOL*, p. 9.

9   Ibid., p. 23.

10 Ibid., p. 24. Of course, an allusion to Oscar Wilde's novel *The Picture of Dorian Gray* can be seen here.
11 Ibid., p. 101.
12 Ibid., p. 75.
13 Ibid., p. 82.
14 Ibid., p. 76.
15 Ibid., p. 47.
16 'He was always skinny … A beanpole. A scarecrow. More fat, said Eileen, on a butcher's knife': ibid., p. 9.
17 Ibid., p. 83.
18 Ibid., p. 106. Surprisingly enough, a Jewish character refers here to the Gospel. Did McCann ask himself the questions raised by the writer in the following story: 'Is that feasible? Is it even possible?': ibid., p. 152.
19 Luke 15.
20 McCann, 'Thirteen Ways of Looking', *TWOL*, p. 112. Mendelssohn feels betrayed when he mentions his 'treacherous son': ibid. pp. 20, 133.
21 McCann, 'Thirteen Ways of Looking', *TWOL*, pp. 86, 105.
22 The father humorously mentions the means used by his son to keep bloodthirsty creatures away: 'A silver bracelet on his wrist. To keep the vampires away': ibid., p. 87.
23 The colour of Elliot's mouth is reminiscent of wine, symbolically of blood: 'his wine-colored mouth': ibid., p. 111.
24 Ibid., p. 77.
25 Another mirror effect can be seen in common first names: Pedro Jimenez is Peter Mendelssohn's alter ego.
26 Like 'Thirteen Ways of Looking', 'Treaty', the last short story of the book, is full of references to mirrors that allow the protagonist to watch others indirectly: staying in 'a place of mirrors' (McCann, 'Treaty', *TWOL*, p. 212), Beverly examines her 'sisters' in the rearview mirror of the car (ibid., p. 211), watches her torturer 'in the shop-window reflection' (ibid., p. 234), and 'spies the reflection of the shopkeeper in the window' (ibid., p. 242).
27 It is also in Connecticut that Colum McCann was assaulted in 2014 after going to the aid of a woman he believed to be involved in a domestic dispute. The woman's husband knocked him to the ground. Ironically, McCann had been in New Haven, Connecticut to attend a conference on empathy. That has fuelled *Thirteen Ways of Looking*, which further explores, and tests, the limits of empathy.
28 This verb is also present in Stevens' poem.
29 McCann, 'Thirteen Ways of Looking', *TWOL*, p. 136.
30 Ibid., p. 56.
31 The adjective 'indecipherable' is mentioned in the sixth stanza of the poem.
32 McCann, 'Thirteen Ways of Looking', *TWOL*, p. 19.
33 By the same token, the spaces between sections are breaks that can be compared to pauses.
34 'They (detectives) work in much the same way as poets: the search for random

word, at the right instance, making the poem itself so much more precise': Colum McCann, 'Thirteen Ways of Looking', *TWOL*, p. 26.

35   'Just as a poem turns its reader into accomplice, so, too, the detectives become accomplice to the murder. But unlike our poetry, we like our murders to be fully solved: if, of course, it is a murder, or poetry, at all': ibid., p. 73.

36   Ibid., p. 80.

37   McCann, 'Step We Gaily, On We Go', *FTSBR*, p. 64.

38   'Or was it Eve who ate the apple?': McCann, 'Thirteen Ways of Looking', *TWOL*, p. 50; 'Or was that Mr Synge?': McCann, 'Step We Gaily, On We Go', *FTSBR*, p. 73.

39   See McCann, 'Thirteen Ways of Looking', *TWOL*, p. 61; McCann, 'Step We Gaily, On We Go', *FTSBR*, p. 60.

40   McCann, 'Thirteen Ways of Looking', *TWOL*, p. 63; McCann, 'Step We Gaily, On We Go', *FTSBR*, p. 71.

41   McCann, 'Thirteen Ways of Looking', *TWOL*, p. 56.

42   Ibid., p. 62.

43   Exodus 34:7.

44   'Elliot, son, you could clear a room quicker than the Black Death': McCann, 'Thirteen Ways of Looking', *TWOL*, p. 111.

45   Elliot has 'a dark mark in the center of his forehead' (ibid., p. 241), which recalls the one put by God on Cain (Genesis 4:15).

46   Ibid., p. 47. Just after this quotation, the text mentions 'the old gray man with his walking stick' (p. 47). The old man walking with a stick is part of the riddle set by the sphinx, which no one before Oedipus was able to answer.

47   'he will never recover from the shock': McCann, 'Thirteen Ways of Looking', *TWOL*, p. 139.

48   Sophocles, *Oedipus the King*, ll. 893–4, 1,191 (Oxford: Oxford University Press, 2016).

49   McCann, 'Thirteen Ways of Looking', *TWOL*, pp. 130–1.

50   'It is his own son he has slain': W.B. Yeats, *On Baile's Strand* [1904], in idem, *Collected Plays* (London: Macmillan, 1992), p. 276.

51   Ibid., p. 257.

52   Genesis 2:24.

53   The short story 'Thirteen Ways of Looking' mentions the names of Heaney, Muldoon, Whitman, Burroughs, Kant and Simone de Beauvoir (McCann, 'Thirteen Ways of Looking', *TWOL*, pp. 11, 14, 55–6, 86), and evokes or quotes the works of Dante, Shakespeare, Joyce, Huxley and Pasternak (ibid., pp. 10, 13, 21, 29, 33, 36).

54   Colm Tóibín, *Mothers and Sons* (London: Picador, 2006).

55   'He must talk to his second mother in Afghanistan from the kitchen of his first mother's house': McCann, 'What Time Is it Now, Where You Are?', *TWOL*, p. 153.

56   'She used to imagine … something maternal she could jolt from him': McCann, 'Treaty', *TWOL*, p. 209.

57   Ibid., p. 203.

58   Ibid., p. 158.

59 Ibid., p. 150. Mendelssohn also lives on that street: ibid., pp. 13, 43.

60 'he could' is repeated seven times in the eleventh section.

61 Ibid., p. 157.

62 Ibid., p. 148, my emphasis.

63 Ibid., p. 147, my emphasis. The association of these two words is also noticeable in the following sentence: 'Though he still has little *idea* of what exactly she might say, she is *beginning* to become a little more complex for him': ibid., p. 150.

64 McGahern's story narrates Eva's desire to write an imaginary life of Chekhov from the latter's short story 'Oysters'.

65 John McGahern, 'The Beginning of an Idea', in idem, *Getting Through* (London: Faber & Faber, 1978), p. 24.

66 'Two weeks passed … She got nothing written': ibid., p. 24.

67 'In late May he settled down to sketch out a few images that might work, but soon found himself struggling, adrift. For a couple of weeks in early summer he cast about, chased ideas and paragraphs, left a few hanging, found himself postponing the assignment, putting it to the back of his mind. Occasionally he pulled his notes out again, then abandoned them once more': McCann, 'What Time Is it Now, Where You Are?', *TWOL*, p. 147.

68 'She left on New Year's Eve for Spain': McGahern, 'The Beginning of an Idea', p. 20. 'What Time Is it Now, Where You Are?' is described as 'a New Year's Eve story': McCann, 'Thirteen Ways of Looking', *TWOL*, p. 147.

69 McGahern, 'The Beginning of an Idea', p. 23.

70 McCann, 'Thirteen Ways of Looking', *TWOL*, p. 156.

71 James Joyce, 'The Dead', in idem, *Dubliners* [1914] (London: Penguin, 1983), p. 242. A reference to the Apostles' Creed can also be seen here, insofar as the formal statement of Christian religious belief stipulates that Jesus Christ 'will come again to judge the living and the dead'.

72 In view of the polysemy of the word 'rifle', a sentence such as 'What sort of feeling will *rifle* through her blood when she hears Kimberlee's voice?' is somehow anticipating Sandi's death: McCann, 'What Time Is it Now, Where You Are?', *TWOL*, p. 157, my emphasis.

73 Ibid., p. 157.

74 James Joyce, 'The Dead', p. 216. 'Let Me Like a Soldier Fall' is a song from *Maritana*, an opera by the Irish composer and musician William Vincent Wallace, written and performed in London in 1845.

75 McCann, 'Hunger Strike', *EITCM*, p. 95.

76 Ibid., pp. 135–6.

77 McCann, 'Sh'khol', *TWOL*, p. 167.

78 'a yellow kayak went swiftly by': ibid., p. 167.

79 'The kayak glided out … a bright yellow speck on the grey cloth of the sea': McCann, 'Hunger Strike', *EITCM*, p. 42.

80 'Her hair was dark': McCann, 'Sh'khol', *TWOL*, p. 163. 'His mother sighed and twisted a lock of her hair around her finger. Her hair was extraordinarily black': McCann, 'Hunger Strike', *EITCM*, pp. 59–60.

81   McCann, "Sh'khol', *TWOL*, p. 162; McCann, 'Hunger Strike', *EITCM*, p. 44.

82   Kevin looks at people 'from under a stray lock of hair': McCann, 'Hunger Strike', *EITCM*, p. 129; Tomas' hair is described as 'thick and long': McCann, 'Sh'khol', *TWOL*, p. 195.

83   It must be noted that the same verb is used in both texts: 'He *bent* himself *over* at the waist to calm down his erection' (McCann, 'Hunger Strike', *EITCM*, p. 94); 'He *bent over* to try to disguise himself against the fabric of his shorts': McCann, 'Sh'khol', *TWOL*, p. 195, my emphasis.

84   'the boy pulled on an extra shirt – it had once been his father's – and inside there was still room for a whole boy more': McCann, 'Hunger Strike', *EITCM*, p. 43; 'She looked down at Tomas' trousers. Denims. Too large by far. A man's denims': McCann, 'Sh'khol', *TWOL*, p. 192.

85   McCann, 'Hunger Strike', *EITCM*, pp. 52, 63, my emphasis.

86   McCann, 'Sh'khol', *TWOL*, p. 193, my emphasis.

87   McCann, 'Stolen Child', *FTSBR*, p. 102.

88   At bedtime, Rebecca reads to Tomas in Irish from a cycle of ancient Irish mythology: McCann, 'Sh'khol', *TWOL*, p. 170.

89   The Scottish legend of the selkie is referred to here: searching for Tomas, the policemen can see something moving in the water, shout to one another, but notice it is only a seal: 'Rebecca knew well the legend of the selkie': ibid., p. 183.

90   Ibid., p. 182.

91   Ibid., p. 169.

92   Ibid., p. 188.

93   Nadezhda Mandelstam, *Hope Abandoned* (London: Macmillan, 1981). The two volumes of the memoir are respectively titled *Hope Abandoned* and *Hope Against Hope*. The title is based on a pun, the Russian word for 'hope' being 'nadejda'.

94   McCann, 'Hunger Strike', *EITCM*, p. 54.

95   McCann, 'Sh'khol', *TWOL*, p. 187.

96   McCann, 'Hunger Strike', *EITCM*, p. 120; McCann, 'Sh'khol', *TWOL*, p. 171.

97   'On one of his fingers he had, months ago, begun to tattoo a single word but had stopped when he wasn't quite sure what the word should be. All that appeared now was a single straight line where he had stuck a hot needle into his forefinger and smudged blue ink upon it': McCann, 'Hunger Strike', *EITCM*, p. 46. 'Once he had bitten her finger while asleep, and she had given herself two stitches ... There was still a scar on her left forefinger: a small red scythe': McCann, 'Sh'khol', *TWOL*, p. 171. The injured finger, together with the bruises on the body of a Russian kid suffering from a disability, against the backdrop of the Chernobyl disaster, are specific details recalling the Irish novel by Darragh McKeon, *All That Is Solid Melts Into Air* (Toronto: HarperCollins, 2014), the back cover of which reports Colum McCann's praise for this debut.

98   McCann, 'Hunger Strike', *EITCM*, p. 65.

99   McCann, 'Sh'khol', *TWOL*, p. 170.

100 McCann, 'Hunger Strike', *EITCM*, p. 86, my emphasis.

101 McCann, 'Sh'khol', *TWOL*, p. 182.

102 In 'Hunger Strike', Kevin remembers a poem from school: '*Death once dead, there's no more dying then*': McCann, 'Hunger Strike', *EITCM*, p. 86. The text does not specify the origin of the line, which proves to be the conclusion of Shakespeare's sonnet 146 in which the poet incites 'a poor soul' not to forget the mortality of beauty, the corruption of flesh, and to be aware of profound realities. As long as death is not dead, it will have the last word, as the ultimate distich of the sonnet puts it: '*So shalt thou feed on Death, that feeds on men,/And, Death once dead, there's no more dying then*'. The connection with McCann's story 'Hunger Strike' is significant insofar as the semantic field of food can be noticed in the poem: the verb 'feed' – echoing 'eat' – is repeated three times. This specificity induces Henri Fluchère to see in Shakespeare's sonnets a poetry of flesh and blood, 'une poésie de chair et de sang': William Shakespeare, *Œuvres complètes*, vol. 1, introduction (Paris: Pléiade Gallimard, 1959), p. lxiv. Sonnet 146 is also based on opposites – *within/without*, *poor/rich* and, of course, *live/die* – death being a major motif both in the poem and in the short story, as the four occurrences in the distich above clearly show.

103 McCann, 'Hunger Strike', *EITCM*, p. 134.

104 McCann, 'What Time Is it Now, Where You Are?', *TWOL*, p. 156, my emphasis.

105 Genesis 24.

106 McCann, 'Treaty', *TWOL*, p. 217.

107 'six months in all': ibid., p. 209.

108 The motif of death and the maiden peaked in Renaissance German paintings, but it has been taken up in other artistic disciplines: for example, in 1824 Franz Schubert set Matthias Claudius' poem 'Death and the Maiden' to music in a string quartet. This piece of poetry had already inspired his *lied* in 1817.

109 McCann, 'Treaty', *TWOL*, p. 226.

110 Ariel Dorfman, *Death and the Maiden* (New York: Penguin, 1991), I.iv (p. 22).

111 McCann, 'Treaty', *TWOL*, p. 210.

112 Dorfman, *Death and the Maiden*, I.iv (p. 23).

113 McCann, 'Treaty', *TWOL*, p. 237.

114 Ibid., p. 240.

115 Dorfman, *Death and the Maiden*, II.i (p. 28).

116 Ibid., I.ii, p. 18.

117 Ibid., II.i, p. 32.

118 Ibid., II.ii, p. 39. 'Treaty' mentions 'the ghost of his face': McCann, 'Treaty', *TWOL* p. 209.

119 McCann, 'Treaty', *TWOL*, p. 232.

120 *Esquire*, Aug. 2015.

121 'Forgive: yes, forget: no', says Gerardo: Dorfman, *Death and the Maiden*, III.i (p. 43).

122 McCann, 'Treaty', *TWOL*, p. 207.

123 The hostage of her rapist, Beverly feels horror at the thought of a possible pregnancy: 'She wondered what might happen if she ever conceived a child. One time, the clock of her body stopped for two months. It terrified her, then she bled again': ibid., p. 223.

124   http://colummccann.com/narrative-4-main-page/ (accessed 6 April 2016). Narrative 4 was founded in 2012 by artists and activists who believe that stories and storytelling can help reshape the world around us, and that these stories can become a call to action.

Conclusion

1   'The best way to protect a tradition is to attack and subvert it': Declan Kiberd, *Inventing Ireland* (London: Jonathan Cape, 1995), p. 605.

2   The ironist jokes over values because he believes in them, according to Vladimir Jankélévitch: 'L'ironiste badine sur les valeurs parce qu'il croit aux valeurs': Vladimir Jankélévitch, *L'Ironie*, p. 167.

Bibliography

Fiction by Colum McCann

Novels
TransAtlantic (London, New Delhi, New York, Sydney: Bloomsbury, 2013)
Let the Great World Spin (New York: Random House, 2009)
Zoli (London: Weidenfeld & Nicolson, 2006)
Dancer (London: Weidenfeld & Nicolson, 2003)
This Side of Brightness (London: Phoenix, 1998)
Songdogs (London: Phoenix, 1995)

Short stories
Thirteen Ways of Looking (London: Bloomsbury, 2015)
Everything in this Country Must (London: Phoenix, 2000)
Fishing the Sloe-black River (London: Phoenix, 1994)

Other publications
The Book of Men (ed.) (New York: Picador, 2013)

Short stories published in periodicals/anthologies
'The Word Shed', *New Yorker*, 22 December 2014
'Ice', *Esquire*, vol. 157, nos. 6–7 (June–July 2012)
'Aisling', *Paris Review*, no. 193 (summer 2010)
'What Is it Called, Your Country Behind the Mountain?', in David Marcus (ed.), *The Best New Irish Short Stories of 2005* (New York: Carroll & Graf, 2005)
'All That Rises, All That Falls', *Esquire*, December 2003
'Whirligig', *Portal*, 3 August 2000
'Sumac', *Story*, no. 47 (spring 1999)
'As if There Were Trees', *Story*, no. 48 (autumn 1999)
'The First Snow', *Grand Street*, no. 63 (1998)
'As Kingfishers Catch Fire', in David Marcus (ed.) *Phoenix Irish Short Stories* (London: Phoenix House, 1997)
'Tresses', in Ciaran Carty and Dermot Bolger (eds), *The Hennessy Book of Irish Fiction* (Dublin: New Island Books, 1995)

Selected non-fiction by Colum McCann
'Beneath the Streets of New York: when poverty drives people below', *Literary Hub*, 8 September 2015
'A Love Letter to Ireland', *Travel and Leisure*, 22 April 2015

'Ireland's Troubled Peace', *New York Times*, 15 May 2014

'Northern Ireland's Peace is Delicately Poised: it needs to look forward', *Guardian*, 16 May 2014

'Irish Identity Is Work of Art, Not Political Expediency', *Irish Times*, 16 March 2013

'"Je Viens Vivre Tout Haut". Défense du roman social: un essai sur Emile Zola', *Les Assises internationales du roman*, no. 102, 'Le Roman: hors frontières' (Paris: Christian Bourgois, 2009), pp. 29–45

'My Ugly Lovely Town: an essay by Colum McCann', *Stinging Fly*, vol. 2, no. 20 (winter 2011–12)

'Do National Writers Still Exist?', *Daily Beast*, 28 November 2010

'But Always Meeting Ourselves', *New York Times*, 16 June 2009

'"I Am Here to Live Out Loud". In defense of the social novel: an essay on Emile Zola', http://www.colummccann.com/zola.htm (accessed 26 October 2011)

'The Heavens Be His Bed', *Irish University Review*, special issue: Benedict Kiely, vol. 38, no. 1 (2008), pp. 64–71

[With Aleksandar Hemon] 'The Writer Sees in the Dark Corners Swept Clean by Historians', *Guardian*, 30 June 2003

'The International Bastards', *Irish Echo Supplement*, March 1998

'The Tunnels Under New York City', *Fotoshoot Magazine*, 5 February 1995

Selected interviews with Colum McCann

Bantick, Christopher, 'A Voice That Was Other Than Irish', *Canberra Times*, 10 May 1998

Birnbaum, Robert, 'Colum McCann', *Morning News*, 3 May 2007, http://www.themorningnews.org/article/colum-mccann (accessed 6 April 2016)

_____, 'Colum McCann Talks With Robert Birnbaum', *Reader's Progress* (Boston), 25 February 2003

Bolick, Katie, 'Some Strange Vessel', *Atlantic Online*, 16 July 1998

Camelio, Stephen V., 'An Interview with Colum McCann', *Nua: Studies in Contemporary Irish Writing*, vol. 3, nos. 1–2 (2002), pp. 89–100

Clancy, Luke, 'Writer and Wanderer', *Irish Times*, 21 June 1994

Cryer, Dan, 'The Burning Season', *Long Island Newsday*, 19 November 1995

Deignan, Tom, 'The CRAIC: notes from the new Irish', *Irish Voice*, 21 March 2000

Donnelly, Pat, 'Empathizing with "the Other"', *Gazette* (Montreal), 20 October 2007

Dunn, Adam, 'Dancer from the Dance', *Publishers Weekly*, 13 January 2003

_____, 'Interview with Colum McCann', *San Francisco Chronicle*, 3 July 2009

Fisher, Mark, 'People Who Live Down Below', *Herald* (Glasgow), 29 July 1999

Lennon, Joseph, 'An Interview with Fiction Writer Colum McCann', *Poets and Writers*, 14 March 2003

_____, 'Colum McCann on Rudolf Nureyev and Writing Toward the Unknown', *Poets and Writers Magazine* (New York) 14 March 2003

Levasseur, Jennifer and Kevin Rabalais, 'Interview with Colum McCann', *Glimmer Train*, no. 69 (winter 2009), pp. 56–73

Mackin, Thomas E., 'Universal Truths', *World of Hibernia*, no. 6 (summer 2000), p. 156

Marchand, Philip, 'Writers Without Borders', *Toronto Star*, 5 October 2000

Maudet, Cécile, 'Deux entretiens avec Colum McCann', *Transatlantica*, no. 1, 'Expatriation and Exile', 2014, http://transatlantica.revues.org/6940 (accessed 6 April 2016)

McDermott, Peter, 'The Wanderer', *Irish Echo Online*, 7 February 2007
Metcalfe, Anna, 'Small Talk: Colum McCann', *Financial Times*, 29 August 2009
Miller, Farah, 'A Conversation with Colum McCann', *O: The Oprah Magazine*, July 2009
Rabalais, Kevin, 'A Moment of Grace', *Australian*, 31 July 2009
Welch, Dave, 'There Goes Colum McCann, Telling His Bonfire Stories Again: an interview
    with Colum McCann', http://www.powells.com/post/interviews/there-goes-colum-
    mccann-telling-his-bonfire-stories-again (accessed 6 April 2016)

Selected works on Colum McCann
Books

Brown, James S. and Jack W. Weaver, *Exile and Identity in Colum McCann's* Fishing the
    Sloe-black River (Rock Hill: Winthrop University, 2004)
Cahill, Susan and Eoin Flannery (eds), *This Side of Brightness: essays on the fiction of Colum*
    McCann (Bern: Peter Lang, 2012)
Cusatis, John, *Understanding Colum McCann* (Columbia, SC: University of South
    Carolina Press, 2011)
Flannery, Eoin, *Colum McCann and the Aesthetics of Redemption* (Dublin: Irish Academic
    Press, 2011)
Hones, Sheila, *Literary Geographies: narrative space in* Let the Great World Spin (New York:
    Palgrave Macmillan, 2014)

PhD theses

Garden, Alison, 'Empathy, Alterity and the Transnational Imagination in the Work of
    Colum McCann', University of Edinburg, Scotland, 2014
Maudet, Cécile, 'L'Autre, l'autrefois et l'ailleurs: Poétique de la rupture dans l'œuvre lit-
    téraire de Colum McCann', Université Rennes 2, France, 2015

Articles

Cahill, Susan, 'Corporeal Architecture: body and city in Colum McCann's *This Side of*
    Brightness', *Etudes irlandaises*, nos. 32–1 (Lille: Presses Universitaires du Septentrion,
    Printemps 2007), pp. 43–58
Cardin, Bertrand, "Hunger Strike' de Colum McCann ou la fluctuation des frontières',
    in Bertrand Cardin and Claude Fierobe (eds), *Irlande, Ecritures et réécritures de la*
    Famine (Caen: Presses Universitaires de Caen, 2007), pp. 165–80
Fierobe, Claude, 'Colum McCann, des coyotes, des saumons et des hommes', *L'Atelier du*
    roman, no. 36 (Décembre 2003), pp. 74–82
Flannery, Eoin, 'Rites of Passage: migrancy and liminality in Colum McCann's *Songdogs*
    and *This Side of Brightness*', *Irish Studies Review*, vol. 16, no. 1 (February 2008),
    pp. 11–25
____, 'Terrorised Youths: Colum McCann's *Everything in this Country Must* and the
    Northern Irish Troubles', in John Strachan and Alison Younger (eds), *Essays on*
    Modern Irish Literature (Sunderland: University of Sunderland Press), 2007,
    pp. 169–83
____, 'Troubling Bodies: suffering, resistance and hope in Colum McCann's "Troubles"
    short fiction', *Irish Review*, nos. 40–1 (winter 2009), pp. 33–51

Fogarty, Anne, 'Contemporary Irish Fiction and the Transnational Imaginary', in Eamon Maher (ed.), *Cultural Perspectives on Globalisation and Ireland* (Bern: Peter Lang, 2009), pp. 133–47

Gabinsky, Andrzej, 'Challenging History: past reconstruction in Colum McCann's *Songdogs*', *Estudios Irlandeses/Journal of Irish Studies*, no. 2 (2007), pp. 44–56

Healy, John F., 'Dancing Cranes and Frozen Birds: the fleeting resurrections of Colum McCann', *New Hibernia Review/Iris Eireannach Nua: A Quarterly Record of Irish Studies*, no. 4 (autumn 2000), pp. 107–18

Mari, Catherine, 'Tell-tale Ellipsis in Colum McCann's *Everything in this Country Must*', *Journal of the Short Story in English/Les Cahiers de la nouvelle*, no. 40 (spring 2003), pp. 47–56

Mianowski, Marie, 'Down-and-outs, Subways and Suburbs: subversion in Robert McLiam Wilson's *Ripley Bogle* (1989) and Colum McCann's *This Side of Brightness* (1998)', in Ciaran Ross (ed.), *Subversions* (Amsterdam: Rodopi, 2008)

_____, 'Skipping and Gasping, Sighing and Hoping in Colum McCann's "Aisling": the making of a poet', *Journal of the Short Story in English*, special issue: The 21st Century Irish Short Story, ed. Bertrand Cardin, no. 63 (autumn 2014), pp. 25–38

Mikowski, Sylvie, 'Landscapes in Movement: cosmopolitanism and the poetics of space in Colum McCann's Fiction', in Marie Mianowski (ed.), *Irish Contemporary Landscapes in Literature and the Arts* (Basingstoke: Palgrave Macmillan, 2012), pp. 119–29

_____, 'Figures de la migration dans la fiction de Colum McCann', in Pascale Amiot-Jouenne (ed.), *Irlande: insularité, singularité?*, Actes du colloque de la SOFEIR, Perpignan, 23–24 March 2001 (Perpignan: Presses Universitaires de Perpignan, 2001), pp. 157–68

_____, 'Nomadic Artists, Smooth Spaces and Lines of Flight: reading Colum McCann through Joyce, and Deleuze and Guattari', in Susan Cahill and Eoin Flannery (eds), *This Side of Brightness: essays on the fiction of Colum McCann* (Bern: Peter Lang, 2012)

Slack, John S., 'Telling Sots: photography in/as/and literature in Colum McCann's *Songdogs*', *Nua: Studies in Contemporary Irish Writing*, vol. 4, nos. 1–2 (2003), pp. 77–85

Wall, Eamonn, 'Winds Blowing from a Million Directions: Colum McCann's *Songdogs*', in Charles Fanning (ed.), *New Perspectives on the Irish Diaspora* (Carbondale, IL: Southern Illinois University Press, 2000), pp. 281–8

Selected essays on the Irish novel

Cahalan, James M., *The Irish Novel* (Dublin: Gill and Macmillan, 1988)

Cairns, David and Shaun Richards, *Writing Ireland: colonialism, nationalism and culture* (Manchester: Manchester University Press, 1988)

Cardin, Bertrand, *Miroirs de la filiation: parcours dans huit romans irlandais contemporains* (Caen: Presses Universitaires de Caen, 2005)

Corcoran, Neil, *After Yeats and Joyce: reading modern Irish literature* (Oxford: Oxford University Press, 1997)

Deane, Seamus, *Celtic Revivals: essays in modern Irish literature, 1880–1980* (London: Faber & Faber, 1985)

_____, *A Short History of Irish Literature* (London: Hutchinson, 1986)

_____, *Strange Country: modernity and nationhood in Irish writing since 1790* (Oxford: Clarendon Press, 1997)

Donoghue, Denis, *We Irish: the selected essays* (Brighton: Harvester Press, 1986)

Fierobe, Claude and Jacqueline Genet, *La Littérature irlandaise* (Paris: Armand Colin, 1997)

Foster, John Wilson, *Colonial Consequences: essays in Irish literature and culture* (Dublin: Lilliput Press, 1991)

Harte, Liam and Michael Parker (eds), *Contemporary Irish Fiction: themes, tropes, theories* (London: Macmillan, 2000)

Kiberd, Declan, *Inventing Ireland* (London: Jonathan Cape, 1995)

Martin, Augustine, *Bearing Witness: essays on Anglo-Irish literature* (Dublin: UCD Press, 1996)

Mercier, Vivian, *The Irish Comic Tradition* (Oxford: Oxford University Press, 1962)

Mikowski, Sylvie, *Le Roman irlandais contemporain* (Caen: Presses Universitaires de Caen, 2004)

Owens-Weekes, Ann, *Irish Women Writers: the uncharted tradition* (Lexington, KY: Kentucky University Press, 1990)

Smith, Gerry, *The Novel and the Nation: studies of the new Irish fiction* (London: Pluto Press, 1997)

Welch, Robert, *Changing States: transformations in modern Irish writing* (London: Routledge, 1993)

_____ (ed.), *Irish Writers and Religion* (Gerrards Cross: Colin Smythe, 1992)

Selected essays on the Irish short story

Cardin, Bertrand (ed.), 'Introduction', *Journal of the Short Story in English*, special issue: The 21st Century Irish Short Story, no. 63 (autumn 2014)

Dunn, Douglas (ed.), *Two Decades of Irish Writing: a critical survey* (Cheadle: Carcanet Press, 1975)

Genet, Jacqueline (ed.), *La Nouvelle irlandaise de langue anglaise* (Lille: Presses de l'Université du Septentrion, 1996)

O'Connor, Frank, *The Lonely Voice: a study of the short story* (London: Macmillan, 1963)

O'Faolain, Sean, *The Short Story* (London: Collins, 1948)

Rafroidi, Patrick and Terence Brown (eds), *The Irish Short Story* (Gerrards Cross: Colin Smythe, 1979)

Selected essays on Irish history, culture and society

Brown, Terence, *Ireland: a social and cultural history, 1922–2002* (London: Harper Perennial, 2004)

Carlson, Julia, *Banned in Ireland: censorship and the Irish writer* (London: Routledge, 1990)

Kearney, Richard (ed.), *The Irish Mind: exploring intellectual traditions* (Dublin: Wolfhound Press, 1985)

_____ (ed.), *Across the Frontiers: Ireland in the 1990s* (Dublin: Wolfhound Press, 1988)

Maignant, Catherine, *Histoire et civilisation de l'Irlande* (Paris: Nathan, 1996)

Other works cited

Bakhtin, Mikhail, *The Dialogic Imagination* (Austin, TX: University of Texas Press, 1984)

Barthes, Roland, 'The Death of the Author' [1968], in Barthes, *The Rustle of Language* (Berkeley, CA: University of California Press, 1989)

Bloom, Harold, *The Anxiety of Influence: a theory of poetry* (Oxford: Oxford University Press, 1973)

_____, *The Anatomy of Influence: literature as a way of life* (New Haven, CT and London: Yale University Press, 2011)

Borges, Jorge Luis, *The Total Library: non-fiction, 1922–1986* (London: Penguin, 2007)

Compagnon, Antoine, *Literature, Theory and Common Sense*, New French Thought series (Princeton, NJ: Princeton University Press, 2004)

_____, *La seconde Main ou le travail de la citation* (Paris: Seuil, 1979)

Dällenbach, Lucien, *The Mirror in the Text* (Oxford: Polity Press, 1989)

Eagleton, Terry, *Literary Theory: an introduction* (Oxford: Basil Blackwell, 1983)

Eco, Umberto, *Interpretation and Overinterpretation* (Cambridge: Cambridge University Press, 1992)

Frye, Northrop, *The Anatomy of Criticism* (Princeton, NJ: Princeton University Press, 1957)

Genette, Gerard, *Paratexts: thresholds of interpretation* (Cambridge: Cambridge University Press, 1997)

_____, *Palimpsests: literature in the second degree* (Lincoln, NE: University of Nebraska Press, 1997)

Hannoosh, Michele, *Parody and Decadence* (Columbus, OH: Ohio State University Press, 1989)

Hutcheon, Linda, *A Theory of Parody: the teachings of twentieth-century art forms* (Chicago, IL: University of Illinois Press, 1985)

_____, *A Poetics of Postmodernism: history, theory, fiction* (New York, NY and London: Routledge, 1988)

Kristeva, Julia, *Strangers to Ourselves* (New York: Columbia University Press, 1994)

_____, *Desire in Language: a semiotic approach to literature and art* (New York. NY: Columbia University Press, 1980)

Oates, Joyce Carol, *In Rough Country: essays and reviews* (New York: Harper Collins Publishers, 2010)

Riffaterre, Michel, *Text Production* (New York: Columbia University Press, 1985)

Index